# Passports to Success in BPM

## Real-World, Theory and Applications

Nathaniel Palmer, Peter Schooff, Lloyd Dugan,
Charles Farina, Pedro Robledo, Frank Kowalkowski,
Prof Mark von Rosing, *et al*

Published in association with the
Workflow Management Coalition

*Workflow Management Coalition*

**Edited by**
## LAYNA FISCHER

## Excellence in Practice Series

Future Strategies Inc.
Lighthouse Point, Florida, USA

# Passports to Success in BPM:
# Real-World, Theory and Applications

Copyright © 2014 by Future Strategies Inc.

**ISBN13: 9780984976492**

Published by Future Strategies Inc., Book Division
3640-B3 North Federal Highway, #421, Lighthouse Point FL 33064 USA
954.782.3376 / 954.719.3746 fax
www.FutStrat.com email: books@FutStrat.com

*For bulk orders, resellers, academic orders and extracts, please contact the publisher.*

# Passports to Success in BPM:
# Real-World, Theory and Applications

p. cm.
Includes bibliographical references and appendices.

1. Business Process Management. 2. Organizational Change. 3. Technological Innovation. 4. Information Technology. 5. Total Quality Management. 6. Management Information Systems. 7. Office Practice Automation. 8. Knowledge Management. 9. Workflow. 10. Process Analysis

Fischer, Layna. (ed)

*NEW! We know that our many readers love their print books, but that they don't necessarily want to carry them around with them all the time.*

The **Digital Edition** is automatically bundled with this **Print Edition** and is completely FREE to download to your mobile device.

Instantly download the complete book to your eBook reader or mobile device in one of the following formats: **epub, mobi/prc, or pdf.**

## How does it work?

1. Download the free **BitLit** app for Android or IOS
   **Android app**: http://goo.gl/ik8Q84
   **IOS app:** http://goo.gl/R5eLEq
2. Write your FULL NAME in upper case in the space shown below.
3. Then, use the app to take a picture of this WHOLE page.
   This proves that you are the legal owner of this book.
4. Get the **complete** Digital Edition of the Print book instantly.

A **bundled** eBook edition is available with the purchase of this print book

Write your full name here

CLEARLY PRINT YOUR NAME ABOVE IN UPPER CASE

**Instructions to claim your eBook edition:**
1. Download the BitLit app for Android or iOS
2. Write your name in **UPPER CASE** above
3. Use the BitLit app to submit a photo
4. Download your eBook to any device

**ISBN: 978-0-9849764-9-2**

# Passports to Success in BPM:
## Real-World, Theory and Applications

© Published by Future Strategies Inc., Book Division
3640-B3 North Federal Highway, #421, Lighthouse Point FL 33064 USA
954.782.3376 / 954.719.3746 fax
www.FutStrat.com email: books@FutStrat.com

# Table of Contents

FOREWORD     7
*Keith Swenson, WfMC Chair and Fujitsu America Inc., USA*

INTRODUCTION: PASSPORTS TO SUCCESS IN BPM     13
*Layna Fischer, Future Strategies Inc.*

## Section 1:  Understanding BPM

THE TOP 5 REASONS WHY A BPM PROJECT FAILS     23
*Peter Schooff, BPM.com, USA*

THE BPM SUCCESS MANIFESTO     27
*Nathaniel Palmer, BPM, Inc. (BPMI), USA*

HOW STRATEGIC ARE YOUR BPM INITIATIVES? FOUR QUESTIONS TO ASK YOURSELF     57
*Charles Farina, Essroc Cement Corp., USA*

BPM EMPOWERS THE DIGITAL ENTERPRISE     63
*Pedro Robledo, BPMteca.com, Spain*

EXPLOITING BUSINESS ARCHITECTURE FOR PROCESS EXCELLENCE     71
*Lloyd Dugan, BPM, Inc. (BPMI), USA*

USING ANALYTICS TO IDENTIFY PROCESS OPPORTUNITIES     83
*Frank F. Kowalkowski, Knowledge Consultants, Inc., USA*

LEARNING FROM THE LEADERS     97
*Prof. Mark von Rosing, Maria Hove, Henrik von Scheel, Global University Alliance*

## Section 2:  Using BPM

BANK DHOFAR     105
Award: Banking and Financial Services: Loan Origination
*Nominated by Newgen Software Technologies Limited, India*

HCL IBS, UNITED KINGDOM     117
Banking and Financial Services, Back Office Optimization
*Nominated by Corporate Modelling, UK*

HML, UK     129
Finalist: Financial Services
*Nominated by IBM, UK*

LIBERTY UNIVERSITY, USA 137

Finalist: Education
**Nominated by BizFlow, USA**

PRINCE SULTAN MILITARY MEDICAL CITY, SAUDI ARABIA 145

Finalist: Healthcare and Medical
**Nominated by Bizagi, UK**

PSCU, UNITED STATES 157

Award: Banking and Financial Services, Service Request Management
**Nominated by OpenText, Canada**

REFINERY OF THE PACIFIC, ECUADOR 165

Finalist: Manufacturing
**Nominated by AuraPortal (AURA), USA**

RIGHT OF WAY, DEPARTMENT OF TRANSPORT OF ABU DHABI, UAE 175

Award: Public Sector Planning and Permitting
**Nominated by DoT, United Arab Emirates**

SWISS FEDERAL RAILWAYS SBB 191

Award: Transportation and Logistics, Agile Development
**Nominated by ti&m AG, Switzerland**

U.S. DEPARTMENT OF VETERANS AFFAIRS, USA 199

Award: Public Sector, Benefits Enrolment
**Nominated by Living Systems Technologies, USA**

VITENS, THE NETHERLANDS 211

Award: Public Sector- Customer-centric Transformation
**Nominated by You-Get, the Netherlands**

## Section 3: Appendix

WFMC STRUCTURE AND MEMBERSHIP INFORMATION 223
AUTHOR APPENDIX 227
INDEX 237
FURTHER READING: BPM AND WORKFLOW 239

# Foreword

Twenty four years ago Michael Hammer published the article "Reengineering Work: Don't Automate, Obliterate" in the Harvard Business Review in which he encouraged people to eliminate needless business processes before inventing time in automating them. Even then, the focus for business process management was understanding, scrutinizing, and fundamentally reworking business processes, and not to assume that the process you have is the one that you want or need, and certainly not to blindly automate it.

Since then, when the Business Process Management movement came out in the first years of the new century, the meanings attributed to the term BPM varied extensively. Some say BPM as a new kind of programming, focused entirely on automation, and server integration.

Yet others stayed true to the ideal that business process is something people *do*, not a program, not a programming language, and not a system for programming. There was for years significant confusion about what different vendors and practitioners really meant.

This year, a number of experts came together on line, and worked out a comprehensive definition for BPM. The following result has contributions from dozens of notable people in the field:

> **Business Process Management (BPM) is a discipline involving any combination of modeling, automation, execution, control, measurement and optimization of business activity flows, in support of enterprise goals, spanning systems, employees, customers and partners within and beyond the enterprise boundaries.**

This definition is designed to be short enough to use regularly, without gratuitous words. There is a trade-off: a longer definition might make it clearer, and at the same time more cumbersome. Here is clarification of what we mean by these words:

- **BPM is a discipline**; it is a practice; it is something you do.
- **Business** stems from the state of being busy, and it implies commercially viable and profitable work. A business exists to provide value to customers in exchange for something else of value.
- **Process** means a flow of business activities and seeing those activities as connected toward the achievement of some business transaction. Flow is meant loosely here: the order may or may not be strictly defined.

A person doing BPM must consider a process at the scope of interrelated business activities which holistically cooperate to fulfill a business objective. This is the key difference from a functional view of business where each function might be optimized independent of the other functions.

In a complex system like a business, it is well known that local optimization of part of the system will rarely lead to good overall results. A BPM practitioner must consider the metrics of the entire system when evaluating a specific process.

- **Modeling** means that they would identify, define, and make a representation of the complete process to support communication about the process. There is no single standard way to model, but the model must encompass the process.

- **Automation** refers to the work that is done in advance to assure the smooth execution of the process instances. In many cases this means writing software, but it might include building machinery or even creating signage to direct participants.
- **Execution** meaning that instances of a process are performed or enacted, which may include automated aspects. Conceptually, the process instance executes itself, following the BPM practitioner's model, but unfolding independent of the BPM practitioner.
- **Control** means that the there is some aspect of making sure that the process follows the designed course. This can be strict control and enforcement, or it might be loose control in the form of guidelines, training, and manual practices.
- **Measurement** means that effort is taken to quantitatively determine how well the process is working in terms of serving the needs of customers.
- **Optimization** means that the discipline of BPM is an ongoing activity which builds over time to steadily improve the measures of the process. Improvement is relative to the goals of the organization, and ultimately in terms of meeting the needs of customers.
- **Enterprise** is used here simply to mean a business organization; any organization where people are working together to meet common goals; it does not need to be exceptionally large, and it does not need to be for profit.
- **Enterprise goals** is included here to emphasize that BPM should be done in the context of the goals of the enterprise, and not some small part of it. This might seem a bit redundant in one sense: any improvement of a process must be an improvement in terms of the enterprise goals – anything else would not be called an improvement.
- **Within and beyond the enterprise boundaries** recognizes that the enterprise is part of a larger system. Customers are part of the business process. Their interaction, along with those of employees should be considered as part of the end-to-end interaction.

The definition needs some explaining about exactly how the words are used. Here are some things we can say about BPM to help understand what definition intends to mean.

### BPM is an activity; a practice

Predominant in the definitions is the idea that BPM is something you do, not a thing you own or buy. It is described in many definitions as a practice. There was wide agreement on this, well over 90% of the participants expressed this view.

### BPM is about improving processes

It presumes the idea that you view business as a set of processes, and BPM is the act of improving those processes. This is important: "skill" is different from "skill improvement". This can be confusing.

For example in competitive situations the two ideas are often intertwined – what is the act of playing tennis, if not also the act of trying to improve the way you play tennis? However, in other contexts it is easier to distinguish –

the activity of driving is different than taking a driving course to improve the way you drive.

The implication is that BPM is not about automating business process (in the 'paving the cowpaths' meaning) but about improving them. The same way that 'reengineering' a process is about not simply automating what is currently there. Some will say that automation by itself is an improvement over a manual process.

The BPM is the activity of discovering and designing the automated process, and is done when the finished application is deployed to the organization. The running of the processes is not part of BPM. However, monitoring the process to find areas of improvement would still be an important part of BPM.

### BPM is done by people concerned primarily with improvement of the process

A business process will involve many people, but how many of them are concerned with improving it? Some will insist that improvement is everyone's job. That is, the receptionist should be thinking about how to improve the operations if possible. This interpretation is too broad to be useful. The cook who adds salt to the food making it taste better, motivating more employees to eat in the building, cutting down on waste of time driving to an outside restaurant, and improving the amount of information interaction between worker, and resulting in better performance is NOT business process management by any account.

Everybody in a business is working to do their best job, and every good job helps the business, but all of this is not BPM. BPM must be narrowly defined as the activity done by people who *actively* and *primarily* look specifically at the business processes, and trying to improve them. Clearly those people must solicit input from as many others as possible, but those others are not doing BPM.

### Participating in a process is not doing BPM

A manager approving a purchase order is not doing BPM even though that approval is an activity in a process. A bank manager rejecting a loan application is not doing BPM even though this activity is a step in a business process. These people are doing jobs that are part of a process, but they are not doing BPM.

### Implementation (coding) of the process application is not BPM

An application developer designing a form for data entry as a step in a process is not doing BPM at that moment. Once the "to-be" process has been adequately spelled out, the actual implementation of the application that supports it is no longer actively engaged in improving the process. A small caution here: applications are often developed incrementally — show to the customer, get feedback, improve, and iterate — and the process may be improved incrementally as well.

Those incremental improvements should be included as the activity of BPM, but the activity of implementation of the application is not BPM. The criteria are clear: if you are actively and primarily engaged in improvement of the process, then it is BPM, otherwise it is engineering.

### Making a suggestion for process improvement is not BPM

This means that there is a distinction between many people who make suggestions, and those who then actually do the BPM. When a process analyst is involved in BPM, it is expected that they will solicit lots of information about what is and is not working, as well as suggestions on how it might work. Those people who give the feedback are helping the BPM work, but not themselves doing BPM.

### *Improving a single step of a process is not BPM*

Some have the mistaken idea that any possible action that improves a process is BPM no matter how small. A person doing BPM needs to have some kind of big-picture view of the process. It has been described as an "end-to-end view" of the process.

Optimizing one step in a process, without knowledge of the entire process, is exactly what Hammer and Champy were warning about: to understand the correct optimizations we need to consider those optimizations within the context of a complete business process.

A workman smoothing gravel on a road is improving all of the process that involved driving on that road, but it is not BPM because he does not have visibility of the whole process. The engineer finding a way to double the bandwidth of a fiber optic cable is improving all the processes that require communications, but this is not BPM either.

An office worker who finds that OpenOffice4 helps to create documents faster than some other word processor is improving all the processes that involve writing documents; this is not BPM either. In order to have a discussion about BPM, we can consider only those activities by people who have a view to, and consider the effect on, the entire end to end process.

## MISREPRESENTATIONS OF BPM

Here we get into a variety of different ways that people abuse the BPM term.

**BPM is not a product** - There is a category called "BPMS" which is a BPM Suite or BPM System. Gartner has introduced a new product category called "intelligent BPMS." What is included depends very much on the vendor. Analysts have attempted to list features and capabilities that are necessary, but those features change from year to year. For example, in 2007 analysts commonly insisted that BPM Suites must have a BPEL execution capability, but today this is entirely ignored or forgotten.

Most products designed to support BPM also include a lot of other capabilities beyond just those the BPM practitioner requires. Particularly they generally include a lot of application development and data integration capability. It is very convenient to offer all this in a single package, while other vendors bundle collections of offerings together to get the same benefit. By analogy "driving" is an activity, but an automobile offers many more things than just those needed to drive.

**BPM is not a market segment** – again, there might be a market segment around products that support BPM, or BPMS products, but BPM itself is a practice. Vendors may be labeled as a "BPMS Vendor" which simply means they have some products which can support the activity of BPM, among other things.

**An application does not do BPM** – the application might be the result of BPM activity. Once finished, it either does the business process, or support people doing the business process. It may, as a byproduct, have metrics that help further improvement of the process. In this sense it supports BPM in the same way that receptionist may support BPM by coming up with good ideas, and that is not enough to say that the application, or the receptionist, is doing BPM.

**BPM as a Service is not application hosting** – We use the term business process as a service (BPaaS) to mean applications hosted outside the company that supports more than one function of a business process. Like the application above, it does the process, but it does not do BPM.

**Entire organizational units don't do BPM** – To say that a company is doing BPM is simply a way of saying that there are some people in the company that are doing BPM. This kind of abstraction is normal. It should be obvious that when a company or division claims to be doing BPM, the majority of the people there are not actually doing BPM.

**BPM is not anything that improves business** – some argue that every activity is part of a process – because a process is just a set of activities. Then, any action taken to improve any activity is BPM. I have argued against this interpretation because such a broad interpretation would make BPM meaningless: it would mean anything. There is broad acceptance that BPM is a practice of methodically improving a process that supports business, and that improvements in part of the process must be done only after the consideration of the entire end to end process.

**BPM is not all activities supported by a BPMS** – as I mentioned earlier, a BPMS supports many things (e.g. application development) which is not BPM. A BPMS that only supported the exact activity of BPM would not be as useful as one that bring a lot of capabilities together. It is however a common mistake for people to say that because a BPMS supports something, it is then an aspect of BPM.

While it is true that someone who does BPM needs to document a process, it is not true that anyone who documents a process is doing BPM. While it is true that many BPMS support designing a screen form, it is not true that design a screen form is BPM. The activity of BPM is fairly well defined, but a BPMS support a much wider set of activities.

**Because you can do something with a BPMS does not mean you are doing BPM** – A BPMS is designed to support the activity of BPM. However there are many things a BPMS can do that are not BPM.

[1]It is fitting that as we reach the stage of maturity for BPM, where the approach is accepted and widely used, that we settle on this definition, and these explanations, as we begin to explore the rest of the space of possibilities known as Business Process Management.

*Keith Swenson, WfMC Chair*
*Vice President of R&D, Fujitsu America Inc., USA*

---

[1] Many thanks to everyone who helped with the definition, most notably the following people: Alexander Samarin, Karl Walter Keirstead, Kiran Garimella, John Morris, Scott Francis, Lloyd Dugan.

# Introduction: Passports to Success in BPM

## Layna Fischer, Future Strategies Inc.

Is your BPM project set up for success or failure?

Knowing what your BPM success will look like before you even begin will help you achieve it. As will knowing what are the most common causes of failure. We learn more from failure than success, but it's easier, cheaper and quicker to learn from others' mistakes rather than go through the pain personally.

BPM projects fail more often as a result of missed expectations than inadequate technology. In this book you will learn how to create and present a credible business case and plan for success, starting with the chapter "BPM Success Manifesto."

The value of BPM is realized through planning and measurement, and the business case needs to be developed with transparent success criteria and "real world" metrics.

In addition to the highly insightful and instructional white papers contributed by industry thought leaders, this book provides compelling award-wining case studies written by those who have been through the full BPM experience.

These case studies describe successful ROIs and competitive advantages gained through BPM and the writers also generously share solid advice on how to avoid the pitfalls they personally encountered– and overcame. These examples present great learning opportunities for you (and a lot more inside the book):

- ✓ *Ensure representation from all relevant departments during process study and planning, including the IT department*
- ✓ *Don't attempt to establish perfect specifications of a process without prototyping*
- ✓ *Removing paper doesn't mean you have gone "paperless." Make sure to capture data as well as routing data along with documents enables true workflow automation*
- ✓ *BPM is extremely fast and flexible which drives the business and IT to try to use BPM for solutions that aren't true processes.*
- ✓ *Managing Demand – without a solid governance and prioritization process the BPM backlog can get unmanageable*
- ✓ *Don't underestimate the true number of process steps (some may not be apparent in legacy world)*
- ✓ *Use an experienced Agile Coach: Projects which "try to be agile" may fail easily. Make sure you have enough experience and commitment of customers, business analysts and developers before you start.*

BPM is essential to a company's survival in today's hyper-speed business environment. BPM done right empowers an enterprise to compete at the highest level in any marketplace. BPM done right delivers continuous business transformation.

So it is absolutely essential to understand how to avoid doing BPM wrong: in fact, your business depends on it.

# Section 1: Understanding BPM

FOREWORD
**Keith Swenson, WfMC Chair**
**Vice President of R&D, Fujitsu America Inc., USA**

This year, a number of experts came together on line, and worked out a comprehensive definition for BPM. This definition is designed to be short enough to use regularly, without gratuitous words. Keith Swenson also offers substantial clarification on what BPM *is* – and is *not*.

THE TOP 5 REASONS WHY A BPM PROJECT FAILS
**Peter Schooff, Managing Editor, BPM.com, USA**

BPM is essential to a company's survival in today's hyper-speed business environment. But BPM often requires business transformation, and that's really just another word for business change. Anyone with any business experience will tell you, anything that requires business change involves a high risk of failure. And the hard truth is, the greater the need for BPM in an organization, the greater the risk for failure. So why do projects fail? This chapter looks at the top five reasons.

THE BPM SUCCESS MANIFESTO
**Nathaniel Palmer, BPM, Inc. (BPMI), USA**

Business Process Management (BPM) is a discipline involving any combination of modeling, automation, execution, control, measurement and optimization of business activity flows, in support of enterprise goals, spanning systems, employees, customers and partners within and beyond the enterprise boundaries. This is the first consensus-led definition of BPM to emerge since it emerged as an identifiable software segment more than a decade ago. Yet it goes to the heart of what is driving interest in BPM today – the ability to improve and automate how we manage both our business processes and the information that supports them.

Nathaniel Palmer discusses impact of new technologies, the mandate for greater transparency, and how the ongoing aftershocks of globalization have collectively removed nearly any trace of predictability within the business environment. As a result, sustainable competitive advantage no longer comes from scale and efficiency but adaptability – the ability to process streams of information flows, make sense of these, and rapidly translate these into effective responses designed for precision rather repeatability.

HOW STRATEGIC ARE YOUR BPM INITIATIVES? 4 QUESTIONS TO ASK YOURSELF
**Charles Farina, Essroc Cement Corp., USA**

Gone are the days when process excellence was just about standardization, cost cutting, or quality. In today's businesses, process is about enabling business strategy. So how sure are you that your BPM program stacks up?

One way to start addressing this question is to evaluate what you're doing with respect to the characteristics of **Strategic BPM.** With these requirements in place, your BPM actions will be integrated with your company's organizational objectives – resulting in *strategic alignment!*

The author emphasizes that BPM is not something that you do on top of everything else. It's a key part of how you manage the business.

BPM EMPOWERS THE DIGITAL ENTERPRISE
**Pedro Robledo, BPMteca.com, Spain**

The Digital Economy, globalization, social and environmental problems, natural disasters, the threat of terrorism, migration waves... are conditioning companies to make urgent situation analysis exercises and strategic processes to be competitive and to maintain their companies with solvency. Aspects such as delinquency management, debt control, control margins, risk management... are highly relevant and priority processes.

Pedro Robledo reviews disruptive technologies arising from SMACT - Social, Mobile, Analytics, Cloud, Things - and details how organizations with a management approach should document, automate, analyze and monitor business processes, but not in terms of functions (marketing, sales, production, customer service...) but in terms of processes from start to finish and across all functional boundaries; understanding business processes as a sequence of activities to support the strategy, analyze operational effectiveness and facilitating the establishment of performance measures for continuous improvement.

## EXPLOITING BUSINESS ARCHITECTURE FOR PROCESS EXCELLENCE
### *Lloyd Dugan, BPM, Inc. (BPMI), USA*

Business Process Management (BPM) is a term that has regrettably come to mean too many different things to too many different but related practitioner communities, including process automation, process modeling, process improvement, business or enterprise architecture, etc. Worse still is that none of these communities fully and consistently define BPM as something that unifies and integrates its interdisciplinary nature. Instead, provincial interests have led some communities to balkanize (or fragment) what BPM means in order to assert methodological superiority or to gain market share or both.

Lloyd Dugan discusses, how, in many ways, BPM as a practice area is at a crossroads, wherein it, too, can give way to a successor concept (as BPM itself was to workflow) or it, as the preferred alternative, can evolve to be all of what it should have been in the first place, aka BPM 2.0.

## USING ANALYTICS TO IDENTIFY PROCESS OPPORTUNITIES
### *Frank F. Kowalkowski, Knowledge Consultants, Inc., USA*

Because processes are critical to business execution, process performance management and improvement have become two key aspects of BPM for improving business performance. These two key process approaches form the basis of enterprise transformation, integration and consolidation within the enterprise. They also support integration across enterprises and form the foundation for e-commerce, e-government and enterprise excellence. Organizations are good at assessing due diligence regarding financial, market and legal issues. However, studies (Michael Porter and others) show that most structural changes requiring integration fail due to operational (read process) and/or cultural incompatibilities. Both of these issues can be addressed with some core process and cultural analytics.

Frank Kowalkowski shows how all this leads to a need for process management that achieves a lean, compliant and more flexible enterprise. Process management and process methodology can provide process analytics at specific points in the methodology to reduce the failure rate. Management of processes should also include analytics that form the basis of monitoring continuous improvement of the enterprise as well as the processes through a process performance reporting system, often via business intelligence tools.

## LEARNING FROM THE LEADERS
### *Prof. Mark von Rosing, Maria Hove, Henrik von Scheel*

When you take the time to compare your own knowledge to that of others, you become better at learning. This is not a new phenomenon or concept; this is a basic reason why so many organizations want their employees to work together, to collaborate, and/ or to create the circumstances for them to share knowledge. The growing amount of software that supports collaboration to enable effective mutual learning is a confirmation of this trend. This chapter looks at why it's important to read the BPM case studies in this book, what we can learn from them and how we can take the most of them.

# Section 2: Using BPM

## BANK DHOFAR

Award: Banking and Financial Services: Loan Origination
### *Nominated by Newgen Software Technologies Limited, India*

Established in 1990, Bank Dhofar commenced operations with two branches, in Muscat and Salalah. Today it is one of the fastest growing Banks in the Sultanate of Oman, with a strong presence in Corporate Banking, Consumer Banking, Treasury Banking and Project Finance. The bank realized that to facilitate and manage the growth of its retail assets, it needed to enhance its operational capacity, productivity, and ability to scale-up operations. Automation of key business processes was identified as a key imperative. The bank decided to automate two of its key business processes, Retail Loan Origination (covering Home Loan & Personal Loan), and Credit Card Processing.

The Loan Origination process is highly regulated and data-intensive, requiring input and feedback at multiple steps throughout the loan cycle. The bank realized that there was a strong need for a solution that could effectively digitize and handle the effective flow of the documents from across the process life-cycle. Further, to keep up with the demands of the ever-increasing customer-base, the bank needed a solution for end-to-end automation and centralization of its credit card processing and approval systems.

After evaluating a host of solutions, Bank Dhofar decided to go with a solution comprising a proven Business Process Management (BPM) platform, an Enterprise Content Management (ECM) platform, and a Scanning and Digitization suite, for end-to-end automation of its Retail Loan Origination and Credit Card Approval processes. The solution offered enhanced business flexibility, better credit risk management, and rules-based processing, resulting in improved business performance for the bank.

## HCL IBS, UNITED KINGDOM

Banking and Financial Services, Back Office Optimization
### *Nominated by Corporate Modelling, UK*

HCL IBS is an outsourcer carrying out policy administration and affiliated services in the UK closed book Life Assurance and Pensions market place. We deliver those services to demanding commercial SLAs, cheaper than the insurance companies with whom we contract. Our client contracts are on a "per policy" basis so revenue from those contracts reduces year on year in line with the attrition of each book of business. HCL IBS also have to meet stringent and emerging UK regulatory requirements. In 2009, as a response to this challenge we began a journey to deliver immediate reductions in operations costs (c.30%) and ongoing ability to control costs whilst improving people productivity.

We have benefited from more than a 15% increase in the number of transactions processed per person (FTE). This has been a key enabler to delivering more for less. Within the first year, we also realized a progressive reduction in overall operating costs of c. 15%. These savings have enhanced our competitive standing and reputation allowing us to profile new opportunities to gain market share. In addition, upcoming releases and implementation of improved and additional workflow functionality will cause further savings putting us well on track for our targeted 30% reductions.

## HML, UK

Finalist: Financial Services
***Nominated by IBM, UK***

HML responds faster to customer communications, streamlining workflows for incoming correspondence with IBM Business Process Manager. When your business depends on your clients' trust, you need to make sure that you meet their expectations, not just most of the time, but all the time. To ensure that it is serving customers effectively, HML works to strict service level agreements (SLAs), which are agreed individually with each client. The company constantly looks to improve its performance in this area. HML receives up to 30,000 letters, 50,000 emails and 5,000 faxes from customers or a diverse range of third parties each month. Each item of correspondence will initiate one of 80 corresponding processes, depending on the type of request received.

Customer correspondence is now processed in an efficient manner allowing for improved response times. Saved £400,000 from reduced manual processing and £150,000 from consolidating processing onto a single platform. Flexible solution enables new functionality to be developed quickly, with no need to invest in additional software.

## LIBERTY UNIVERSITY, USA

Finalist: Education
***Nominated by BizFlow, USA***

Liberty University is the largest private, nonprofit university in the United States. It has grown more than 1000% since 2003 and 100% since 2010. In order to both enable and support such growth, Liberty has invested heavily in technology infrastructure and automation. Liberty uses BPM to continually improve process efficiencies, user effectiveness, and overall customer services with students and staff.

In this paper, Liberty describes how it started with BPM and BPM Suites and where it has implemented BPM beginning with Student Financial Aid. To date, Liberty has reduced Verification record processing 42% from 12 minutes per record to 7 minutes per record while increasing the number of records processed by 25% (13,826 to 18,349 records). More than 10 other processes have been fully automated.

## PRINCE SULTAN MILITARY MEDICAL CITY, SAUDI ARABIA

Finalist: Healthcare and Medical
***Nominated by Bizagi, UK***

Prince Sultan Military Medical City (PSMMC) formerly known as The Riyadh Military Hospital (RMH) is located in Riyadh City and considered as one of the most advanced medical centres in the Middle East. PSMMC is the Medical Services Department (MSD) for the Ministry of Defense (MOD). The hospital now has a capacity of more than 1,400 beds and employs over 12,000 staff.

Key challenges faced by the hospital were related to patient safety. These included identifying the right patient, providing the right treatment to the right patient and preventing identification fraud and misuse of medical services by patients.

Existing legacy system used by the Patient Affairs department could not address these challenges. A BPM system was introduced to streamline and manage the improved processes of various departments associated with Patient Affairs. PSMMC has already had a positive experience after the Family and Community Department, Al-Wazarat Health Centre (WHC), was automated with over 70 processes last year. The system delivered end to end patient care for over 2,000 outpatients. The success of the first BPM initiative encouraged the PSMMC management team to consider the same BPM solution for this much larger initiative which required the end-to end automation of a 1400 bed hospital, serving the big part of the city.

Key drivers for both projects was to deliver a highly intuitive system that medical professionals can use daily and easily and that helps to improve patients care and reduce costs.

## PSCU, UNITED STATES

Award: Banking and Financial Services, Service Request Management
### Nominated by OpenText, Canada

PSCU is one of the largest credit union services organizations in the U.S., representing close to 700 credit unions. PSCU implemented OpenText Assure in 90 days, enabling them to realize significant cost savings, improve customer service and satisfaction, and increase efficiencies, The Assure application factory provides out-of-box, industry best practice components to ensure a quick time-to-value and continuous process improvement. PSCU Customer Service Agents use the Assure Work Center to manage requests and resolve issues very quickly. The PSCU customers at the credit unions use the self-service portal to log requests and monitor the status of requests in real-time.

The BPM CoE team was instrumental in delivering a successful solution in such a short time frame. This team combined BPM and Six Sigma specialists to bridge the gap between IT and the business and build trust and collaboration, which was a huge advantage. After implementing Assure, PSCU was able to increase customer satisfaction levels as was noted in recent customer surveys, and by using the out-of-the-box reporting tools, they can now identify trends, predict issues, and proactively identify new service needs. Assure allows PSCU to respond faster and more efficiently to customer requests, process double the amount of requests with the same amount of staff, and has eliminated 90% of the paper in the process, saving them over $300,000 annually. This is a competitive advantage that PSCU is able to offer free-of-charge to the credit unions.

## RIGHT OF WAY, DEPARTMENT OF TRANSPORT OF ABU DHABI, UAE

Award: Public Sector Planning and Permitting
### Nominated by DoT, United Arab Emirates

The Department of Transport (DoT), in line with the overall strategy for the government of Abu Dhabi, has identified the need to improve customer care as a key objective. They consider their customers one of their greatest assets. One of the key drivers for this project was the improvement of customer care through the identification and implementation of a leading NOC application and approvals procedure to create clear impact on both internal and external customers.

All contractors, consultants and developers in the emirate of Abu Dhabi of the United Arab Emirates are required to obtain No Objection Certificates (NOCs) from the DOT for any intended construction within the Emirates' Rights of Way.

As outlined in this document the main objective was to significantly improve the application process required to obtain the Departments approval for third parties to undertake work within the Rights of Way. This was achieved through the development of the online NOC System as a single contact point for receiving NOC applications and to facilitate the expediting the issuing of consolidated NOCs on behalf of the DOT.

## REFINERY OF THE PACIFIC, ECUADOR

### Finalist: Manufacturing
### *Nominated by AuraPortal (AURA), USA*

Refinery of the Pacific Eloy Alfaro is a mixed economy institution created to build, operate and sustain a complex 300 MDB refinery, through a strategic alliance between PDVSA and Petroecuador. This alliance contemplates the implementation of process units with profound conversion technology, required for the production of gasoline, distillates, LPG and chemical bases.

Refinery of the Pacific has successfully implemented BPM Methodology supported on a Business Process Management suite (BPMS) for the operational and administrative management of its processes on a corporate level.

This Case Study is based on the first process to be implemented; the Public Procurement Management process. This is a complex process made up of eight sub processes for each type of procurement, which include the intervention of several departments: Administration, Management, Finance, Accounts, Technical Commission and Internal Control. The implementation of BPM methodology has led to an effective automation of Refinery of the Pacific's processes and a drastic reduction in human error.

## SWISS FEDERAL RAILWAYS SBB

### Award: Transportation and Logistics, Agile Development
### *Nominated by ti&m AG, Switzerland*

The Swiss are world champions in using their railways - on average a Swiss citizen travels 2258km per year on the railway network. As a consequence the railway system is heavily used and the quality of service has to be high according to Swiss standards which also means the processes for rail network operation have to be efficiently controlled.

The BPM project 'SIP' (SBB Infrastructure Portal) automates incident processes with a workflow system. In the project, one unified BPM system was used for very diverse process management and we would like to emphasize how we managed complexity. Imagine a tree that has fallen on a railway track. It damages rails, power lines and even telecom wires. A complex mixture of processes and organizations (civil engineering, power services, IT, external companies) has to be mastered by different technical control centers in order to efficiently react to the incident and finally make the joint decision to give the green light once all impediments have been resolved.

## U.S. DEPARTMENT OF VETERANS AFFAIRS, USA

Award: Public Sector, Benefits Enrolment
### Nominated by Living Systems Technologies, USA

This case study details the experience of transforming a highly political, overburdened and mostly manual governmental claims processing system into a highly efficient and effective system via the application of world-class solution architecture and information technologies products. It examines the direct benefits of following a structured approach that effectively decomposes the business layer into a collection of requirements backed by BPMN 2.0 process models, followed by the subsequent composition of the solution through the application and technology layers.

An emphasis on correctly positioning layered architecture principles is crucial to the formation and evaluation of an appropriate solution architecture. Of particular importance, once a layered architectural perspective is adopted, it becomes possible to cleanly abstract a process layer, whose functionality can be fulfilled via model-driven execution.

## VITENS, THE NETHERLANDS

Award: Public Sector- Customer-centric Transformation
### Nominated by You-Get, the Netherlands

With over 5M customers, Vitens is the largest water company of the Netherlands, with the goal to be the best service provider of the Netherlands and additionally have the lowest integral costs per connection. The Customers department of Vitens, responsible for all communication (including invoicing and collection) realized that the key in achieving this lies in more efficient and effective business processes followed the BPM Maturity Model steps, in combination with proven Best Practices.

The starting point has been the business processes documentation and optimization, followed by a BPMSuite automation project (IBM BPM) and completed with an organization structure adjustment. First the organization is made process aware, then (to secure the proactive and continuous improvement of the processes) Process Improvement teams and a BPM CoE (Center of Excellence) has been set up, including defined KPIs. Vitens now has a flexible and efficient matrix organization, with real-time process monitoring and continuously visible process performance, and is working towards all end-to-end processes being visible, in control and continuously improving.

## HOW TO SUBMIT AN ENTRY IN THE ANNUAL AWARDS
The annual WfMC **Awards for Global Excellence in BPM** are sponsored by WfMC.org and BPM.com. The prestigious annual Awards are highly coveted by organizations that seek recognition for their achievements. These awards not only provide a spotlight for companies that truly deserve recognition, but provide tremendous insights for organizations wishing to emulate the winners' successes.

General information and guidelines for submissions are at www.bpmf.org

# Section 1

# Understanding BPM

# The Top 5 Reasons Why a BPM Project Fails

## Peter Schooff, BPM.com, USA

### Introduction

BPM is essential to a company's survival in today's hyper-speed business environment. But BPM often requires business transformation, and that's really just another word for business change. Anyone with any business experience will tell you, anything that requires business change involves a high risk of failure.

And the hard truth is, the greater the need for BPM in an organization, the greater the risk for failure.

### The Importance Of Identifying BPM Failure As Early As Possible

Various studies have put the failure rate of BPM project at anywhere between 25 and 55 percent. Gartner released a report back in in 2012 titled, *Organizational Politics Will Prevent at Least One-Third of BPM Efforts Through 2016*[1]. That's the percentage just from company politics alone, and that figure does not include the projects that were delayed or did not fully deliver on promises.

Whatever the rate of failure, because of the business-critical nature of BPM, any rate of failure for BPM is too high. Therefore, it is absolutely necessary to understand and identify the places where BPM can go wrong as early as possible, and thereby avoid making the same mistakes.

---

[1] http://www.gartner.com/newsroom/id/1914714

As Managing Editor of BPM.com, I have the extraordinary opportunity to raise what I believe are important issues around BPM and have some of the best, most experienced minds in the industry weigh in on them.

The main Forum discussion I reference for this chapter was the one where I asked: **What Is the First Sign That a BPM Project Is Going to Fail?**

## TOP REASONS FOR BPM FAILURE

### 1. Treating BPM as a Project

The unanimous number one reason for BPM failure is treating it as a project. The reasoning is simple: business often views a project as something that is external to the daily business of a company.

A project is often seen as something that has a definite start date and end date. Also, many people view a BPM project as something that involves outside analysts and consultants that one day march into the company, do their fact finding, deliver the results, then march right back out again.

Truly successful BPM should be fully integrated into the everyday business of the company. It should become part of a company's DNA!

As Emiel Kelly, a Dutch BPM trainer/coach, so often likes to repeat on the Forum (and is worth repeating again): **BPM is daily business!**

Or, as Peter Johnston, a Management Consultant with Gluu, stated so well: **BPM is about continuous improvement – P stands for Process, not for Project, and processes, in theory, go on forever.**

*Please note*: I am well aware that when I refer to BPM in this chapter, I also call it a project. The fact is, companies unfamiliar with BPM have to start somewhere, and they often start BPM as a project. It's where you go with BPM that counts!

### 2. Poor Communication

Poor communication is the second key reason BPM fails. Let's face it, poor communication can derail almost any business initiative. I believe that the quality of communication in a company is the direct reflection of a company's management. And to me, management, or the M of BPM, is often one of the most overlooked aspects of BPM.

What I first started thinking about this topic, I was initially going to title this chapter: *Underestimating the Human Element of BPM*. But then it hit me, the best way to fully understand and factor in the human element of BPM is through communication. Or to put it in IT terms: communication is the user interface of the human being.

As Ken Schwarz, the Director of BPM and Case Management Product Marketing at Pegasystems, said so well:

**Projects rarely fail for "technical" reasons. Usually, things go seriously awry when you have sponsorship problems, lack of clarity around roles and responsibility, or breakdowns in communication.**

Another important aspect of BPM that Tom Baeyens, the CEO of Effektif, brings up is:

**One of the big values (of BPM) always has been to establish a common language, improve communication between business people and IT and offer more control to business people where they needed it.**

Implementing BPM can and does improve communication within and across departments. But the commitment to communication has to start at the very beginning through clear roles, clear goals, and clear timelines.

### 3. Treating BPM as an IT Project

There's that word again: Project. But in this case, it's 'IT Project.'

There is a persistent belief among enterprises that BPM is supposed to be an IT project. This is mainly due to BPMS (business process management suite) being used as a tool of automation, and while process automation is still a key factor, BPM is much more than that.

There has long been a deep divide between business and IT departments at most companies. That gap has been closing, but not fast enough. Also, it has been said that one of the keys to successful BPM is getting buy-in from the business user. One of the quickest and easiest ways to fail at user buy-in is to put IT in charge of the initiative.

As Steve Weissman, Principal Consultant of the Holly Group, said in answer to the question:

**What are the Biggest Myths of BPM? That BPM is a technology. It's not; it's a business practice that can be ably enabled and supported by the proper set of technologies (plural).**

Or, as Stephen Zisk from Pegasystem wrote to the same question:

**BPM is about making the business itself work better by using a process-based view of the business to understand, measure, and improve business interactions. Yes, it has to involve IT as a key player...but fundamentally, the process "owner" is the business line or function that is responsible for the success of the process.**

The language of BPM needs to become the language of the organization, and that is much more than just an IT project.

### 4. Lack of Commitment

All businesses deal from a deck of limited resources. Whether that resource is time, money, personnel, or the focus of top management, how a company commits these limited resources determines how and at what that company will succeed (or in this case, fail).

When I asked the question on the Forum, *What One Thing Most Often Makes the Difference Between Success and Failure With BPM*, of the 14 answers I received, the near unanimous choice was executive-level sponsorship. Sponsorship speaks directly to executive-level commitment, and without executive sponsorship many BPM endeavors will simply fail to launch.

Time is also a key commitment to BPM success. As Tim Bryce, a Management Consultant, wrote on the Forum:

**When you hear developers say, 'We don't have time to do it right.' Translation: 'We have plenty of time to do it wrong.'**

That says it all to me. If the cost seems too high to get it right, think of the cost to get it wrong. And the single most effective way to assure continuous executive commitment (as well as effective communication) is with BPM governance.

### 5. Bad Business Architecture

Business architecture is often viewed as something external to BPM. The problem with this viewpoint is that bad business architecture can drag down almost any big tech initiative in a company.

Bad business architecture silos business units, threatens end-to-end processes, and orphans services and data. And while a BPM project might succeed at some level with poor business architecture, the truly big, lasting gains will only come from BPM that is in line with solid business architecture.

As Dr. Alexander Samarin, an independent consultant, wrote:

*If you already have (BPM and/or BPMS) and still cannot evolve your business as fast as you want then you need a better architecture for BPM.*

Looking ahead, with the further fracturing of business units through mobile, and with the growth of customized business processes, along with the amount of data that's being kicked off by every business unit, business architecture is becoming more important than ever to both business and BPM.

### CONCLUSION

BPM done right empowers an enterprise to compete at the highest level in any marketplace. BPM done right delivers continuous business transformation.

So it is absolutely essential to understand and avoid the key ways of doing BPM wrong: in fact, your business depends on it.

## REFERENCES

BPM Forum at http://bpm.com/my-bpm/forums

# The BPM Success Manifesto

## Nathaniel Palmer, BPM, Inc. (BPMI), USA

## 1. INTRODUCTION

Business Process Management (BPM) is a discipline involving any combination of modeling, automation, execution, control, measurement and optimization of business activity flows, in support of enterprise goals, spanning systems, employees, customers and partners within and beyond the enterprise boundaries.

This is the first consensus-led definition of BPM to emerge since it emerged as an identifiable software segment more than a decade ago. Yet it goes to the heart of what is driving interest in BPM today – the ability to improve and automate how we manage both our business processes and the information that supports them.

The impact of new technologies, the mandate for greater transparency, and the ongoing aftershocks of globalization have collectively removed nearly any trace of predictability within the business environment. As a result, sustainable competitive advantage no longer comes from scale and efficiency but adaptability – the ability to process streams of information flows, make sense of these, and rapidly translate these into effective responses designed for precision rather repeatability.

Today we are in what many see as the third phase of BPM, marked by *Intelligent BPM Systems* or *iBPMS*, which builds upon the previous two generations, yet extends into directions previously out of reach. "Intelligent?" you may ask, "as opposed to Dumb BPM?" No, not dumb, per se, but blind. Whereas previous generations of BPM offered limited ability to make sense of business activity flows, iBPMS is distinguished foremost by a "sense and respond" orientation. This notion frames the Phase Three of BPM in terms of the synergistic combination of three groups of capabilities:

- **Phase One** – separating systems (application logic) from the processes (business logic) which they support;

- **Phase Two** – presenting a flexible architecture that supports adaptable, goal-driven process models by maintaining the intelligence for how to access information and application resources without having the bind this into a rigid process model; and

- **Phase Three** – building on the first two sets of capabilities while delivering visibility and feedback which shows what is going on within a process, as well as what will likely occur in the near future.

The first two phases of BPM have set a solid foundation for enabling adaptable systems, allowing BPM adopters to respond with far greater agility than ever before – moving away from the command-and-control structure which has defined management systems for the last 30 years.

For the first several years of the BPM market, these sorts of applications dominated. This also limited the potential market for BPM software, however, because for most firms the exception is the rule. The vast majority of business processes are dynamic, not standardized, and thus require the business systems (e.g., deployed software) that support them to adapt quickly to changes within the business environment. As a business technology, the greatest value of process management software is delivered not through automation and integration alone, but by introducing a layer between users and existing IT infrastructure to allow business systems to adapt and keep pace with the constant found in most business environments. Fully realizing the ability offered through orchestration, however, requires the 'situational awareness' necessary to adapt business systems to a changing business environment – the ability to sense and respond. By taking the lid off the black box of automation, the Phase Three of BPM offers a framework for continuously validating and refining an understanding of business performance drivers, and adapting business systems accordingly.

This will require a new level of transparency of processes and operations that is sure to present cultural and human factors challenges. But this is nothing new for BPM. At the end of the day BPM is only slightly about technology. It is, instead, mostly about the business and the people. What is indeed new, however, and at the center of the Phase Three opportunity, is the ability now to adapt systems continuously to match the ever-changing business environment. The model most frequently referenced throughout this chapter, this continuous loop of visibility and adaptability offers one of the first real leverage points for transforming business through adaptability.

## 2.  THE EVOLUTION OF INTELLIGENT BPM

To understand the opportunities offered by Intelligent Business Process Management, it's helpful to consider the phases of maturation solutions have gone through over the last decade. During technology expansion of the mid- to late-1990s, the management of business processes was typically limited to the repetitive sequencing of activities, with rigid, "hard-wired" application-specific processes such as those within ERP systems. Any more sophisticated degree of workflow management generally imposed a significant integration burden, frequently accounting for 60-80% of the project cost with little opportunity for reuse. Still, integration was typically limited to retrieval of data or documents, similarly hard-wired with one-to-one connection points.

These early process management initiatives often focused on integrating and automating repetitive processes, generally within standardized environments. Whether focused on Straight-Through Processing transactions or a discrete process such as Account Activation, these are applications where the flow and sequence of activities is predetermined and immutable. The role of exception handling here is to allow human intervention to quickly resolve or correct a break in the flow of an otherwise standard process.

By the end of the 1990s, however, BPM had emerged as an identifiable software segment, a superset of workflow management distinguished in part by allowing process management independent of any single application. This was enabled by managing application execution instructions separate from process flows, so processes could be defined without limitation to single application, as well as through support for variable versus hard-wired process flow paths.

The first wave of BPM deployments were typically aimed at bridging the island of automation described above, such as closing gaps in existing ERP deployments. Early BPM solutions were differentiated by integration-centric functionality, such as application adapters, data transformation capabilities and product-specific process definitions (e.g., an order-to-cash process). Eventually, the introduction of standards such as Web Services and advances in the development tools within BPM suites lowered the cost and complexity of data integration. This began to shift the fundamental value proposition of BPM from discrete capabilities to enabling the management of business logic by business process managers, without threatening the integrity of the application logic (the infrastructure that is rightfully managed and protected by IT personnel).

The availability of standards-based protocols significantly lowered the burden on BPM adopters for building and maintaining integration infrastructure, freeing time and resources to focus on the process and business performance, rather than being consumed with plumbing issues. Over time this facilitated a refocus of process management software from that of automation and integration to orchestration and coordination, bringing BPM into the realm of business optimization. Business environments are dynamic, requiring the business systems that support them to be so as well. This means that systems must be able to easily adapt to changing business circumstances.

Phase Two of the BPM opportunity was presented through making orchestration a reality – the ability to connect abstracted application capabilities across orchestrated business processes, thereby transforming existing automation infrastructure into reusable business assets. What separates orchestration from automation is presented by a fundamental shift in perspective, from thinking of processes as a flow of discrete steps, to understanding processes in terms of goals and milestones.

## 3. BEYOND INTEGRATION TO ORCHESTRATION

Orchestration allows systems to mirror the behavior of the rest of the business environment (one defined in terms of objectives rather than scripts). Over the last decade, orchestration has introduced a visible shift in the axis of business computing. As firms realize the opportunities presented by orchestration, it offers (arguably mandates) a wholesale rethinking of the role of applications and information systems.

Orchestration has already had a visible impact on the direction of the BPM market, enabled by standards protocols (notably XML and the core Web Services stack of SOAP, UDDI, and WSDL), the emergence of Service-Oriented Architectures (SOA) has provided a new level flexibility and simplicity in resolving integration issues. In fact it has to such an extent that it almost seems redundant to discuss in the context of forward-looking perspective of modern BPM.

Now we can nearly take for granted that the underlying systems of record are decoupled from how we access them – that access is enabled through a services layer rather than a programmatic interface that requires integration at the code level (i.e., "tightly-coupled"). What SOA provides for BPM and other software environments is a common means for communicating between applications, such that connections do not need to be programmed in advance. As long as the BPM environment knows where to find information and how to access it. This is critical to dynamic processes where the specific information, activities and roles involved with a process may not be predetermined but identified as the process progresses.

Of course this does require, however, that the information and infrastructure sought to be accessed is exposed as services. For example, core system capabilities can be exposed as containerized Web services with a WSDL description, able to be invoked by any Web services compliant application, or increasingly with a RESTful interface allowing integration points and data variables to be defined at design time, but resolved at run-time, eliminating the inherent problems of hard-wired integration.

## 4.   LEVERAGING CONTENT AS A SERVICE: INTEGRATING UNSTRUCTURED INFORMATION

While the evolution of Service-Oriented Architecture has dramatically improved the accessibly of structured information through standardized interfaces, access to unstructured information can be far more challenging. Consider for a moment where customers reside in your firm. The answer is most likely "everywhere" – records, transactions, profiles, project data, recent news, and other sources of structured and "semi-structured" information (such as correspondence and other documents without uniform representation). For many firms it would take years to rationalize all the places where customer data might be found. But by instead knowing where to find it and how it is described, it can be left intact yet used for multiple purposes.

Following the same strategy as is presented by SOA for accessing structured information, a relatively new standard called "Content Management Interoperability Services" or more commonly "CMIS" enables a services approach to "content middleware" by exposing information stored within CMIS-compliant content repositories, both internally and externally managed sources. As content is captured or otherwise introduced to a process, it can be automatically categorized and indexed based on process state and predefined rules and policies. This presents a virtual repository of both content and meta-data that describes how and where content is managed at various stages of its lifecycle. Meta-data is exposed to the system and process nodes, but invisible to users who instead are presented with the appropriate content and format based on their identity the current state of the process.

## 5.   SHIFTING FROM EVENT-DRIVEN TO GOAL-DRIVEN

The notion of orchestration has changed the role of BPM from that of a transit system designed to shuttle data from one point to another over predefined routes, to that of a virtual power user that "knows" how to locate, access and initiate application services and information sources. In contrast with more easily automated system-to-system processes and activities, "knowledge worker" processes characteristic of manual work involve a series of people-based activities that may individually occur in many possible sequences.

This transition in computing orientation can be described as the shift from *event-driven* where processes are defined in terms of a series of triggers, to *goal-driven* where processes are defined in terms of specific milestones and outcomes (goals) and constant cycles of adaptations required to achieve them. In event-driven computing, systems respond to a specific event – a request for information is received and the appropriate information is sent, or a process step is complete and so the results are recorded and the next step is initiated. In most cases, the nature of event-driven computing requires explicit scripting or programming of outcomes.

Goal-driven processes, however, are far more complex. A process that has only 20-30 unique activities, a relatively small number for most knowledge worker processes, may present over 1,000 possible permutations in the sequencing of activities. This of course presents too many scenarios to hard-code within linear process flows in advance, or to create a single process definition, which helps explain the difficulty traditionally faced in the automation of these types of goal-driven processes. Rather, this capability is enabled through the application of goals, policies and rules, while adjusting the flow of the process to accommodate outcomes not easily identifiable.

### Goal-Driven Scenarios

In many cases each subsequent step in a process is determined only by the outcome and other circumstances of the preceding step. In addition, there may be unanticipated parallel activities that occur without warning, and may also immediately impact the process and future (even previous) activities. For these reasons and the others described above, managing goal-driven processes requires the ability to define and manage complex policies and declarative business rules – the parameters and business requirements which determine the true "state" of a process. Goal-driven processes cannot be defined in terms of simple "flow logic" and "task logic" but must be able to represent intricate relationships between activities and information, based on policies, event outcomes, and dependencies (i.e, "context.")

Such a case is the admission of a patient for medical treatment. What is involved is in fact a process, yet the specific sequence and set of activities most does not follow a specific script, but rather is based on a diagnostic procedure which likely involves applying a combination of policies, procedures, other rules, and the judgment of healthcare workers. Information discovered in one step (e.g., the assessment a given condition) can drastically alter the next set of steps, and in the same way a change in 'patient state' (e.g., patient goes into heart failure) may completely alter the process flow in other ways.

The patient admission scenario described earlier is an example of this. What is needed to successfully execute an admission process is either a super user who knows both the medical protocols to make a successful diagnosis and the system protocols to know where and how to enter and access the appropriate information. Alternatively, BPM can exist as the virtual user layer, providing a single access point for the various roles involved, while assuming the burden of figuring out where and how access information.

Yet what really differentiates this as a goal-driven system is the ability to determine the sequence of a process based on current context. For example, a BPM system can examine appropriate business rules and other defined policies against the current status of a process or activity to determine what step should occur next and what information is required.

### Facilitating Better Decisions vs Mandating Actions

Often the flow and sequencing of a goal-driven process is determined largely by individual interpretation of business rules and policies. For example, a nurse who initiates a patient admitting process will evaluate both medical protocol and the policies of the facility where the healthcare services are administered. Similarly, an underwriter compiling a policy often makes decisions by referring to policy manuals or his own interpretation of rules and codes. As a result, what may be an otherwise 'standard' process will be distinguished by exceptions and pathways that cannot be determined in advance, but at each step each activity must nonetheless adhere to specific rules and policies.

## 6. PHASE THREE: INTELLIGENT BPM

The first two phases of BPM laid a solid foundation for enabling adaptable business systems, by allowing business logic (processes, policies, rules, etc.) to be defined and managed within a separate environment, as well as using an open approach to communicating with other systems (Web Services). This has provided a level of adaptability that allows BPM adopters to respond to changes in the business environment with far greater agility than ever before.

This shift towards goal-oriented computing has laid the path for Phase-Three BPM, which combines integration and orchestration with the ability to continuously validate and refine the business users' understanding of business performance drivers, and allowing them to adapt business systems and process flows accordingly. The effect of Phase Three BPM is to 'take the lid off' what has for years been a black box shrouding automation.

With the third phase of BPM, visibility combines with integration and orchestration to enable business process owners and managers to discover the situation changes which require adaptation. Phase Three of BPM offers a framework for continuously validating and refining an understanding of business performance drivers, and adapting business systems accordingly. This should represent in a new and significantly greater level of interest and adoption of BPM software, by attracting firms seeking to optimize business performance, rather than integrating and automating systems and tasks.

Part of the recent evolution towards iBPMS technology is inclusion of more sophisticated reporting capabilities within the BPM environment itself. This is both enabled and in many way necessitated by the greater flexibility of the architectures introduced with the BPM suites that define Phase Two. With these environments, the ability to support non-sequential, goal-driven models is greatly increased, requiring more feedback (reporting) to enable success execution of this type of less deterministic process models.

With few exceptions, reporting on process events and business performance was previously done only after a process had executed, or otherwise within a separate environment disjointed from the process. This obviously prevented any opportunity to impact the direction or a process, but was based on a limitation of system and software architectures. Specifically with regard to BPM, process models were most commonly defined as proprietary structures, and in many cases compiled into software. Thus, changes either required bringing down and recompiling an application, or were otherwise limited to discrete points in the process (such as exceptions and yes/no decision points).

## 7. BPM AND SOCIAL MEDIA

In an era when an aberrant Tweet can in a matter of minutes costs shareholders millions, it is the meta-context of business events across a spectrum of structured, unstructured, and semi-structured information that defines the larger perspective of business activity. The impact of mobile and social capabilities in enterprise systems, as well as external social networks is having a very real material impact on business. It has become critical (even if comparatively smaller but clearly growing) piece of the business event stream.

Most workers have access to outside information, and already no doubt incorporate this to their existing work patterns. They do this because the information available through Google, Wikipedia, and specific blogs is no doubt more comprehensive, more current, and likely more accurate than internal sources when it comes to topics and events occurring outside of the organization, and in some cases even those happening on the inside. This is because these sources benefit from socialization – the continuous scrutiny, fact-checking and updating offered by the surrounding social network.

Here trust and reputation represent the critical leverage points for the value of information, as there is no top-down governance nor authentication of information would otherwise be expected in a corporate setting. The information in question is only as valuable as the trust in and reputation of its authors – and typically not the originators but the network in place to vet.

Trust and reputation hardly play any role at all in the command-and-control world of process automation. A control flow token travels down a predefined path from one node and another, and with passes control without bias or prejudice. Often a manager sits above multiple running processes, detached from front lines, and may engage in 'load balancing' by shifting work items from one subordinates queue to another. Perhaps just as common an occurrence is circumstances where work performed on a given activity is preceded by the labor of someone else, with having no specific awareness nor concern of the others' reputation, nor any opportunity to act on it if they did. The modeled processes that provide the foundation of BPMS environments today, rarely take into account either the existence or lack of trust and reputation in the design of routing logic.

In social media, however, trust and reputation are key. It is these two factors that offer the crucial leverage point for the success of any social endeavor. Within a social network we pick and chose our partners not on firsthand experience typically, but rather on their respective positioning within a broader framework of familiar relationships. We make decisions about accepting links, becoming 'friends' and passing on information based who they know that who we know. It is highly unlikely anyone would respond favorably to a request from any individuals with whom there is no means to validate reputation or any other basis to establish trust.

Can you believe everything you read on the Internet? No, of course not. Yet this is the very point of social media – that the network of 'antibodies' represented by the crowd of linked individuals, in many cases with no more association than their affinity or membership to that particular network, will systemically attack and expunge any infection of misinformation. Through this socialization, like a well-functioning immune system, only accurate details are spared, or otherwise the infected data is sufficiently discredited such that it is immediately obvious what is credible and what is not.

The way that social computing can have the greatest impact on the execution of work is by applying the same social computing and social media concepts to business processes. Specifically, it is the ability to leverage the collective insight of a group, network or 'crowd' of individuals. In this way the network functions as an organizational immune system, not as controlled group, managed by top-down authority, but rather as a social community. The value and validation offered through this type of intra-organizational socialization can be grouped into one of three forms:

- **Social Modeling** -- leveraging social media conventions within process discovery and modeling to engage stakeholders or otherwise deliver better validated results than possible through traditional analysis.

- **Social Collaboration** – leveraging internal social networks to form goal-driven, virtual teams who collaborate and 'socialize' around a given activity or set of activities.

- **Social Chatter** – leveraging collections of events and event data from either or both internal and external networks to inform decisions or otherwise generate actionable information within a business process.

Social Modeling is one of the first recognizable instances of leveraging enterprise social software within BPM, a practice that is has been for at least a decade prior to the emergence of contemporary social media. For example, the "*Collaborative Distributed Scenario and Process Analyzer (ColD SPA)*" was a research project launched over a decade ago, premised on the notion that involvement of key personnel during process modeling is necessary for both model accuracy and gaining stakeholder buy-in, yet despite this models are most commonly developed by small teams due to inherent the complexity and difficulties involved in the modeling process.

Specifically, both the methods behind process modeling and the tools used to support it impose an inevitable learning curve, which either leaves out key stakeholders or otherwise requires meditation by "modeling professionals" who must interpret and explain details, thereby both slowing the process and risking biasing the result. The *ColD SPA* prototype was developed to demonstrate how a web-based tool could be used to facilitate the engagement of stakeholders directly within the modeling and discovery process.

### The Cathedral and the Bazaar

It is often said that process models have three states – the "as-is," the "to-be," and "the way it is really done." When modeling is left to subject matter experts, only a limited view of potential improvements is presented. Worse yet, the reality-based view of how things actually work in practice is typically omitted, leaving only an idealized (and often naively ignorant) definition of the as-is state. Without an accurate baseline, the desired to-be state will be more difficult to win support for and likely difficult to realize in the practice.

Simply adding to the mix a rarified group of chieftains (political stakeholders versus actual end users) to weigh-in with their opinions and observations may offer a better understanding of things, but falls short of true socialization. It is unlikely to provide for the serendipitous discovery of potential process improvements, or new processes, which arise from normal interaction (i.e., not as a part a formal discovery session) of workers within a social network. A model for this is presented in how Open Source Software (OSS) is developed, as described by Eric Raymond in his seminal work, "The Cathedral and The Bazaar." Raymond distinguishes between the traditional model of *The Cathedral*, where software is managed by a formal governance model, where access between releases is limited to discrete group of anointed stakeholders, as the case with project-led modeling efforts; and *The Bazaar* where electronically connected, yet otherwise officially unacquainted users offer continuous scrutiny and, in the case of OSS development, add periodic improvements (patches, bug fixes, et al.) as a currency for encouraging other contribution.

The result is a shift away from the centrally managed, command-economy model that governs traditional development practices, to a market-based approach where broader functionality and higher quality software is realized through many small contributions and improvements offered by the larger pool of software consumers. This is essentially the same concept pursued by the first wave of social-enabled BPM platforms, which provide not just a platform for collaborative modeling, which alone does little to transcend the cathedral model, yet also enable 'the bazaar' by connecting a much larger pool of users to connect through private and public communities.

These platforms allow users to post events in a familiar *Facebook Wall* medium, which allow other users to comment on and otherwise identify either existing or proposed process models, post documents and other information, as well as to compose working models based on 'snippets' of prebuilt software functionality.

### Beyond the Virtual Water Cooler

The term "Social Collaboration" may at first appear redundant. After all, what collaboration isn't social? The answer is found, however, not in how collaboration is delivered, but how collaborating parties connect in the first place. It is in this regard that BPM offering Social Collaboration depart from other forms of Computer-Supported Collaboration (CSC) such as 'chat' and email, which require pathways to be preordained and typically lack any business process context. Today's more robust BPM environments provide the ability identify and connect with the relevant experts, not already integrated within the business process flow, but to do so within the work space of the BPMS (i.e., to enable ad hoc collaboration within the execution of a business process task.)

A business user can leverage internal social networks as well as a ranked organization chart to enlist the help of individuals outside of the standard process flow to complete a given task. This may include creating a temporary collaboration space organize individuals and related information around the completion of a given task.

Ideally, and an important distinction between BPM-enable Social Collaboration and generic white-boarding, what occurs within this space should remain as part of the permanent audit trail of the process instance, including even a virtual representation of the space itself and all accessed information saved in the form of a case folder.

This latter ability is an example of how BPM enables Case Management, with regard to both the capture of process context and information, as well as the ability to invoke guidance at any given time in the process through the identification and engagement of outside experts. The ability to recall through the audit trail individuals proven helpful in similar circumstances (but not otherwise associated with a given process task) illustrates how trust and reputation can be leveraged in the completion of a business process managed within a BPMS environment. Ideally, individuals' past performance and/or ranking by past collaboration partners is captured by the platform and represented as part of the social network hierarchy.

### Divining Business Process From Business Activity Streams

A founding principal of business process management is that business activities must occur within the process itself to be manageable. This thinking originates in the Taylorist meme that you cannot improve what you cannot measure, and by extension you cannot measure what occurs within the ad hoc, unstructured realm outside of the process model. Yet it is a fact that much if not most of business activity occur in the white space outside the boundaries of a predefined process model.

Streams of discrete activities or events collectively represent the "Social Chatter" that define backdrop of every business. Yet the ability to capture, filter, analyze and ultimately leverage collections of such events and/or associated event data to inform decisions and otherwise generate actionable information within a business process is a notable value point of BPM. This capability is premised on the "Wall" concept that was first popularized by Facebook and is now arguably the most recognized (and in demand) aspects of social computing. The event stream allows users to subscribe to events, which may be either manual (individually authored) or automated (machine generated) event entries, as well as to filter these by various categories corresponding to event tags.

The event stream represents an efficient way to quickly communicate business data to business users, typically including the ability to deliver the same format to mobile devices. Leveraging social interaction within the BPM user interface extends the reach of BPM beyond the traditional worklist metaphor and desktop environments common to previous generations of business software, supporting real-time view into business activity.

Why does this matter? Because a fundamental value point of all BPM is the ability to accelerate response time to business events. Early modality process improvement focused on the low hanging fruit of automatable activities. Yet most events today occur outside of the realm of what can modeled in advance. The next wave of performance improvement will come from generating real-time analytics from business activity streams (both internal and external) and connecting these to the type of closed-loop environment offered by BPM. Although the exact metrics vary between specific events and individual organizations, in virtually every case the value realizable through response to event declines sharply as soon as the event occurs. The faster the response, the greater the realizable value. The total reaction time from the discovery of an event to the moment that that action is taken can grouped into three categories:

✓ **Data Latency** - *delays capturing event from operations*

✓ **Analysis Latency** - *delays translating events into analytics*

✓ **Decision Latency** - *delays acting on analytics*

Traditionally, the greatest loss of value occurs in the delay in capturing the event (such as recording the event in a transactional system.) Here significant value can be preserved by capturing the event in real-time, such as by using a Social Chatter capability as illustrated on the previous page. Reducing latency here offers the greatest historic benefit, however, value is also lost in the analysis and time elapsed before action is taken.

In the context of BPM with social capabilities, an event can be actionable almost as soon as it occurs. This again involves tagging the event at the source, so that context is preserved, and as a result the need for additional analysis is diminished. The event appears within a stream on your handheld device, and with it context linked to either an individual or another point of origin that allows you to quickly assess the best response. From that event you may launch a corresponding process, or leverage Social Collaboration to enlist the support of experts within your network.

### *Time-based Value of Business Event Response*

Regardless of the specific circumstances involved, the value of the response is greater closest to the moment of the complaint, diminishes over time and after a certain period in time, any response is going to be of little value. There is not a single set of hard metrics for all organizations, or all events, but in every case, there is predictable value gained from the ability to capture an event. It could be related to a sales opportunity, or field maintenance, or terrorist threat, in every case the faster the response the greater the value.

It can be assumed that the ability to take action on a specific event will always involve some delay. Yet there is a similar inevitability that the value lost as a result of that delay will follow a utility curve, not a straight line. Thus, the greatest source of value will always come from faster notification and action-ability, rather than faster decision-making.

The value of faster decisions (automating the function of knowledge workers in the decision-making process) offers little value, particularly when compared to the cost of poor decisions made in haste. Because of the greater the delay in notification and actionability, there is greater pressure on making decisions sooner rather than losing further value. Yet the opportunity lies in reducing Infrastructure Latency. By getting actionable information into the hands of knowledge workers sooner, iBPMS systems offer a predictable source of business value and clear differentiation from passive systems (i.e., notification only, without the ability to facilitate a response.)

Yet clearly not all events by themselves alone are actionable. By using event filtering and associating metrics based on the relative trust and reputation of event originators, collections of events can be grouped into meaningful patterns which may in aggregate represent an actionable outcome not otherwise visible through the examination of events individually.

## 8. WHY BPM IS CRITICAL TO HOW WE MANAGE CONTENT

Over the last decade most, small and medium, and certainly nearly all large enterprises have invested in some combination of Electronic Document Management (EDM), Web Content Management (WCM), and/or Enterprise Content Management (ECM). As these environments are increasingly converging, we will refer to them collectively as "ECM."

ECM offers a critical tool by helping organizations keep pace with the explosive growth of unstructured information; an ever-expanding volume of content that shows no signs of letting up. ECM has become a popular source for introducing workflow management to the organization. Typically this includes document routing and approval workflows, capturing the steps involved in creating a document, or automating a basic process such as a travel request or expense report.

What ECM provides is governance and integrity of content and data. Outside of controlling access and authorization (i.e., who gets to see what), what ECM doesn't provide is *governance of work* – managing how that content and data is used in the course of business. For this reason, if you've got ECM, then inevitably what you also have is a workflow management capability, but to optimally improve and automate how you manage content and your business processes, what you need is BPM.

BPM provides the means for connecting the content from within ECM and other System of Records (SORs) to an underlying process where that content is both used and created. In this way, BPM provides a transactional thread for managing this information across processes that inevitably span different applications, and often organizational boundaries. It allows for control of not necessarily the content and information, but rather how it is used in business operations.

For example, in common business processes such as "order to cash" and "procure to pay" there is a combination of (SORs) involved. Data and information (i.e., both structured and unstructured content) define the order in terms of financial details and customer, as well as other information likely stored within an ECM repository and other SORs. Yet none of these systems alone has the complete picture, end-to-end across the process lifecycle. In contrast, what BPM provides is a consistent transactional "thread" enabling end-to-end management and visibility out of reach by any of the underlying systems.

BPM in essence is the practice of managing business operations in terms of processes, which span application, departmental, and even organizational boundaries, and which are specifically managed within a "BPMS" or "Business Process Management System". During earlier days of business computing and enterprise IT, it was recognized that the practice of managing data within the applications where it was used presented significant business risk. In particular, breaks in the continuity of data between applications, and the potential for corruption or lack of concurrency. For this reason is it was determined early in the history of IT that data should be managed separate from applications, as part of a common Database Management System or DBMS.

This notion has been fundamental to IT architecture for the last 40 years. Yet just as the notion of abstracting data from applications has defined traditional IT, modern Enterprise Information Management (EIM) understands the need to abstract processes and business logic in the same way with a BPMS layer.

BPM systems offer an ideal platform for process automation, in particular with regard to repetitive processes involved with well-defined structured data, creating *efficiency* through automation and *effectiveness* through consistent performance. These types of processes are generally characterized as rarely changing, with their integration points well-established, and often associated with existing transactional systems.

Combining BPM with existing application-specific workflow automation allows the combination of organized process structures with backend interfaces, creating a system of record for both business data entities and the content involved. From an information management point of view, the resulting fully auditable log includes the complete context and history of the evolving data flow. It is this same consolidation of elements – content, policies/rules, and information access – that distinguishes BPM from other information software systems and allows the representation of the entire process lifecycle.

In this way, BPM provides the core platform through which various information sources and repositories can be integrated. As communications have become increasing digital (or digitized) and as interaction with customers are now more often taking place within an electronic media, ensuring consistency of communication across multiple application environments and back repositories (e.g. ERP, CRM, ECM, WCM, etc.) is critical.

Again, it is not only likely you have ECM already but chances are there are multiple domain-specific SORs in place for specific business areas, such as *Procurement, HR, regulatory filings*, or discrete business areas. In addition it

is likely there are departmental and even potentially redundant ECM repositories. Across all of these, BPM offers a consistent transactional thread for
teams to collaborate transparently and securely through the organization of
structured and unstructured business data and content – following the process lifecycle rather than sticking within the confines of application silos. This
also means having a consistent user experience, following the same transactional thread and end-to-end process with a common user interface.

## 9. BPM AND CASE MANAGEMENT

The ability to deliver a common user interface and user experience across
multiple applications is a critical advantage of BPM over ECM and workflow.
Further, the end-to-end process lifecycle is both information-intensive and in-
herently data-driven. It inevitably involves the capture of information that
leads to actions being taken and decisions made that can be fully anticipated
in advance.

It requires a balance between that which can and should be predefined and
automated. This approach is a reflection of the increasing complexity and un-
predictability of knowledge work, which is what we increasingly referred to as
"Case Management." Although there is sometimes confusion of the use of this
term, case management as a general notion and application type has been
around for decades, however, in this case we are referring to the modern man-
ifestation, typical called "Adaptive" or "Dynamic Case Management", which today represents an essential capability of modern BPM platforms.

Where workflow automation and even the first generation of BPM systems follow specifically a pre-defined process route, a predefined path for each item –
modern BPM supports the combination of workflow automation with facilita-
tion of ad hoc or collaborative knowledge work (e.g., not predefined or structured) that has been out of reach to work management software.

In this way BPM and Case Management enable great transparency into collaborative processes, as well as more effective prioritization of tasks when
managing activities across multiple cases and workloads. BPM facilitates this
by presenting a more unified interface across application silos, offering a sin-
gle-access-point to information trapped within legacy systems, but needed by
knowledge workers, or even customers, with modern "anywhere, any device"
expectations.

The key to successful automation is to provide a balance between relieving the
burden of repetitive drudgery and "busy work" (e.g., to reduce this through
automation) without being overly restrictive over the aspects of work that
should otherwise allow for user control and input. BPM offers the combination
of offloading repetitive and predictable tasks to automation, while allowing
knowledge workers to make smart choices and apply best practices in their
decision-making that is the essence of the value being created.

BPM offers an opportunity for evolution and modernization in order to keep
pace with rapid advances in mobile, social and cloud computing; an opportunity to build bridges between the current islands of automation by utilizing
the case focus to combine isolated processes. It presents a realistic and practical "future-proofing" for enterprise IT. Below is a summary table which highlights some of the core differences between ECM and Workflow and BPM and
Case Management, in particular with regard to how information is shared and
capabilities are delivered.

|  | ECM and Workflow | BPM and Case Management |
|---|---|---|
| **Scope** | Single application, document or form; data and object model specific to application or document, not shared. | Common UI and transactional thread spanning multiple applications and process lifecycle; data structures based on process definition (process instance data) and separate from "payload" or applications where work is performed. |
| **Security** | Application-specific security, or authorization based on document-specific or form-specific processes. | Security bound to roles defined by process swim lanes and the activities they contain; role-based security applied to case folder, content, as well as fine-grain control of work items. |
| **Analytics** | Work item specific reporting, limited to a single document, repository, or application. | Advanced analytics enable identification and reuse of patterns and exceptions, operational visibility. |
| **Data Integration** | Typically data is based on form fields (specific fields within and electronic form) or otherwise application-specific data fields. Data is typically entered or viewed via these forms and not accessible as a shared service or system-to-system resource. | Connectors are provided to integrate external data into the virtual case folder and case record; Data can be manipulated (extracted and transformed or "CRUD" operations) if data structures are defined in the process or as part of external services. |

## 10. GETTING STARTED

The starting point for any BPM initiative is typically the most critical event in determining the project's success. It can also be one of the most challenging and frustrating periods as teams grapple with issues such as which process to target, what politics are involved, and often simply how and where to get started in the first place. Certainly no one plans to fail. Yet with any type of project, IT-oriented or otherwise, success is by no means a certainty, and in fact for BPM in particular, it occurs less than half the time. Last year BPM.com released market research which showed that BPM-related initiatives succeeded less than 50% of the time, which is consistent with other analysts' cited failure rates.

To be clear, this should in no way detract from the potential value of BPM, nor is this failure rate necessarily higher than other business and technology areas. This is particularly true with the introduction of technologies with similarly far-reaching impact on business operations, as seen with BPM. In all such cases, providing a specific plan for success in the form of a Project Charter and mutually understood success criteria is essential. For BPM specifically, however, the BPM.com research offers further guidance for getting it right when getting started, by avoiding the common pitfalls most commonly associated with failed projects. Listed in order of frequency of mention, these are:

1. Failure to Define Realistic Boundaries

2. Resistance by End Users and Stakeholders

3. Lost Executive Sponsorship

Sponsorship can be lost through attrition or a significant change of assignment. Yet the fact is that executives have short attention spans, and if they're not seeing the results they were looking for they will move on to something or someone else. Traditionally the most common issue dooming any new initiative is cultural resistance; stakeholders and end users don't want to participate or feel they were left out of the process and they rebel. You built it, but they didn't come. One of the critical factors for this is ensuring they are engaged from the outset. Yet the most common pitfall is found in failure to define realistic expectations and boundaries at the outset. Scope creep dooms any project. With BPM typically this is an overshoot for processes where the processes and associated rules are too far-reaching, too complex and it becomes politically intractable to reach agreement on how the process(es) should be defined and performed.

When getting started with any new BPM initiative, avoiding these common pitfalls is not simply a matter of luck, but should be a deliberate strategy – there should be a well-defined and explicit plan for success. This success place should be part of a charter established at the outset. Whether a formal "Project Charter" or simply written memo setting expectations with stakeholders and the project sponsor, the charter will set the direction and tone for the project, and should be documented in clear and specific terms, identifying how and why the project will succeed, as well as how and when success will be measured. In order to offer the best chances for success, there are **seven best practices** that should be followed when getting started with BPM.

### *Practice #1: Select the Right Starting Point*

Selecting the right starting point is critical to project's success. Yet this less about the process itself, but rather about the momentum created by demonstrating early proof-points and benefits. As a starting point, **avoid** processes that are *already well-defined*, are *overly complex*, or are *politically-charged*.

Instead, seek out identify opportunities and processes that are characterized as *paper-intensive*, involving tasks done on a *frequent basis* (daily), lacking a rigid or controversial definition, and that offer an *immediate* and *measurably positive impact* on stakeholders and end users.

Once you have the momentum, proof-points, and the wisdom of experience from initial success, then go back and tackle the more difficult process improvement opportunities. Your starting point is the solid platform on which everything that follows will rest; it needs to make perfect sense in terms of your project aims and goals, offer a basis for the value you're looking for and (naturally) you need enough of the right resources to make it work. And as you're unlikely to be doing this solo, don't forget stakeholder engagement; the process you choose has to be compelling – if it doesn't grab the interest, it won't garner the support.

Filter your options by asking yourself a few 'reality' questions: Is this process something that is so politically impractical that you couldn't touch it? Is it something that you're going to be able to use again? Is it visible and likely to make stakeholder's lives better? Lastly, will successful transformation make heroes of those engaged in the process throughout the organization? Don't underestimate the importance of the last point. The ideal starting point will generate excitement and momentum because stakeholders will understand what's in it for them, and will work with your project team to help ensure your success. This is also why it is important to engage them in the prioritization process, as outlined below.

### Rank Process Targets with Stakeholders

Work with stakeholders in a white-boarding session (or some other visual means) to identify and prioritize processes, ranking them in terms of both the impact and value they offer if addressed effectively, as well as the relative complexity involved in doing so. You're striving for a target area that is likely to generate excitement and demonstrable value, yet is not so complex that it will otherwise set you up for failure.

Consider the difficulty of each process option – but not in terms of the effort involved in performing the process, but rather how resistant people will be to changing it. Asking that will reveal aspects of how change will be implemented. Can you define the vision for how it will be different? Are there mutually agreeable metrics for improvement, such as cycle time reduction, quality improvement, greater capacity or lower resulting costs?

Ultimately the goal is to strike a balance between demonstrability and achievability. It must be clearly visible and offer real value, yet do so within a time frame short enough to keep stakeholders engaged and on board.

### Practice #2: Set Process Boundaries to Control Scope

Keeping in mind that the most commonly cited pitfall was the failure to set realistic boundaries, defining the end-points of the process is critical from the outset. This is important both for the likelihood of success, as well as for the ability to demonstrate that success. It is also possible that the original target process is later determined to be excessively complex. In this case, look for ways to separate out an addressable proportion of the larger process, work with that to demonstrate proof-points for the benefits of BPM, and then use that as a leverage point to go after the other process equivalent.

### Practice #3: Starting With Words Before Pictures

One of the common misperceptions of Case Management is that there is no upfront modeling involved. This is far from the truth; you will need to engage in a considerable amount of modeling of business rules, data models, and screenflows.

There will also be modeled workflows, including both automated processes for structured, repetitive tasks, and conceptual process models that may not be explicitly scripted within the system but are nonetheless an important part of the requirements definition. Of course the same is true for BPM, where most of the system's capabilities will be defined within process models.

Yet when you're trying to find the real starting point, you can't begin by drawing diagrams with boxes and lines. The starting point to the starting point is a written understanding of the target process; a written narrative. When writing your narrative, you need to answer (among others) the following questions:

What are the outcomes that this process provides? What are the data and the resources that are dry in these processes? What are the specific activities? What are the roles of those who will be involved? A written narrative keeps things clear as you move forward and add the details and additional information during the decision-making process.

### Identifying Goals, Outcomes, Resources, and Participants

In order to narrow down the options, it's time to break things down and draw up a list of what capabilities will be enabled by the solution as a business function. First, begin by specifying the "what" in terms of the expected outcomes and the required capabilities to achieve them. Second, establish the "why" and "how" of the system from the perspective of stakeholders and system interactions. Ask yourself the following key questions: Who's performing it? What data did they create? What data did they need and what are they actually doing with it? What are the actions—the transformations, verbs, actual performers? Differentiating the "who"s and the "what"s of specific roles and specific individuals is a vital part of choosing the right process.

### Practice #4: Asking the Right Questions

The sequence of the questions that you ask is as important as the questions themselves. "What?" questions give you the facts, the realities; answer those first and then it's safe to move on to the "Why?" questions that can otherwise distract you with their baggage, drawing you towards political factors. "Why?" questions must be answered but not until you've gone into the measurable and quantifiable triggers and dependencies that the "What?" questions can give you first.

### Start With What's and Who's

In the narrative, we identify the elements needed to create your own model. A crucial step is to identify the various "who"s, their roles and the role details, then define and expand on those details. Once the first layer is clear, follow the trail to the next "who", their role, and so on. There is always a path of triggers, clues, and rules to be followed and it's that path that will tell you what questions to ask and in what order.

### Then Ask the Why's, When's, and White Space

After the "who"s and the "what"s have been detailed, it's time to move on to the "why"s, "when"s, and white space. Filling in these fine detail gaps is an integral element to understanding the ins and outs of what is occurring within the process.

### Practice #5: Leverage User-Centered Design

Technology is seductive and a common mistake (despite its apparent obviousness) made with BPM initiatives is to focus on the technology and its functionality as opposed to how it is used. Yet the focus on the "how" is critical to understanding the user's perspective. For the user, it's not about what the system does, it's all about how to use it and – more importantly – why they should. Creating personas which represent not just use cases but specifically a "day in the life of" perspective of actual users, will result in a solution which faces far less user and cultural resistance, leading to fewer change management and training requirements and ultimately, significantly improved user adoption rates and productivity.

Identification precedes engagement; first of all, identify the users and stakeholders for your BPM or Case Management project. There are four broad categories in any BPM project: builders, managers, participants, and customers (and in each of those groups there may exist subgroups). Of key importance is that you use this identification or mapping stage to create a unique user experience tailored to the needs of each group. The secret to keeping each group fully engaged is to present them with a 'noise-free' user experience which offers minimal distractions from their own concerns.

### Practice #6: Early Involvement Reduces Overall Risk

One of the most promising approaches for introducing BPM is by leveraging the methods associated with Agile development. Agile emphasizes delivering demonstrable results quickly and in tight, measureable increments that engage business stakeholders.

The emphasis on early and on-going validation allows much greater alignment with the business than is afforded with alternative approaches. In particular on critical matters such as prioritizing the order that capabilities are delivered, as well as the validation of assumptions made during discovery. Early involvement in the project also helps to increase user adoption, because involvement creates a sense of familiarity and shared ownership (and therefore responsibility for success).

Another hallmark of Agile methods is the notion of continuous testing, and combined with stakeholder engagement, the result is to effectively conduct usability testing at each stage, allowing usability issues to be identified much earlier and be more easily resolved. This results in more successful outcomes, as well as more cost-effective effort – not because there is less work per se, but rather less re-work because the consistent validation ensures development is closely aligned with the business stakeholder's goals and expectation. Whether your organization or project team formally embraces Agile, engage stakeholders early and often.

### Conduct a Regular Stakeholder Workshops

While the notion of a "focus group" might sound clichéd, there is still no more efficient way to obtain agreement on the goals and success criteria than face-to-face discussion. Workshops should be held at regular intervals, and specifically from the outset of the initiative, to identify expectations, as well as validate findings during discovery and analysis.

Then, at the focus group, ask the stakeholders to describe to you the high level process; this will enable you to begin to map out the process. The focus group environment also can be used to explore the mission of the group that owns the process, who their customers are, what the inputs and outputs are, and – most importantly – you can begin to identify their goals and prioritize them.

### Practice #7: Measure from the Start

As the old adage says: "You can't improve what you can't measure" so what better time to start measuring than the beginning? However, in order to begin to measure, you need clarity on the project specifications and the expected improvements. Put another way, you need to know how success is defined for your project. And there's the link back to Practice #2, your identified stakeholders, users and sponsors are there to help identify and (importantly) agree to the measures.

By keeping measurement in mind from the start, you ensure that you don't begin your process improvement project with a missing target. Of course, it is equally important that your chosen yardstick correlates with the objectives of the project – the business goals that prompted it in the first place.

### Defining Performance Metrics and Success Criteria

The defining feature of a good metric is its objective and consistent measurability coupled with an easy comprehension by even the least technically-minded stakeholder – improvements should not only be made but be visibly made. It should be simple, elegant and effective. In fact, the more obvious the metric is, the more it effectively becomes the business case. If, by the nature of the measurement, the improvement to stakeholders' and users' lives is self-evident, no more persuasion will be needed.

Linking back to Practice #3, a key enabler in setting metrics and measurements is getting the narrative right. Part of the narrative exercise is developing a common vocabulary for all those involved in the project - a 'controlled vocabulary' or common lexicon. A single shared language is critical to project success and can give you a lateral route to consensus between different stakeholder factions. Focusing too heavily on achieving consensus on how things work can stymie the discovery process. Yet a common vocabulary lays the groundwork for agreement via the more neutral element of terminology. Along the way, as part of the discussions, you'll also be establishing agreement on the parameters of the process, the metrics, measurement techniques, and ultimately, the whole project.

### Identify and Quantify Your Goals

Goal definition drives the design activity. The first step in quantifying and analyzing project goals is to list the possible improvements that can be made. What are the goals, what was the priority that the team assigned to them, and what's the current situation? Then, when you start to map out the new process, factor in the technologies available to you as well as what you can bring to bear to clean up the end user experience. Now you're starting to list your potential proposed solutions. Do so in detail and try to establish a clear picture of the impact of each possibility. To continuously improve and simplify the process, be prepared to revisit your goals and flesh-out work that doesn't not added any measurable value. An often underutilized but highly effective tool, simulation can be used as a means to sell improvements. Simulation can be an effective sales technique for convincing stakeholders of project benefits; making them visible, demonstrable and showing how the process would be improved. It is equally powerful in the discovery phase of the project; highlighting how the process will perform under different workloads, doing well-depth analysis with processes and establishing improvement targets that may have, otherwise, been overlooked. Simulation is objective and moves the spotlight away from any particular user group or set of stakeholder requirements and effectively de-politicizes the project by focusing on design rather than individual bottleneck stages. By avoiding putting the focus on any one group of stakeholders, end users, subject-matter experts and so on, you encourage true collaboration because no one group has more to lose than the rest.

Planning is ultimately the most critical success factor. As we said earlier, no one plans to fail but it is fair to note that many fail to plan well enough to succeed and the three main factors that trip them up are: failure to define the project; end user and stakeholder resistance; and a lack of executive sponsorship. You will inevitably have a project plan, yet beyond the standard Gantt chart and work breakout structure should be a specific plan for success.

This includes having the stated (written) metrics for how and when success will be measured, agreed to and acknowledged by stakeholders and the project sponsor. As part of this plan, you should be prepared to demonstrate value within the first 90 days. Anything beyond this timeframe will be at risk of losing critical momentum, potentially even sponsorship. Your plan should involve the seven practices to counteract the common pitfalls of failing to define realistic boundaries, facing resistance by end users or stakeholders, and the loss of executive sponsorship.

## 11. The 90-Day Action Plan For Getting Started With BPM

In the first 30 days, you will identify the starting point, the scope and boundaries, validate these collaboratively with stakeholders, and define the core goals, outcomes, resources, and participants. The critical outcome of this phase is establishing scope and boundaries. You may adjust the definition of some capabilities or expectations as you proceed, and may descope to some degree (e.g., postpone capabilities for a subsequent development cycle) but under no circumstances should you be expanding scope beyond this phase.

Depending on the scope and goals of your initiative you may "go live" and deploy to production in 90 days, or you may be providing just the first major proof-point of a series of releases. The benefit of both BPM is that it is not a "once and done" proposition but an iterative process for rolling out a series of capabilities. Yet ensuring success for projects small or large requires identifying and sticking to what can be predictably achieved in the first 90 days.

In the next 30 days, you will engage in more discovery to develop a complete narrative, expanding this through more stakeholder workshops to develop the "look and feel" of the solution, working from the users' perspective consistent with user-centered design. During this phase you have the benefit of requirements and scope being fixed, and you now focus on realizing these within the solution. In the final 30 days, you will have the benefit of already having clearly defined expectations for what will be delivered, and focus is now on demonstrating the achievement of the defined goals and visible metrics. You will have defined when the demonstration of capability will take place and how success will be measured. Find the right process and always, always ask yourself the right honest questions. Keep your users and stakeholders at the center of the project and have involvement as your watchword; encourage them to own their input and their influence and watch the project succeed as they buy in. Measurement is key and the right metrics are worth their weight in project gold because they will convince (and keep on board) even the most troublesome stakeholders and sponsors. Knowing what success will look like before you even begin will help you achieve it.

## 12. Common BPM Pitfalls To Avoid

    ×   ***Missing the Opportunity of Repeatability:*** *although much if not all of the business case is calculated based on a single iteration or otherwise a discrete focus of the BPM initiative, the real value comes from developing a repeatable practice area or Center of Excellence; the first phase of the project should be proof-point for future opportunities.*

- × ***Following the Path of Least Resistance****: it is telling if a project lacks sponsors and more than likely it means more time needs to be spent on the business case. Sponsors who do not otherwise scrutinize an incomplete business case are merely setting the project up for failure.*

- × ***Ignoring or Otherwise Neglecting Stakeholders When Validating Process Designs****: one of the best and traditionally underutilized resources for validating the process are the stakeholders themselves, not just business process owners but end users.*

- × ***Letting "Great" be the Enemy of "Good Enough" in the First Pass****: do not fall into the trap of "analysis paralysis" in the first pass of the 'current state' process definition; get something 'good enough' out in front of the stakeholders who can tell you how it really works.*

- × ***Selecting Cheap or Free BPM Technology Over the Ability to Leverage Existing Skill Sets****: sometimes "free" BPM is the most expensive option; look for alignment with resources and objectives over price.*

- × ***Assuming Sponsorship is There When its Not****: too often wishful thinking takes over and project teams assume sponsorship is committed when it is not; do whatever is necessary to eliminate ambiguity surrounding budgets and ownership.*

## 13. GAINING AND MAINTAINING PROJECT SPONSORSHIP

After nearly a decade of market research on what drives BPM implementations, the answer for what *prevents* them is consistently "lack of sponsorship" by upper management. In other words, the single largest hurdle to BPM implementation is cited as finding someone (an executive or a department) to pay for it. Often departmental teams find the opportunity but not the resources to implement a BPM project, and are unable to win management support despite what may be to them an obvious need or potential benefit.

There is no doubt that budget plays a role in whether or not sponsorship is found. Yet another factor is the perception of career endangerment. For many, any new project (particularly those which touch IT infrastructure) is seen at best as a distraction for core business, and worse as a potential career-killer. Who wants to take on another ERP project (and all the inherent risk it carries with it)? Too often, timidity and a lack of available attention span exceeds the spirit of innovation otherwise needed by senior management to spearhead BPM initiatives.

Gaining sponsorship is about building and presenting a credible business case. If sponsorship is lacking, it is almost always so because a cogent business case has not been developed. A lack of sponsorship, even in the face of such compelling benefits as described above, can be a blessing for a prospective project, as it requires its promoters to more carefully scrutinize the business case and in doing so remove much of the potential risk and uncertainty.

In contrast, one of the worst ways to begin a project is by going with any sponsor willing to fund it, but not otherwise demanding a carefully scrutinized business case. Too often, the need for sponsorship and funding forces project leaders to compromise preferred approaches and target areas, leading the BPM initiative to be setup for failure.

The right way to win sponsorship is by using short-term project wins to show proof-points and build credibility, and then to leverage this into large projects areas (i.e., leverage the **incremental** and **measurable** qualities of BPM to achieve **repeatable** success).

## 14. DEVELOPING THE BUSINESS CASE

BPM initiatives succeed or fail based on the business case. It is both the means for gaining and maintaining management support (e.g., sponsorship), and the first major test of the project's success. While it is always possible that a project may not succeed regardless, it is nearly impossible to realize success without the exercise of developing a business case. Even with project sponsorship in place, at some point it will be necessary to present the forecasted benefit anticipated through your proposed BPM deployment. This requires an understanding of the business benefits and how they will be derived. What will you present? The answer is the business case.

### *Developing a Return on Investment Model for BPM*

The Return on Investment (ROI) model quantifies all the benefits captured in Steps 1-4, correlates them with anticipated costs, and identifies the savings potential. The goal of the ROI model is to provide quantified assessment of the anticipated value-added through the BPM deployment, specifically to estimate both the cost and net benefit expected. A secondary goal is to frame expectations for the planning and design of the BPM deployment initiative, in particular as it relates to procurement of BPM software.

ROI in basic terms is *Profit* divided by *Investment*. For the purpose of the business case, it is the total value anticipated to be returned from the BPM initiative minus the anticipated investment required (i.e., "net return") divided by the investment. For some firms *Return on Equity (ROE)* is of greater interest, as this captures the value realized from existing assets. For the purpose of the BPM business case, however, a new investment will be required and thus ROI is the more appropriate metric.

A positive ROI (i.e., when net value exceeds the cost of the investment) is any percent calculated as greater than zero (0%). Because returns and investments are made over a period of time rather than a single year (typically the business case is based on a 3 to 5 year horizon) the calculation of ROI needs to be made in terms of *Net Present Value (NPV)* or a discounted cash flow stream – although it is worth noting that actual cash flow is likely only a fraction of the value measured and you should expect the majority of the business case to be presented in terms of non-cash benefits.

Calculating NPV requires an understanding or estimation of the firm's *cost of capital*. The cost of capital is literally the cost of debt or equity required for obtaining funds and it is generally used as the minimum rate of return a firm requires for any single investment. In general it is the rate of return that is of most interest, since the BPM initiative alone is not likely to directly involve borrowing to pay for it. Organizations use the rate of the return as the hurdle rate for determining the lowest level of acceptable ROI.

For some firms the *Weighted Average Cost of Capital (WACC)* or the average of debt and equity cost is a known and valuable factor and can be used as the driving factor. For firms where this information is unavailable, however, a conservative cost of capital can be estimated (3% is used in the examples which follow). When building an ROI model, typically two scenarios are modeled – the first is labeled as "conservative" and includes minimal projections and easily verifiable data, and the second is labeled "aggressive" and outlines the potential for greater return factoring a wider range of potential benefits and incorporates more optimistic return forecasts. In both scenarios the cost basis is the same. The difference between the two is meant to illustrate the spread of reasonable expectations.

As it would be impractical during the business case stage – that is pre-solution deployment – to analyze all possible BPM benefits, only a discrete number of project areas are factored into the analysis. These should be used to illustrate how BPM benefits can be derived, and should not be presented as the limit of potential value. It should be explained that the potential benefits of the BPM deployment can also be applicable to other project areas, as well as other benefits can be expected not otherwise identified or enumerated.

When identifying quantifiable benefits, an important caveat is to avoid the temptation of simply aggregating lots of tiny time-savings, such as 10 minutes of every employee's schedule everyday. These sorts of micro productivity improvements are expected to be absorbed and of no real measurable benefit. What would you do with an extra 10 minutes a day? Probably not much compared to savings hours at a time. Instead, base ROI calculations where time-savings impact real transaction overhead, such as verifiable labor savings or reduced workload with actual redeployment of resources.

Overall, benefits should be grouped into distinct categories, such as:

- **Hard-Dollar Benefits**: fewer dollars actually being spent, therefore allowing identified monies to be allocated elsewhere; direct and measurable cash flow reductions.

- **Soft Benefits**: bottom line improvement where the impact may be challenging to quantify in dollars or to pinpoint in specific operations; improved revenue from existing operations and increased efficiency of information management functions.

- **Strategic or Operational Benefits**: which are enhanced or enabled by the BPM deployment; these are kept out of the ROI calculation but are part of the business case.

## 15. THE REAL COST OF IMPLEMENTING BPM

When presenting a business case to management, the first question is invariably "How much will this cost?" This is understandably a difficult question to answer during the early stages of a project – especially in the case of a first BPM initiative where a software solution has not yet been selected and there is no experience benchmark for estimating consulting services costs. However, in order to develop a business case, you must establish some estimate of cost. The fact that this will indeed be an estimate further supports the need for a structured yet fluid model, as cost is one of the key variables that will have to be continually refined during the discovery and due diligence process. Often, the greatest cost of BPM is not in the software license and maintenance fees but in the business resources or consulting services required.

The key to avoiding this is to establish strong communications between business users and IT staff early in the project. Process design environments offer a tool to facilitate this collaboration and they play a significant role in the success of BPM. A good graphical process design tool makes processes easier to understand and simplifies their definition, shortening the time taken to define a process while at the same time reducing the risk of misunderstandings and expensive re-work later on in the project.

Business Process Management (BPM) is not new – it is an established, proven discipline that combines a focus on process with an integrated set of specialized software tools to deliver real business results. Organizations around the world and across industries have proven the value that BPM can deliver – greater efficiency, increased visibility, better control, enhanced operational agility, and measurable ROI in the range of 10-300%.

You too can realize this success, but to do so requires focus. That focus starts with learning how to implement a repeatable framework for evaluating processes, defining distinct BPM projects, and building a business case to justify the investment of time, resources, and money.

Developing the business case for the first BPM initiative will be the most time-consuming and the most important because it will include the evaluation, selection, and justification of a BPM software suite to support the implementation. It will also serve as the first proof-point for BPM in your organization. To ensure success, follow the steps outlined in this white paper and keep the tips and pitfalls in mind – the result will be a strong business case and a set of valuable metrics to monitor and measure results during the implementation.

From that point on, you will have a repeatable approach, a solid technology foundation on which to build, and a set of benefits and benchmark ROI numbers to make justifying future BPM initiatives a breeze – putting you the fast path to realizing continuous process improvement and strategic business value from BPM.

## 16. Calculating BPM ROI: Engineering Services Firm Case Study

To illustrate the type of details and calculations that should be include in the ROI model of the business case, we use an ROI assessment performed at an engineering services firm. The first example is that of a *Soft Benefit* calculation, where an identifiable qualitative benefit is developed into a quantitative cost savings. In this case, pipeline assessments are part of a fixed-price operations and management agreement, and thus represent a cost center. Because these involve a number of handoffs and data-checking activities, each cycle introduces redundant "rework" by expensive engineering resources.

The ability to automate Steps and maintain greater continuity between handoffs represents a measurable cost-savings enable by the introduction of BPM. This opportunity was identified during Steps 2 to 4 as described earlier -- based on interviews of personnel it was identified that these handoffs represented a source of process inefficiency, on average costing around 6 out of 40 hours spent on pipeline evaluations. The details for each of these areas of savings are detailed in the table below.

### *Areas of Calculated and Anticipated Savings*

| Pipeline Evaluations | Year 1 | Year 2 | Year 3 |
|---|---|---|---|
| Number of Evaluations Per Year Per Team | 6 | 6 | 6 |
| Man-Hours Per Job | 40 | 40 | 40 |
| Rework Per Job | 15% | 15% | 15% |
| Rework MH per Job | 6 | 6 | 6 |

| | | | |
|---|---|---|---|
| Total Annual Rework Reduction | 36 | 36 | 36 |
| Licensing Man-Hour Cost | $80 | $80 | $80 |
| Cost Savings/Team | $2,880 | $2,880 | $2,880 |
| Number of Team | 8 | 20 | 50 |
| Cost-savings Per Year | $23,040 | $57,600 | $144,000 |

Other areas to examine where benefits can be measured are improvements on the existing metrics such as increasing *inventory turnover* by reducing order processing time and accelerating the order-to-cash cycle. Although, as described before, this may be ambitious for first BPM initiative, this is an area where there are many handoffs involved in the process from the time an order is received to when the product is delivered.

The ability to improve inventory turnover has a direct and measurable impact on financial performance. Other performance metrics involved in order-to-cash include the *order fulfillment rate* or orders delivered to customers in full quantity at the specified time, and the *cash collection rate* or percent of cash collected within standard or otherwise contractual terms.

Based on these assumptions as well the validation of specific metrics such as labor costs and job frequency, a realistic costs savings estimate can be developed. This is not meant as an exercise in re-engineering, and inevitably while improvements will be realized, more analysis and optimization will be required before, during, and after the implementation.

Rather, this is part of the modeling exercise where metrics are defined for the business case and for measuring the success of the project as it evolves. In the business case, each calculated figure such as this should be broken out individually and explained in terms of assumptions and data sources. The same should be done for the cost side, as well as a single table should be developed so it can be view comprehensively at once.

Although BPM does not impose anywhere near the ten-to-one services-to-software ratios imposed by other technologies, it is possible that you could spend $1.20 to $2.00 in services resources for every $1.00 spent on software. This is determined largely by your ability to leverage existing skill sets versus outsourcing to external parties or attempting to hire new skill sets in house.

This is shaped largely by the ability to leverage existing skill sets, and BPM team made of programmers or analysts. Introducing a new discipline (BPM) new development model (Java, etc.) can doom both to failure, and it is a lot easier to teach or hire programming skills than business acumen. Look for solutions which leverage existing skill sets, and hire-out programmers before business experts. A model for the *Total Projected Project Costs* is presented in the table below.

### Total Projected Project Costs Example

| Projected Cost Summary | Year 1 | Year 2 | Year 3 |
|---|---|---|---|
| BPM Administration | $75,000 | $75,000 | $75,000 |
| BPM Development & Customization | $120,000 | $120,000 | $80,000 |
| Training | $50,000 | | |
| *External Professional Services* | | | |
| BPM Process Consulting | $250,000 | $134,800 | $50,000 |

| | | | |
|---|---:|---:|---:|
| Application Development | $308,800 | $150,000 | $40,700 |
| Integration Services | | $152,400 | $30,000 |
| *BPM Software* | | | |
| Software License | | | |
| *Phase 1* (server license) | $300,000 | | |
| *Phase 2* (additional user licenses) | | $75,000 | |
| *Design Tools and Developer SDK* | $100,000 | | |
| Software Maintenance | $32,000 | $38,000 | $38,000 |
| *Hardware/Equipment* | | | |
| Production Servers and Design Stations | $16,000 | $26,000 | |
| **Total Projected Annual Costs** | **$1,251,800** | **$771,200** | **$313,700** |

One of the biggest caveats of BPM cost estimates is that "free" BPM technology can easily be the most expensive option. BPM technology that comes free with other infrastructure can introduce a great deal of operational risk to the project, starting with miscommunication between business and IT.

Another one of the (if not *the*) greatest potential points of failure is found in the transitions between business logic and application logic. Design-time environments play a significant role in the success of BPM, as difficult to understand process models lead to misunderstandings, erroneous assumptions and expensive re-work.

## 17. ROI CALCULATION

When presenting the ROI model in the business case, each cost and benefit should be broken out so that the numbers are transparent and believable, then each number should be rolled up into a single table showing the comprehensive costs and benefits. ROI is calculated as 131% here, meaning that $1.31 is returned on top of the original investment for every dollar spent, or other $2.31 comes back for every $1.00 going out (keeping mind this is not cash-flow specific but value-added through both reduced transaction costs and revenue increases).

One of the biggest sources of value in the model is *Reduction of Current Project Transaction Costs,* representing the BPM deployment's impact on the productivity involved with performing existing project work. They are productivity-based, relating to how the BPM deployment can be leveraged to perform more work with the same resources or perform the same volume of work with greater efficiency.

As such they are presented as *Soft Benefits* rather than *Hard-Dollar* savings or direct cash flow reductions. In each case specific dollar values are identified based on existing processes and validated costs and/or revenue amounts.

In contrast, the *Automation of Engineering Change Orders* led to a significant redeployment of staff, resulting in measurable Hard-Dollar savings by redeploying staff and reducing a considerable amount of outside travel.

### ROI Calculation Example: Aggressive Scenario

|  | Year 1 | Year 2 | Year 3 |
|---|---|---|---|
| **Hard-Dollar Benefits** | | | |
| Reduced Print & Distribution Costs | $21,600 | $33,200 | $49,500 |
| Automation of Change Orders | $240,000 | $336,000 | $470,400 |
| Elimination of Engineering Re-Work | $51,840 | $72,576 | $101,606 |
| **Soft Benefits** | | | |
| Pipeline Evaluation Labor Savings | $23,040 | $57,600 | $144,000 |
| Identified Productivity Gains | $330,000 | $396,000 | $475,200 |
| Reduction of Current Project Transaction | $410,118 | $706,738 | $1,056,100 |
| Revenue Improvement via Collaboration | $82,000 | $127,000 | $324,000 |
| Annual Totals of BPM-Provided Benefits | $1,158,598 | $1,729,114 | $2,620,806 |
| Total Projected Annual Costs | $1,251,800 | $771,200 | $313,700 |
| Annual Payback | ($93,202) | $957,914 | $2,307,106 |

| | |
|---|---|
| Net Present Value of 3 Year Investment | $2,296,481 |
| 3 Year Project Net Present Value | $3,013,327 |
| 3 Year Project ROI | 131% |
| Year in Which Breakeven Occurs | Year 2 |

ROI is calculated as 3 Year Project NPV / 3 Year Investment NPV

Net Present Value (NPV) was calculated using a constant cost of capital of 3% and discounting each year's net benefit after Year 1. The discount factor is calculated as $(1+ \text{the cost of capital})^{\text{Year-1}}$

Thus, Year 2's net benefit is discounted by 3% or $(1.0+0.03)^1$ and Year 3's is discounted by 6% or $(1.0+0.03)^2$

The difference with the *Conservative Scenario* ROI model (see next page) is largely found in the *Reduction of Current Project Transaction Costs,* which is a Soft Benefit based largely on assumptions. Nothing changes in the Hard-Dollar Benefits or the Cost side of the equation, as both of these are developed from verified numbers. In this Conservative Scenario the initiative pays for itself in Year 3 and over the period three years it returns $1.39 in value for every $1.00 invested. This initiative is indeed "profitable" and earns more than 10% annually compared to an alternative investment, so even as a Conservative Scenario it should make a compelling business case.

### ROI Calculation Example: Conservative Scenario

|  | Year 1 | Year 2 | Year 3 |
|---|---|---|---|
| **Hard-Dollar Benefits** | | | |
| Reduced Print & Distribution Costs | $21,600 | $33,200 | $49,500 |
| Automation of Change Orders | $240,000 | $336,000 | $470,400 |
| Elimination of Engineering Re-Work | $51,840 | $72,576 | $101,606 |

### Soft Benefits

| | | | |
|---|---|---|---|
| Pipeline Evaluation Labor Savings | $23,040 | $57,600 | $144,000 |
| Identified Productivity Gains | $110,000 | $132,000 | $158,400 |
| Reduction of Current Project Transaction | $210,118 | $252,142 | $302,570 |
| Revenue Improvement via Collaboration | $82,000 | $127,000 | $324,000 |
| Annual Totals of BPM-Provided Benefits | $738,598 | $1,010,518 | $1,550,476 |
| Total Projected Annual Costs | $1,251,800 | $771,200 | $313,700 |
| Annual Payback | ($513,202) | $239,318 | $1,236,776 |

| | |
|---|---|
| NPV of 3 Year Investment Dollars | $2,296,481 |
| 3 Year Project Net Present Value | $885,915 |
| 3 Year Project ROI | 39% |
| Year in Which Breakeven Occurs | Year 3 |

## 18. THE REAL COST OF IMPLEMENTING BPM

When presenting a business case to management, the first question is invariably "how much will this cost?" This is understandably a difficult question during the early stage of a project, before a software vendor has been selected and before a real assessment of consulting/services costs can be determined. Yet few organizations truly understand the actual cost of BPM initiatives, and are unwilling to share their expectations with prospective suppliers (presumably out of fear that if they overshoot, they will lose negotiating leverage).

For the purpose of developing a business case, some estimate of cost has to be arrived at. This underscores the need for a structured yet fluid model, as costs are one of the key variables which need to be constantly refined during the discovery and due diligence process. Using estimated costs as a benchmark can help move the model along, and it is much more productive to find a starting point and develop this in a workable model than to try to get it 100% at the outset.

## 19. BPM AND THE MYTHICAL MAN MONTH

"The Mythical Man-Month" is a book by Fred Brooks first published in 1975, which illustrates that adding manpower to a late engineering project only makes it later. Brooks first presented this analysis focused on software engineering, however, it has been shown to be true for other "knowledge work" requiring skilled individuals, such as claims processing or mortgage origination.

This notion, commonly referred to as *Brooks' Law*, holds that the productivity of any group is reduced by the number of participants in the process, and is negatively impacted by the introduction of new works. This is based on the need for "ramp up" and inefficiency of communication (thus the overhead of coordination) between individuals. This notion also presents a compelling case for the value of BPM, by leveraging the ability to streamline communication, facilitate handoffs, and embed instructions within work items.

For example, when an insurance claim is transferred from a customer service rep to an adjuster, it typically requires further research and information gathering, and then is subject to the interpretation and assumptions of the individuals involved. By managing these handoffs within a BPM suite, much of the uncertainty and inconsistency in work quality can be eliminated through data validation and skills-based routing. For this reason, Brooks' Law presents an opportunity for uncovering and identifying existing soft dollar costs wherever handoffs between roles can be found.

## 20. CONCLUSION

The opportunity for realizing business value from Business Process Management (BPM) initiatives is significant and unlike virtually any other area of software. This is due in part to the intimacy and interplay between BPM systems and core business activities within which they exist.

When done right, successful BPM initiatives (herein referring to projects involving business process analysis and the implementation of business process management software) change the entire notion of applications, by allowing core systems to respond to process context, rather than driving processes around application limited. In this way BPM changes the nature of application management and the notion of "applications" altogether.

**BPM is Incremental**: one of the core advantages of BPM is that it need not require boiling the ocean to deliver results. Rather projects can start small, yet still make a large impact. As management sage Peter Drucker observed in his seminal work *Management Challenges for the 21st Century*, "Continuous process improvements in any one area eventually transform the business. They lead to innovation. They lead to new processes. They lead to new business." To paraphrase, it is less important to start with the perfect process candidate than it is to establish a leverage point from which to extend into other opportunities.

**BPM is Measurable**: BPM is unique among technology-based initiatives in its ability to incorporate metrics and measurement parameters at the outset of the project. BPM presents the opportunity for an immediate and material impact on business performance and visibility. Ultimately, the real value of BPM is delivered through what you can gain when you have access to data you never had before and tools that enable you to change and adapt your business.

**BPM is Repeatable**: BPM presents a compound benefit where the skill set and competencies gained from the first process optimized can be leveraged on multiple processes through the organization.

BPM projects fail more often as a result of missed expectations than inadequate technology. Yet a greater number of BPM projects fail to launch at all due to the inability to be a credible business case. The value of BPM is realized through planning and measurement, and the business case needs to be developed with transparent success criteria and "real world" metrics. Yet any business case is only as good as the validity and trueness of the project's architecture and assumptions.

Prioritization and validation of assumptions is part process (methodology) and part tools (simulation and modeling). An iterative should be taken to enable closed-loop analysis or a "round-trip" approach for comprehensive modeling, validation, implementation and refinement or continuous process improvement.

All successful BPM initiatives require executive sponsorship, based on realistic expectations. This should be clearly defined and measurable success criteria with incremental proof-points, and should begin with clearly understood prioritization of process targets (where to begin and where to go next).

Using short-term project wins to build credibility, successful BPM initiatives start at manageable scope and are leveraged into larger projects areas, taking advantage of the incremental and measurable qualities of BPM to achieve repeatable success.

# How Strategic are Your BPM Initiatives? 4 Questions to Ask Yourself

## Charles Farina, Essroc Cement Corp., USA

Gone are the days when process excellence was just about standardization, cost cutting, or quality. In today's businesses, process is about enabling business strategy.

So how sure are you that your BPM program stacks up?

One way to start addressing this question is to evaluate what you're doing with respect to the characteristics of **Strategic BPM.**

Strategic BPM is a system of management that allows us to answer...

- *What's important to our customers and other key stakeholders?*
- *Are our business processes fully addressing these requirements?*
- *Which improvement projects should we be working on and with which priorities?*
- *How do we know that our improvement efforts are creating tangible and sustainable value?*

...and deliver results that matter most to...

- *Customers – products, services, relationships, etc. » the overall customer experience with our company.*
- *Senior Management – business outcomes, e.g., revenues, profits, market share, growth, etc.*

With this description of Strategic BPM in mind, we can take note of several critical requirements needed for its success in driving strategic value.

- Senior management leadership – the buy-in, support, engagement, etc. that demonstrate top-down commitment by what's said, but most importantly by their actions.
- Emphasis on future-oriented successful customer outcomes – How can we make our customers successful in their business?
- Continuous improvement initiatives that begin and end with the customer.
- Use of customer metrics to guide behavior and decision-making in the right directions.
- Understanding of the company's core business processes that directly help to achieve its strategic objectives.

With these requirements in place, your BPM actions will be integrated with your company's organizational objectives – resulting in *strategic alignment!*

In simpler terms, BPM is not something that you do on top of everything else. It's a key part of how you manage the business.

Let's consider four basic questions that can help you understand if your BPM activities are strategic.

### 1. ARE YOUR BPM INITIATIVES MAKING A SIGNIFICANT AND MEASUREABLE IMPACT ON YOUR COMPANY PERFORMANCE?

All too often BPM initiatives can end up as an exercise in documentation. Processes are mapped and standardized. Perhaps the process design team also came up with a series of measures that are added to the lengthy list of KPIs that the company tracks and reports. We may also have spent significant fees on consultants that helped us produce these details. Then these consultants leave, and the process maps and KPI reports are filed away in a big binder of good intentions destined to gather dust for the remainder of existence. It may have consumed significant time, effort, and resources to produce, but the end benefit for the company is negligible. Has anyone really used this information to drive improvement actions in your critical processes? If they did use the information, how would they know that the actions produced the desired outcomes?

BPM initiatives need to have a significant business impact and produce hard benefits that can be quantified. Sure, you should get a lot of soft benefits – such as end-to-end process awareness or eliminating unnecessary work – along with your initiative as well, but your first toll gate should be whether you can really wrap your hands around what you're expecting to achieve from all that hard work. To the extent you can relate these improvements to the types of outcomes that are of interest to senior management (see page 1), you will find a more willing audience to understand and support your BPM improvement actions.

### 2. ARE YOUR BPM INITIATIVES SUSTAINED AND SUSTAINABLE?

BPM is not just a one-off thing, like a training session or software implementation. We don't ever really "finish" BPM, because there will always be areas for improvement, automation, and change.

Equally, when the original leader of your BPM initiative leaves or moves onto the next thing, does everything go back to the way it was before? There are several good examples of companies with solid BPM capabilities and meaningful process improvement results who abandoned or dismantled this approach when the senior executive who sponsored them left the senior management position. The successor either had a different strategy, agenda, and game plan or simply did not believe in the benefits of a successful BPM program.

The diagram on the next page shows that there are several ways in which to deploy and integrate BPM throughout an organization. These are not mutually exclusive, and top-down driven efforts tend to be more effective than those solely from the bottom-up in terms of sustaining BPM and delivering significant results. A combined, integrated approach involving all four aspects can result in the strategic alignment you want on a sustained basis.

Many companies have made successful use of Lean Six Sigma practices including specific tools like process maps, statistical process control, root-cause analysis, etc. However, without the top-down direction and strategic guidance aligning these methodologies and tools to the higher-level needs, the benefits achieved may be localized and they may not contribute to the strategic objectives across the entire company.

The top-down direction coming from an appropriate management philosophy and business model can focus these improvement actions and align them to the strategic and significant opportunities that the company faces.

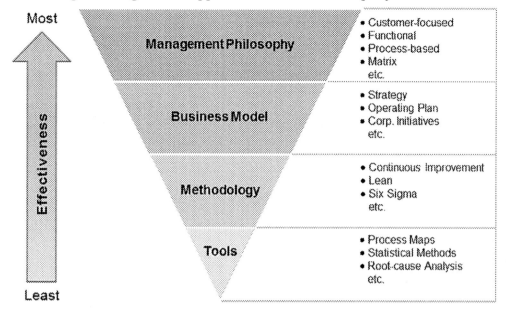

### Sustaining BPM

The only way that BPM will be successful in the long run is by embedding these capabilities within the organization and ensuring that employees are engaged and bought into the new processes and ways of doing things. Management direction, support, and reinforcement of the improved methods of getting work done are critical. In some cases, software can provide the enablement as it's aligned to and enforces the new ways of getting the work done.

If not, you're achieving nothing more than the equivalent of producing a bunch of unused process maps and process measures, because the process is not living, breathing, evolving and adding value.

### 3. ARE YOUR BPM INITIATIVES FOCUSED ON DELIVERING VALUE TO THE CUSTOMER?

There are always lots of opportunities for improvement within an organization. But who will they benefit most? Those initiatives that focus on delivering customer value are more likely to make a more significant impact on revenue and long-term business performance than those that focus merely on internal operations. This is not to say that cost savings are bad, since improvements such as these contribute to the company's bottom line as hard benefits. However, there needs to be a balance between cost reduction opportunities and those opportunities that truly add value to your customers.

It's not practical for a company to excel at *all* of its business processes. It's also not necessary to excel at all things in order to be successful. Consider instead those end-to-end, cross-functional business process that deliver value to your customers.

Think about your company's operations with a focus on what the customer sees...

- What are your "deliverables" to your customers, e.g., products, services, support, information, etc.?

- What are the cross-functional business processes that produce these deliverables?
- What are your customers' expectations for these processes on the basis that these deliverables contribute to successful customer outcomes?
- Who are the touch-points within your company and/or your suppliers who interact directly with your customers? Do they understand what the customers' expectations are, and do they understand how they fit into the overall process?
- Who are the effective owners of each of these processes, and are they held accountable for the outcomes of these processes?
- Do you have meaningful process metrics that measure process performance as the customers see it? The preference is for leading indicators of process performance as compared to lagging indicators (typically those that are after-the-fact and focused on throughput). A good consideration for your process measures is to ensure they capture accuracy, content, and/or timeliness.
- What are the process measures telling you as far as where improvement actions need to be established and prioritized? If there's a critical customer-facing process without any meaningful measures, figure out how to come up with some in order to understand process performance.

It's likely that you'll find only a handful of critical business processes that are crucial to your customers' success. Some of these processes may already have effective process performance measures in place and have long been the focus of management attention. Other processes may not be at this level. These, collectively, are the business processes at which you need to excel so that you consistently deliver successful customer outcomes and meet the strategic objectives of your company.

One particular tool that's useful in explaining which of your company processes deliver value to customers is a strategy map. The information developed in answering the questions above results in a lot of written content that may overwhelm most readers. The strategy map is a good way to tell this story by drawing a picture and telling the story about how the company interacts with its customers through these processes.

The understanding of process performance from the customers' perspective allows you to begin improvement actions. These problem-solving efforts can first address the problems or the symptoms of inadequate process performance followed by root-cause analysis and the elimination of what's causing the problems in the first place.

Upon figuring out the problems, it may also be necessary to implement some short-term fixes – i.e., stop the bleeding – before the long-term solutions can be put into place. The corrective actions that eliminate the root-causes and prevent them from happening can only be validated by your on-going process measures. Has there been a meaningful improvement in the process performance – as the customer sees it?

Growing, acquiring, and keeping customers are the key parts of any successful business – make sure your BPM efforts are focused on supporting that.

## 4. Do your BPM initiatives have senior leadership support?

Leadership has been in the forefront of business excellence initiatives for many decades. Of particular interest is a quotation from Joel Barker...

> *"A leader is person you will follow to a place you wouldn't go by yourself."*

Unfortunately, a company will not follow you as the BPM professional to this future state. The challenge for you is how to influence and shape those in leadership positions to drive Strategic BPM actions. It can be difficult to first get and then keep your executive leadership teams to be focused on BPM. They've got near-term earning pressures and an entire business to keep an eye on. But you can bet your bottom dollar that if it's clear your BPM program is helping them get to where they want to go, you'll have their support in making your efforts a reality.

As we noted on page 1, there's a certain language that these senior leaders use, and it doesn't include terms like process maps, process cycle time, or process capability index. Instead, it will be important for you to prove the value-added of BPM improvements in the terms that are meaningful to them. Show them how your process improvement actions can produce hard benefit results. It's one thing to propose an improvement action that's positioned to deliver these hard benefits. It's another to report on the actual benefits you achieved as this team's work gets done.

If you're early in the implementation of BPM capabilities at your company, it may be likely that your most senior leaders do not share with you the buy-in and passion for BPM that you have as a process excellence professional. Even when speaking their language, it may prove difficult to get their attention. You simply can't expect a leap of faith from senior leaders for BPM. As an alternative, consider the engagement of other senior managers who may be one or two levels below that of the most senior leaders.

It may be easier to get their direct commitment to an improvement opportunity, one that's aligned to the company's strategic objectives and also of particular interest to them. Ensure their commitment by having them as an active member of your process improvement actions. With the success of that opportunity, you'll have an ally to promote the benefits of BPM and get higher levels of management support for future improvement actions. You'll also be grooming a direct supporter of BPM as that individual's career leads to more senior responsibilities.

So if your senior leaders don't buy into your BPM plans, are you sure that your initiatives are really supporting the strategic direction of the company?

### Acknowledgements

Jim Boots, "Does your BPM Initiative Deliver Strategic Value?" – posted on the PEX Network, January 4, 2013 and webinar, January 30, 2013.

Diana Davis, editor at PEX Network, in collaboration for the original article "How Strategic are Your BPM Initiatives?" – posted on the PEX Network, July 8, 2014.

Process Strategy Group for the excerpt from their "Process as a Strategy" webcast.

Brad Power, FCB Partners, for guidance on linking process to strategy, examples of companies unable to sustain earlier successes in BPM, and the use of strategy maps.

Steve Towers, BP Group, for insights on customer experience and the Outside-In view.

# BPM empowers the Digital Enterprise

## Pedro Robledo, BPMteca.com, Spain

## 1. INTRODUCTION

The Digital Economy, globalization, social and environmental problems, natural disasters, the threat of terrorism, migration waves... are conditioning companies to make urgent situation analysis exercises and strategic processes to be competitive and to maintain their companies with solvency. Aspects such as delinquency management, debt control, control margins, risk management... are highly relevant and priority processes. Managers must have all the necessary tools for making decisions and it will only be possible if they decide to implement appropriate technologies in their businesses. Companies should consider tactical plans for the urgency to solve, but mostly it will put focus on the company for the long term through a strategic plan if they wish to overcome the current crisis and the coming future adverse situations.

The solution involves reacting to the inefficiency arising from departmental organizations, with their niches and their concern to achieve individual goals. If we promote the concept of the transverse process, along with resources aligned with strategic business challenges with a clear vision and objectives to external and internal customers, ensure compliance thereof, maintaining operational efficiency and competitiveness of the organization. Organizations with a management approach, should document, automate, analyze and monitor business processes, but not in terms of functions (marketing, sales, production, customer service...) but in terms of processes from start to finish and across all functional boundaries; understanding business processes as a sequence of activities to support the strategy, analyze operational effectiveness and facilitating the establishment of performance measures for continuous improvement.

Traditionally, the business organization is based on departmental units and its pillars are the hierarchy, control and bureaucracy, limiting staff performance and the obsession with assigning responsibilities, which influences the ability to fully meet the requirements of flexibility demanded by today's enterprise. However, process-oriented organization is based on the management and flow system (not as heterogeneous functions), tasking by "processes" (transferring functional barriers) and definition of performance indicators and targets to increase the improvement and aligned, in real time, with the strategic objectives and take into account the needs and expectations of customers.

Companies have to adapt to meet the business challenges to be able to achieve their goals and develop their innovation capabilities if they want to survive to the global economic changes and customer expectations. To do this, they need to be able to make changes quickly, i.e., have the operational agility, which is conditional on the ability of organizations to modify business processes looking to get benefits and reducing risks.

But in addition to that, traditional industries are being disrupted every day by new business models and technology which is empowering the consumer like never before.

## 2. WHAT IS DIGITAL ENTERPRISE OR DIGITAL BUSINESS?

Gartner defines Digital Business (Lopez 2014) as the creation of new business designs by blurring the digital and physical worlds. Digital business promises to usher in an unprecedented convergence of people, business and things (physical objects that are active players and contribute to business value) that disrupts existing business models to drive revenue and efficiency. A digital business includes these main attributes: things are agents for services that are requested and delivered through people; the business is dynamic based on the current context; intelligent things are incorporated into end-to-end processes; there are communication and collaboration among things, business and people.

Neil Sholay, Head of Oracle Digital in EMEA defines Digital Business as the use of any digital technology to promote, sell and enable enhanced and innovative products, services and experiences, and he clarifies that Digital Business isn't about digitalizing everything in sight, but leveraging digital technologies where they add value or allow innovation.

A study conducted in 2013 by MIT Sloan Management Review and Capgemini Consulting focuses on digital transformation, which we define as the use of new digital technologies encompassed by the term SMACT (social, mobile, analytics, cloud and internet of things) to enable major business improvements (such as enhancing customer experience, streamlining operations or creating new business models). The study finds that companies now face a digital imperative: adopt new technologies effectively or face competitive obsolescence. The Enterprises are using Digital for Customer Experience (44%), Operational Improvement (30%) and for new business models (26%). (Fitzgerald 2013)

As Forrester principal analyst James McQuivey has recently written in his book Digital Disruption (McQuivey 2013), digital disruption is about to completely change how companies do business. Digital tools and digital platforms are driving the cost of innovation down to nearly zero, causing at least 10 times as many innovators to rush into your market while operating at one-tenth the cost that you do. Multiply that together and you face 100 times the innovation power you did just a few years ago under old-fashioned disruption.

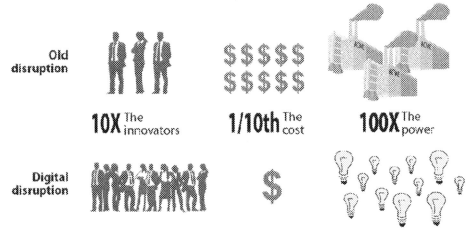

***Figure 1. Digital Disruption is Better, Stronger and Faster.
(McQuivey 2013)***

The digital revolution is a phenomenon that transcends the technology; it is transforming the social ecosystem making in a context of digital relationships, where relationships between individuals sharing interests, between consumers and suppliers of goods and services between citizens and administration are done through digital media. It is no longer just about IT but to innovate in the digital stage for organizations to make more accurate and real-time decisions. Companies have the opportunity to innovate and for surviving we need to make decisions in real time, aligning people, processes and systems, in order to turn our company into a digital one.

Gartner positions the Digital Enterprise as the third big wave in IT. And since there is a gap between Traditional and Digital Enterprise Business, companies must innovate to achieve:

- Scalable IT based on the five disruptive forces (Cloud, Mobility, Social, BigData and Internet of Things)
- End-to-end business processes, based on collaboration and real-time KPIs
- Social interaction with employees, customers and partners
- 360°customer unlimited information in real time.
- Personalized marketing strategy
- Multiple channels of delivery and customer service
- Customized products.

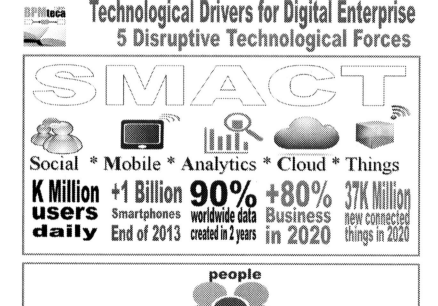

***Figure 2: Technological Drivers for Digital Enterprise
(BPMteca, 2014)***

Technology (social media, mobile, analytics, embedded devices, smart things, 3D printing...) enables new digital business processes, models and moments. Enterprises must become more technologically capable and sophisticated to be digital.

## 3. THE DIGITAL JOURNEY

The journey to digital business is the key theme of Gartner, Inc.'s "Hype Cycle for Emerging Technologies, 2014." (Gartner 2014). Gartner said that as enterprises set out on the journey to becoming digital businesses, identifying and employing the right technologies at the right time will be critical.

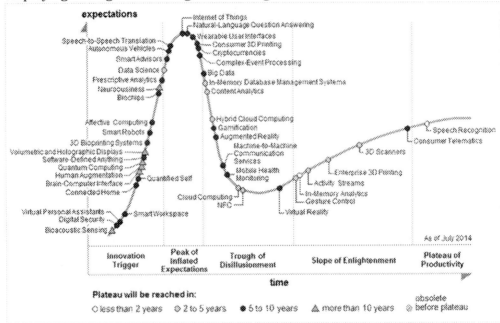

**Figure 3. Hype Cycle for Emerging Technologies, (Gartner 2014).**

Enterprises can identify with today status and to which they can aspire in the future, and to prepare the digital journey that mostly supports the following three stages:

- Digital Marketing stage, where enterprises are focus on new sophisticated ways to reach customers using mobile devices, social networks, cloud services and analysing information in real time to be more proactive.
- Digital Business stage which is focused on the convergence of people, business and things.
- Autonomous stage which provides humanlike or human-replacing capabilities

## 4. THE ROLE OF BPM

Business management evolves to adapt to changes (economic, technological, social, political, environmental...) and digital journey. But can companies maintain current organizational structures to deal with changes in the environment quickly and flexibly, so that it does not impact the results and to meet their strategic objectives? Definitely not, they need a paradigm shift in Business Process Management (BPM).

BPM discipline (including methods, tools and technology) is oriented to continuous improvement of the business processes of an organization, which orchestrates the traditional participants (people, systems, applications and data) and the new smart digital objects which are connected via internet to exchange information to be processed in a reactive or proactive manner, taking decisions in real time automatically according to business rules for compliance with business objectives.

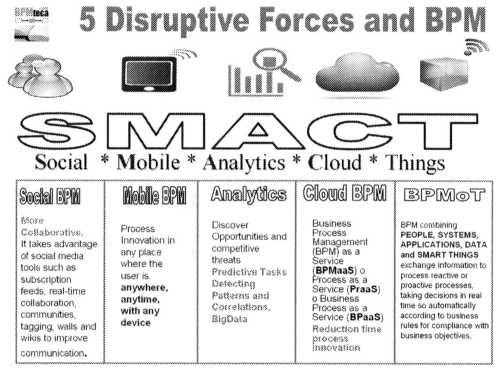

**5 Disruptive Forces and BPM**

**SMACT**

Social * Mobile * Analytics * Cloud * Things

| Social BPM | Mobile BPM | Analytics | Cloud BPM | BPMoT |
|---|---|---|---|---|
| More Collaborative. It takes advantage of social media tools such as subscription feeds, real-time collaboration, communities, tagging, walls and wikis to improve communication. | Process Innovation in any place where the user is. **anywhere, anytime, with any device** | Discover Opportunities and competitive threats Predictive Tasks Detecting Patterns and Correlations, BigData | Business Process Management (BPM) as a Service (**BPMaaS**) o Process as a Service (**PraaS**) o Business Process as a Service (**BPaaS**) Reduction time process innovation | BPM combining **PEOPLE, SYSTEMS, APPLICATIONS, DATA and SMART THINGS** exchange information to process reactive or proactive processes, taking decisions in real time so automatically according to business rules for compliance with business objectives. |

*Figure 4. Five disruptive forces and BPM, (BPMteca 2014).*

The five disruptive technology trends (SMACT) impact on processes and process management truly offer competitive advantages through new business opportunities unprecedented innovation. BPM provides methodology, tools and technology to help companies in the digital journey providing:

### 1.- *Operational Effectiveness:*

BPM provides the ability to achieve the desired or expected effect, allowing:
- Getting full traceability of activities offering an absolute control of what is happening and want to happen in each process.
- Achieving performance improvement resources involved in the process to achieve the desired objectives.
- Will redirect human resources to higher value activities
- Allow integrate and coordinate information systems with processes.

### 2.- *Operational Efficiency:*

BPM provides the ability to achieve a certain effect, allowing:
- To have agility and flexibility to adapt to market changes and the environment.
- To have faster decisions and appropriate information for each process in real time

- Successfully combine people, processes and technology to improve productivity and the value of any operation, reducing costs to the desired level.
- To have the ability to achieve the best results in terms of quality, service satisfaction, profitability and productivity, using appropriate resources, streamlining and simplifying processes and controlling spending.
- To be focus on the work of human resources by avoiding bad outcomes.
- To contribute to the achievement of a specific goal complying with the corresponding strategy.
- To automate processes to achieve the best result.
- To create separate processes that people execute, achieving continuity and solidity.

### 3.- Operational Excellence:

BPM provides top quality perfection and outstanding features, and getting:
- To increase productivity and competitiveness through automation and management of business processes.
- To increase productivity by detecting and correcting inefficient use of resources (downtime, bottlenecks ...)
- Participation of business users. People who actually do the work offer a new perspective on how to look at what they do in their jobs, and have a vision process easy to understand.
- Measure, evaluate and control the processes by identifying critical points and solutions for continuous improvement.

### 4.- Operational Success:

BPM gets achieving positive outcomes, obtaining:
- Increased quality of the products and services of the company.
- Satisfy internal and external customers to improve care, their requirements and respond proactively resolving issues that arise.
- Comply with the new regulations (laws and regulations).
- Competitively position the company creating sustainable processes in time.
- Resolution time savings.
- Financial savings.
- Achieving expected results

### 5.- Operational Strategy:

BPM gets the achievement of business objectives by focusing on:
- Facilitating the adoption and implementation of a strategy, allowing preventive or corrective actions in a timely manner.
- Alignment of all business units with the strategic objectives.
- Work together in achieving the same strategy.
- Meet the systemic view of the organization and its processes, facilitating business management.
- Determine and implement technological and organizational requirements for the implementation of the processes according to the strategic objectives.

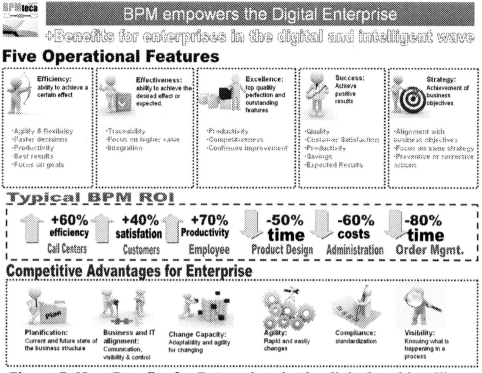

*Figure 5: More Benefits for Enterprises in the digital and intelligent wave (BPMteca, 2014)*

The implementation of process management has emerged as the most effective tool of business management for all types of organization. Many examples confirm the validity of this management discipline. Thus, companies are able to reduce design time product by 50% by improving the "time-to-market" more competitive and more profitable products; improve the efficiency of call centres by 60%, reducing costs, increasing customer satisfaction and improving the management of resources; reduce order processing time by 80% with cost savings, increasing customer satisfaction and earning higher returns; 50-60% reduced administrative costs in almost any process, obtaining a significant financial savings.

## 5. CONCLUSIONS

In order to summarize what has been presented, over the last few years, we've seen an explosion of disruptive technologies such as mobile, cloud, social media, big data and internet of things (the 5 disruptive technological forces). As everything is connected on the network, consumers are increasingly willing to buy goods and services through digital channels. This is the third wave of computing, the vision of "Industry 4.0", the GE's vision of the Industrial Internet, that will transform business, and it is mandatory for any business looking to have future.

Becoming a digital enterprise is critical, is not an option, and it is a journey and there is no finish line as the technology creates a constant change. Companies must transform themselves to provide a proactive customer service, smarter products, agile services, more speed... The evolution of digital technology presents opportunities and threats for all businesses, so digital becomes a top agenda item for most executives.

According to Gartner, the Industrial Digital Economy will be conducted quickly by machine-to-person, person-to-machine and machine-to-machine, through the Internet of Things (IoT) communication. A market that Gartner predicts will eclipse $ 304,000 million in 2020, with over 30 billion "things" (essentially interconnected sensors). These forecasts generate some interesting expectations for business if you have the ability to process in real time all available information from the devices to process (Device-To-Process) and from processes to send instructions (Process-To-Device), and it is possible using Business Process Management.

## 6. REFERENCES

(Aron 2013) Dave Aron and Mark P. McDonald "The Digital Enterprise and Beyond." Gartner CIO Leadership Forum 11-13 March 2013 UK http://www.gartner.com/imagesrv/summits/docs/emea/cio-fo-rum/CIOE-2013-Trip-Report.pdf

(Burkett 2014) Michael Burkett, Jorge Lopez, Patrick Meehan, Don Scheibenreif and Jim Tully. Agenda Overview for Digital Business, 2014

https://www.gartner.com/doc/2689517?ref=ddisp

(Fitzgerald 2013) Michael Fitzgerald, Nina Kruschwitz, Didier Bonnet and Michael Welch. Embracing Digital Technology. A New Strategic Imperative. 2013 Digital Transformation Global Executive Study and Research Project of Capgemini Consulting. MITSloan Management Review.

http://sloanreview.mit.edu/projects/embracing-digital-technology/

(Gartner 2014) Gartner's 2014 Hype Cycle for Emerging Technologies Maps the Journey to Digital Business

http://www.gartner.com/newsroom/id/2819918

(Gartner CIO 2014) "Taming the Digital Dragon: The 2014 CIO Agenda." Insights From the 2014 Gartner CIO Agenda Report.
http://www.gartner.com/imagesrv/cio/pdf/cio_agenda_insights2014.pdf

(Lopez 2014) Jorge Lopez, Patrick Meehan, Stephen Prentice, Mark Raskino, Chris Howard and David A. Willis. Get Ready for Digital Business With the Digital Business Development Path

https://www.gartner.com/doc/2777417?srcId=1-4274487421

(McQuivey 2013) James McQuivey. Digital Disruption. Amazon Publishing (2013) ISBN-13: 978-1477800126

(Streibich 2014) Karl-Heinz Streibich. The Digital Enterprise. Germany: Software AG, 2014. ISBN-13: 978-0989756402

(Willmott 2013) The digital Enterprise Interview to McKinsey director Paul Willmott

http://www.mckinsey.com/insights/business_technology/the_digital_enter-prise

# Exploiting Business Architecture for Process Excellence
## Lloyd Dugan, BPM, Inc. (BPMI), USA

## 1. INTRODUCTION

Business Process Management (BPM) is a term that has regrettably come to mean too many different things to too many different but related practitioner communities, including process automation, process modeling, process improvement, business or enterprise architecture, etc. Worse still is that none of these communities fully and consistently define BPM as something that unifies and integrates its interdisciplinary nature. Instead, provincial interests have led some communities to balkanize (or fragment) what BPM means in order to assert methodological superiority or to gain market share or both.

The principal sources of obfuscation and confusion over what BPM means are the BPM System (BPMS) vendors and their enablers, the industry analyst services, who have conspired to have BPM be mostly understood as an automation platform wherein all of the relevant BPM concepts come together. This is, of course, a false claim, but it is a pervasive perception that – in conjunction with legitimate areas of persistent ambiguity that still beg for clarification – has contributed to a woeful lack of generalized competency and consistency in BPM efforts. In many ways, BPM as a practice area is at a crossroads, wherein it, too, can give way to a successor concept (as BPM itself was to workflow) or it, as the preferred alternative, can evolve to be all of what it should have been in the first place, aka *BPM 2.0*.

## 2. THE EVOLUTION OF BPM 2.0

For this evolution to occur, environmental drivers must appear to compel BPM to adapt to new circumstances and thus to improve its impact in application. The first such driver is the failure of BPM to be clearly successful more often than not, the typical cause of which is a toxic mix of a narrow set of defined outcomes (e.g., process automation only), lack of a disciplined seriousness to doing it right (i.e., such as is the case in industrial engineering efforts), and insufficient contextual understanding that results in a failure to adequately align the effort with the business (as understood architecturally). As a consequence, BPM as a management science is undergoing a prolonged period of introspection by its various constituencies and practitioner communities.

The second such driver is the advent of Business Process Model and Notation (BPMN) v2.0 from the Object Management Group (OMG), which formalized the semantics of this standard process modeling language in a meta model and the serialization of model data in the new BPMN XML format (based on the corresponding schema).[1] The modeling power of BPMN and the ability to interchange BPMN models are slowly but surely forcing process modeling, as a core component of BPM efforts, to become more standardized and effective in practice.

---

[1] See http://www.omg.org/spec/BPMN/index.htm for the standard and http://www.bpmn.org/ for additional information about the standard's specification.

The third such driver is the maturation of architecture frameworks, including the separation of Business Architecture (with a purely business focus) as its own set of concepts apart from Enterprise Architecture (that is too often seen as a tool of IT). Through refinement of the mappings of semantic meanings, these frameworks are enabling a more useful incorporation of Business Process as an architectural concept than has been possible in the past, which is making alignment with the business less ambiguous and easier to demonstrate.

The final such driver is the emergence of semantic technologies that enable robust treatment of data concepts, including model and architectural data. These technologies enable the use of a tool-agnostic approach and repository in which architectural mappings can be better captured and analyzed, elevating them to a more actionable form in which the actual data about the enterprise can now be understood as instances of the architecture.

Together, these drivers are changing the methodological, technique, and tooling landscapes for how the modeling and analysis of Business Processes can better fulfill BPM's full potential. This collective result is happening because it is now possible to fully (and more properly) understand a Business Process within the larger, comprehensive context of the business itself, as expressed as formalized architectural data that can be captured, mapped, analyzed, and reconfigured to achieve business objectives.

## 3.  RECONCILING BPM AND BA

Implicit in this confluence of drivers is the need to reconcile two distinct but related disciplines: BPM and Business Architecture (BA). Unfortunately, practitioner efforts in either space have often been mixed inappropriately or even led to one being confused with the other.[2]

A recently-developed but widely-endorsed definition of BPM reflects the pull to have BPM serve a large and diverse community of needs:

> BPM is a discipline involving any combination of modeling, automation, execution, control, measurement and optimization of business activity flows, in support of enterprise goals, spanning systems, employees, customers and partners within and beyond the enterprise boundaries.[3]

This definition captures the totality of BPM's interdisciplinary nature, but can prove to be a lot to embrace at the practitioner level. This is especially true with respect to the implicit treatment of the concept of the Business Process and its principal analytical artifact, the Business Process Model.

On the other hand, a similarly recent but widely embraced definition of BA explicitly states the larger context for understanding the business:

---

[2] Note that much of the material in this section is drawn from either the Author's contribution to a forthcoming position paper from the Business Architecture Guild (http://businessarchitectureguild.org/) on *"Business Architecture & BPM – Differentiation & Reconciliation"* or from the Author's own training material offered through Business Process Management, Inc. (BPM, Inc.).

[3] See the source for this definition at *http://social-biz.org/2014/01/27/one-common-definition-for-bpm/*, which was based on discussions on or with *Linked-In's BPM Guru Group, BPM.COM's Forum, Workflow Management Coalition (WfMC) Members,* and the *Association of BPM Professionals (ABPMP) Forum.* To fully disclose, this definition is formally embraced and used by BPM, Inc. (see at *http://www.bpm.com*), of which the Author of this Chapter is the Chief Architect and had a contributing role in its crafting.

*"A blueprint of the enterprise that provides a common understanding of the organization and is used to align strategic objectives and tactical demands."[4]*

In practice, BA per a defined architectural framework separates out the various concerns of the business in creating value, including the "what," the "who," the "why," the "when," the "where," and the "how," all of which are concepts that are modeled and mapped accordingly.

### Clarifying What Is a Business Process Between the BPM and BA Disciplines

Each discipline generally has the concept of a Business Process, but the definition of what one is and how it should be modeled are not necessarily the same between the two practice areas. This difference emerges from the different contexts in which each discipline operates.

Though generally not formalized as such, BPM's understanding of relevant concepts really comes out of the Operating Model context of the enterprise, which states:

*"An Operating Model is an abstract representation of how an organization operates across process, organization and technology domains in order to accomplish its function."[5]*

On the other hand, BA's understanding generally (and often formally) comes out of the Business Model context of the enterprise, which states:

*"A Business Model describes the rationale of how an organization creates, delivers, and captures value."[6]*

There is enough semantic overlap in the meaning of terms between these two contexts to permit (maybe even to encourage) each discipline to claim its own take on what is a Business Process, and to proceed accordingly in their respective efforts.

Without forcing a resolution in this regard, which is always fertile ground for spawning arguments among architects that only they can appreciate, it is nonetheless possible and prudent to talk about what should not be defined and modeled as a Business Process when better alternative architectural concepts and representations exist. Mutual acceptance of these distinctions will go a long way towards reconciling the disciplines of BPM and BA, simply by permitting a common understanding of such to be shared and applied between them.

While there is no singularly accepted definition for what is a Business Process, there have been definitional flavors that have (more or less) gained widespread acceptance over time. The earliest ones emerged out of the Business Process

---

[4] See *BIZBOK™ Guide* v3.5, Sec. 2.4, p. 115, from the Business Architecture Guild.

[5] See Wikipedia (*http://en.wikipedia.org/wiki/Operating_model#cite_note-1*), cited as coming from Marne de Vries, Alta van der Merwe, Paula Kotze and Aurona Gerber. (2011) A Method for Identifying Process Reuse Opportunities to Enhance the Operating Model. 2011 IEEE International Conference on Industrial Engineering and Engineering Management, and will be incorporated into the forthcoming BIZBOK v4.0 from the Business Architecture Guild.

[6] See Alexander Osterwalder and Yves Pigneur, *Business Model Generation*, Self-Published, 2010, Page 14, which is incorporated into Section 3.3 of the BIZBOK v3.5 from the Business Architecture Guild.

Reengineering (BPR) movement of the early 1990s, which emphasized the perspectives of value-output (as an operational outcome as opposed to something more abstract) and/or functionality (as input-to-output transformations).[7]

More recently, a more *operational* flavor has emerged, as process modeling languages have evolved and become standardized, that further generalized and refined the outcome of the set of related activities to be the realization of business goals and objectives.[8] This more recent flavor is also the one typically embraced by the BPM modeling community that uses BPMN.[9] Some in the architectural modeling community have also embraced the operational flavor, and by convention use BPMN for such.[10] Some architectural frameworks go even further by explicitly incorporating BPMN, albeit with extensions in its semantics and symbology to (purportedly) make the modeling language more effective and useful.[11]

Regardless of the process modeling language used, some concepts of a Business Process are so core that they are shared in some form across different languages and their various usages. In the case of BPMN, these and the rest of its modeling concepts are formally realized in its meta model and serialized as model data in XML form per its governing schema.[12]

**Span of Control** – A Process will have a span of control that defines the controlling context that governs or enforces its flow, application of business logic, assignment of performers, etc. In BPMN, the Participant element is visualized as a Pool, which acts as a Flow Element container. However, a Participant is not required (i.e., it is not necessary to draw a Pool) unless one is seeking to show Collaboration or to otherwise clarify the span of control. Without the use of this concept, the span of control of a Process modeled in BPMN can only be notionally understood as occurring within an encapsulating and defining context. In addition, a Participant can be notionally but not semantically divided into Roles that are visualized as Lanes.

---

[7] "Process is a technical term with a precise definition: an organized group of related activities that together create a result of value to the customer." – From Reengineering the Corporation: A Manifesto for Business Revolution (1993), p. 35, by Michael Hammer & James Champy. "In definitional terms, a process is simply a structured, measured set of activities designed to produce a specific output for a particular customer or market." – From Process Innovation: Reengineering Work Through Information Technology (1993), p. 5, by Thomas Davenport. The concept of value in these definitions is not really the same as is used in architectural frameworks, which is better explored in other chapters elsewhere in this Book.

[8] "A set of one or more linked procedures or activities which collectively realize a business objective or policy goal, normally within the context of an organizational structure defining functional roles and relationships." – From Workflow Management Coalition (*http://www.wfmc.org*), as cited in the *"In OMG's OCEB Certification Program, What is the Definition of Business Process?"* May 2008 (*http://www.omg.org/oceb/defbusinessprocess.htm*).

[9] The operational understanding of a process can be seen in BPMN Modeling and Reference Guide (2008), p. 27, by Stephen A. White, Ph.D and Derek Miers, and in BPMN Method and Style, 2nd Edition, p. 11, by Bruce Silver.

[10] For example, in the Department of Defense Architecture Framework (DoDAF) v2.02, a Business Process can be represented as a set of behaviors in the Event Trace, which is an Operational View formally known as OV-6c (see *http://dodcio.defense.gov/dodaf20/dodaf20_ov6c.aspx*), which is separate from but related to a Capability View.

[11] A good example of this is the Architecture Framework from LEADing Practice (*http://www.leadingpractice.com/*).

[12] The BPMN modeling language meta model, though modeled in UML (multiple inheritances notwithstanding), is really a MOF Level 2 statement, which makes the BPMN model, with the model data in XML form, the associated MOF Level 1. MOF stands for Meta Object Facility, which is from the OMG (http://www.omg.org/mof/), but a good explanation and a helpful diagram can be found at its Wiki site (*http://en.wikipedia.org/wiki/Meta-Object_Facility*).

**Decomposition** – Decomposition of a Process is essentially a decomposition of a span of control, wherein a higher-level expression of execution exchanges with a lower-level one. In BPMN, the Subprocess element contains its own execution context, but it is (more or less) defined as a child in relation to the parent Process. However, a Subprocess is but one Flow Node that can exist in a Process in BPMN, and if it is a Call Activity then it references a Global Process that has its own and separate execution context. Thus, the concept of decomposition in BPMN is not as strong as it is in other process modeling languages, wherein the sum of all children equals the parent.[13]

**Trigger and End States** – A Process when instantiated has a specific set of circumstances that constitutes a definitive beginning, and another that constitutes a definitive end(s). In BPMN, Start and End Events are visualized as Flow Nodes that either start or end a Process sequence. These Events can be typed as having specific behaviors that can include the definition of a payload that upon receipt starts a Process or upon transmission ends a Process, with the ending(s) representing Process outcome(s).

**Exchange Interfaces** – A Process will have interfaces through which exchanges occur between the span of control of a specific process and other Processes. In BPMN, such interfaces generally will occur over Messages (though Signals also constitute a type of information exchange), which are visualized as occurring via Message Events. (BPMN also has an Interface element that provides the implementation detail for how Messages are exchanged.) Exchanges of information can be visualized as Message Flows that connect from a Pool or Flow Node in a Pool to another Pool or Flow Node in a Pool. Thus, interfaces can be implied without further definition whether a Message Flow is drawn or not. This conceptual framework can be used to understand the boundaries of the concept of a Business Process, helping to make the case for what really should be mutually recognized as a Business Process by both the BPM and BA practitioner communities.

## 4. MODELING VALUE STREAMS OR CAPABILITIES IN BA, BUT NOT AS BUSINESS PROCESSES IN BPM

In BA, the concepts of Value Stream and Capability provide the core structure of the actual model for the BA, as defined in the associated architecture framework (typically expressed as a meta model using UML Class Diagrams).

Usually represented as a contiguous (or "chained") sequence of chevrons, a Value Stream is the means for mapping value generation in the enterprise, wherein the chevrons represent decomposed elements of the Value Stream. In a widely used BA framework, it is defined thusly:

"The primary blueprint used to do this is the value map which shows the activities that an organization performs to create the value being exchanged between itself and its stakeholders."[14]

Usually represented as a nested set of decomposed elements, a Capability is the means for mapping functional aspects of the enterprise that have desired results. In the same BA framework referenced above, it is defined thusly:

---

13 Such an example is IDEF0 (see http://en.wikipedia.org/wiki/IDEF0 or
http://www.idef.com/idef0.htm), which was a popular predecessor language to BPMN, especially in the Department of Defense, from which it originated.

14 See the BIZBOKTM Guide v3.5, Section 2.4, p. 115, from the Business Architecture Guild.

*Specifically, the business capability is "a particular ability or capacity that a business may possess or exchange to achieve a specific purpose or outcome.[15]*

While each of these concepts can be (and has been) represented and modeled as a Business Process, there are compelling reasons for not modeling them as such, particularly when the use of a process modeling language such as BPMN is involved. This point will become clear as each of these concepts is evaluated using the conceptual framework proposed earlier. A Value Stream can be decomposed, but has little in common with the concepts of span of control (of which there may be more than one involved in generating value), trigger and end states (which are about control flow in a Business Process, and not about value flow), and exchange interfaces (wherein segments of a Value Stream are fully self-contained, meaning a segment does not exchange with other segments). Notwithstanding these points, a Value Stream can be modeled as a high-level, end-to-end (E2E) Business Process using BPMN, though the result is not a material improvement over the non-standard but fairly ubiquitous chevron notation, as shown in **Figure 1** below.[16]

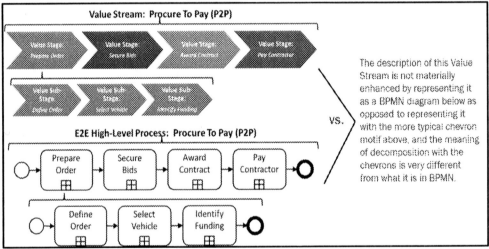

**Figure 1 – Example of Value Stream Using Chevrons vs. Value Stream Using BPMN**

The BPMN diagram indicates sequence and decomposition, while the chevron diagram indicates this as well but also suggests value generation and/or accumulation.[17]

A Capability can be decomposed, but has little in common with the concepts of span of control (of which there may be more than one involved in implementing it), trigger and end states (which are about control flow in a Business Process, and not about functionality), and exchange interfaces (wherein segments of a Capability are fully self-contained, meaning that a segment does

---

15 See the BIZBOKTM Guide v3.5, Chapter 2.2, p. 1, from the Business Architecture Guild.

16 The term "value stage" in the following graphic means that "each value stage of a value map as it moves from left to right creates value for one or more stakeholder," which is excerpted from the BIZBOKTM Guide v3.5, Section 2.4 p. 118, from the Business Architecture Guild.

17 The chevron notation likely owes its origins and ubiquity to Michael Porter's seminal use of it to show his Value Chain (see a reasonable treatment of this in the Wiki entry *http://en.wikipedia.org/wiki/Value_chain*).

not exchange with other segments). Notwithstanding these points, a set of Capabilities can be modeled as a high-level, E2E Business Process using BPMN, though the result is not a material improvement over the non-standard but

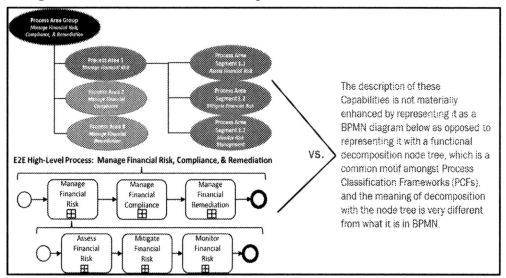

semantically simpler Capability Node Tree notation, as suggested in **Figure 2** below.[18]

### *Figure 2 – Capabilities Using Node Tree vs. Capabilities Using BPMN*

The BPMN diagram indicates decomposition, while the Capability Node Tree indicates this as well while not suggesting the misleading, inappropriate, and incorrect sense of flow across contiguous nodes.[19]

The top-down structure of the Capability Node Tree is reflective of it being a "what" concept and not a "how" concept, and as such it is often developed and standardized for horizontal or vertical segments of an enterprise.[20] These off-the-shelf constructs are generally referred to as Process Classification Frameworks (PCFs) or Industry Reference Models (or something similar). PCFs are helpful in normalizing the naming of process models via a common vocabulary, but they have no concept of flow and thus are not useful as models of operational behaviors. Unfortunately, there is often a mixing of meanings in practice that can be a key source of confusion between BA and BPM, which can be committed by efforts in either community or both communities to their mutual detriment.[21]

In summary, one CAN represent a Value Stream as a high-level E2E Business Process, but such an approach diminishes the effectiveness of the Value

---

[18] The terms "process area group" and "process area" are generic stand-ins for categories common in PCFs.

[19] Alternative and better means of showing decomposition of Capabilities exist, such as the Capability Map, which shows decomposition as nested boxes within boxes instead of node leafs hanging off of node leafs..

[20] General PCFs for different horizontal and vertical segments gathered by the American Productivity & Quality Center (AQPC) can be found at *http://www.apqc.org/*. Industry examples include the telecommunications industry with the eTOM Business Process Framework (see *http://www.tmforum.org/businessprocessframework/1647/home.html*) and the supply chain industry with the SCOR Process Reference Model (see *https://supply-chain.org/our-frameworks*).

[21] For a brief but good discussion of this phenomenon and its impact on modeling processes in BPMN, see BPMN Method and Style, 2nd Edition, pp. 11 - 12, by Bruce Silver.

Stream concept in localizing value generation and consumption in the business for strategic-level analyses and planning. Similarly, one CAN represent a set of related Capabilities as a set of related Business Processes, but such an approach diminishes the effectiveness of the Capability concept in inventorying functional features that are delivered or consumed. Furthermore, the semantics of the process modeling language used generally offer little in the way of greater clarity in describing what is being modeled, while constraining things in ways that are problematic for the overall modeling (such as in the case of decomposition from higher levels to lower levels). Consequently, Value Streams and Capabilities need their own conceptualizations and notations.

For these reasons, it is better to use BPMN to model the operational behaviors of Business Processes, which then can map (in whole or in part) to Value Streams or Capabilities – all as part of the BA model. This approach does not force a misleading mapping of the different granularities for these concepts.

## 5. RESOLVING VALUE STREAM OR CAPABILITY GRANULARITIES VS. BUSINESS PROCESS GRANULARITIES

The granularity of the set(s) of operational behaviors in a Business Process, particularly one modeled in BPMN will not be the same as the granularity of a Value Stream (whole or segments) or of a Capability. However, the mappings between a Business Process and these other, BA concepts do have a cardinality and optionality that can be understood at the meta model level.

A Business Process MAY *consume* value from the segment(s) of the Value Stream(s), which in a BPMN model would be the operational behavior of a BPMN Activity or Event that leverages something else to generate the requisite value as needed in the overall Business Process. This something else could be another Business Process or part(s) of one, or of a Service, a Resource, etc. A Value Stream MUST *be operationalized by* the associated Business Process(es) or part(s) thereof, meaning that the operational behaviors necessary to generate the value are executed by the associated BPMN model elements. Similarly, a Business Process MAY *use* one or more Capability, which in a BPMN model would be the operational behavior of a BPMN Activity or Event that leverages something else to implement the requisite Capability as needed in the overall Business Process. This something else could be another Business Process or part(s) of one, or of a Service, a Resource, etc. A Capability MUST *be operationalized by* the associated Business Process(es) or part(s) thereof, meaning that the operational behaviors necessary to implement the Capability are executed by the associated BPMN model elements. The resulting many-to-many relationships in these mappings are illustrated in **Figure 3** below, which shows how the various granularities can line up.

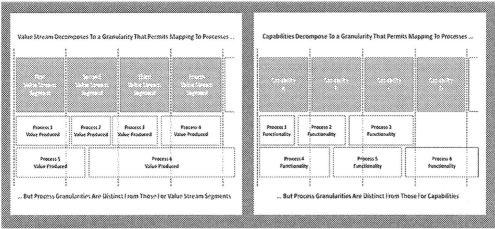

***Figure 3 – Different Granularities for
Business Processes vs. Value Streams or Capabilities***

While the mapping of Business Processes to Value Streams or Capabilities, and vice-versa, is essentially a many-to-many type, a more useful type of mapping requires a stylized approach to UML-based modeling that makes the "in whole or in part" relationship more workable. Such an approach is needed not just because of the granularity differences, but also to account for the imprecision inherent in most process models as well abstract concepts in a BA. This new approach is formally known as "Whole-Part," which recognizes a distinction between "strong" and "weak" types of decomposition[22]:

*Strong decomposition is a relationship that is resultant, with the "part" properties tied to the "whole" (i.e., rigorously decompositional from higher levels to lower ones)*

*Weak decomposition is a relationship that is emergent, with the "part" properties not necessarily tied to the "whole" (i.e., more like a catalog of items).*

By convention, this distinction can be realized through standard UML notation for Class Diagrams, as shown in **Figure 4** on the next page, where strong decomposition is shown using the compositional relationship and the weak decomposition is shown using the aggregation relationship.

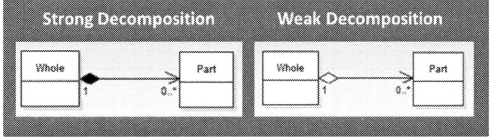

***Figure 4 – Strong Decomposition vs. Weak Decomposition***

---

[22] To see how deep the rabbit hole goes, explore the literature on this topic using Google, e.g., *"The Whole-Part Relationship in the UML: A New Approach"* pre-UML 2.0, the file for which can be found by searching for the title.

The resulting mapping of the Business Process concept (with Business Processes modeled in BPMN) to the Value Stream and Capability concepts (as well as other, related BA concepts) might look something like the meta model relationships show in **Figure 5** below.

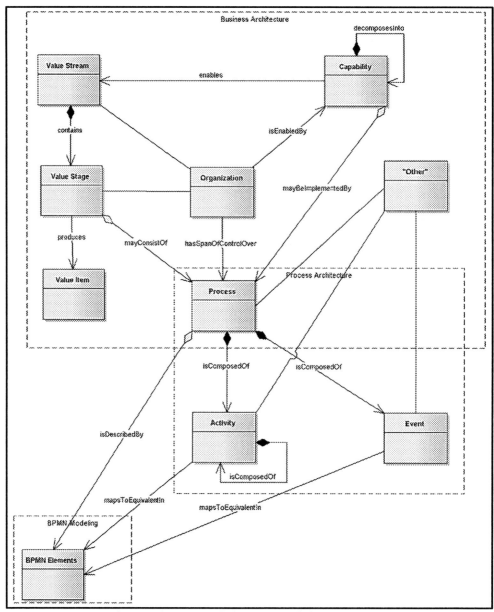

*Figure 5 – Sample Meta Model Mapping of*
*Business Process To BA Concepts*

## 6. WHY THESE MAPPINGS ARE NEEDED

With Business Processes mapped to Value Streams and Capabilities, the operational perspective of the business is blended with the strategic level of the business. This blending is particularly manifested in what is known as a Heat Map, wherein operational assessments of Business Processes can inform assessments of Values Streams and Capabilities, and strategic assessments of

Values Streams and Capabilities can inform assessments of Business Processes.[23] In this way, BPR efforts can be better targeted at areas of true need, and will be done in better alignment with business objectives.

Aside from being used in Heat Maps, these mappings can also surface Capabilities that are redundantly operationalized by similar Business Processes. Such information could be used to explore consolidating similar sets of operational behaviors into a single, reusable Business Process. Or, it could be used to better understand the reasons for any variations in the delivery of Capabilities across the enterprise.

BA gives BPM the architectural context BPM needs to be effective in achieving process improvement. In turn, BPM gives BA the process understanding BA needs to be effective in planning strategic initiatives.

## 7. LINKING BUSINESS PROCESS MODELS WITH FRAMEWORK-BASED ARCHITECTURES USING SEMANTICS

With the ability to now capture and work with model data from Business Processes modeled in BPMN, it is possible to explicitly link the values for concepts in the BPMN models to the values for concepts in the BA. This means that model data from one set of models can be used to populate or align with analogous or related concepts in other models, which either creates a common vocabulary for describing both sets of concepts or (at least) enforces a controlled vocabulary for describing both sets of concepts. The resulting set of linkages might look something like what is shown **Figure 6** on the next page.

With semantic technologies, these models and their linkages can be captured, stored, and queried like any other data. In this fashion, concepts are defined as classes (with attributes) that permit multiple inheritances and mappings between concepts at the instance level, where the values for the classes are actually realized. The key is to transform the model data into semantic form, where it can be understood as belonging to one or more ontology. Being in semantic form consists of being defined by Resource Description Format (RDF) or Web Ontology Language (OWL).[24]

---

[23] A Heat Map (see http://en.wikipedia.org/wiki/Heat_map) is a matrix expression of a mapping between two related concepts, with the intersecting entries color-coded to indicate the nature of the assessment made. Typically, this would be green for entries that are not in need of attention, red would be for entries that are in need of immediate attention, and yellow would be entries that may warrant attention at some point.

[24] RDF and OWL are standard formats maintained by the W3C (see *http://www.w3.org/TR/owl2-rdf-based-semantics/*).

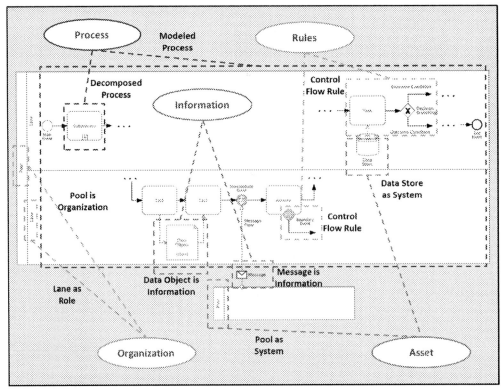

Figure 6 – Sample Linkages Between BPMN Elements and BA Concepts

The related modeling language concepts in the BA and BPMN models, and the associated models themselves, can then be understood as a set of related ontologies and instances. Consisting of RDF-OWL data, the architectural repository can be queried for analytical purposes, including use cases for architectural impact analysis and architectural conformance assessment. Furthermore, when paired up with legacy system data from the enterprise, this analytical reach extends into the realm of business and data analytics because such data can now be seen (and queried) as instance data of the architecture.

The resultant analytical power of this type of treatment goes well beyond what has been typically accepted as baseline feature sets in BPM and BA modeling approaches and tools. Previously, BA lacked meaningful process understanding that BPM-driven process modeling can provide, while BPM lacked the native ability to align with the business understanding that BA-driven architectural modeling can provide. BPM 2.0 answers these shortcomings by explicitly embracing architectural modeling.

This approach sorts out how the concept of Business Process should be distinguished between the two disciplines, and uses mapping concepts to make sure that this treatment is consistent and integrated across the two disciplines. Finally, semantic technologies provide the means to leverage and enforce these mappings in a standard way, making it possible for one set of understandings to automatically and directly inform the other. Such is the promise of BPM 2.0, the next generation of BPM.

# Using Analytics to Identify Process Opportunities

## Frank F. Kowalkowski,
## Knowledge Consultants, Inc., USA

### 1. PROCESS PERFORMANCE AND THE BUSINESS ENTERPRISE

Because processes are critical to business execution, process performance management and improvement have become two key aspects of BPM for improving business performance. These two key process approaches form the basis of enterprise transformation, integration and consolidation within the enterprise. They also support integration across enterprises and form the foundation for e-commerce, e-government and enterprise excellence. Organizations are good at assessing due diligence regarding financial, market and legal issues. However, studies (Michael Porter and others) show that most structural changes requiring integration fail due to operational (read process) and/or cultural incompatibilities. Both of these issues can be addressed with some core process and cultural analytics.

All this leads to a need for process management that achieves a lean, compliant and more flexible enterprise. Process management and process methodology can provide process analytics at specific points in the methodology to reduce the failure rate. Management of processes should also include analytics that form the basis of monitoring continuous improvement of the enterprise as well as the processes through a process performance reporting system, often via business intelligence tools.

BPM really consists of four components, the processes themselves, a methodology to build/change processes, a body of knowledge about processes and a management approach that treats processes like an asset. There are many good tools and tool suites that support these components. However, while some tools contain monetary and quantitative analysis features few tools also contain phrase analytics based on descriptions used to define the structure of the enterprise. Analytics, especially process analytics, are important to both the success of the methodology and the management of the processes.

With studies showing that there are many process project failures, some estimate 75% fail in some manner such as failure to meet quantitative targets like cycle time, error rates or cost as well as functionality gaps. There is certainly room for anything that can improve the success rate. Many new analytic techniques have emerged that make more formal analysis of process architecture and execution possible. For example, methods of determining process rank based on yield versus risk provides a formal, reliable method of process ranking. This provides the guidance to the process staff with respect to the order of process improvement based on opportunity and risk. The technique illustrated here combines quantitative analytic with phrase analytics to get risk/yield ranking insight.

There are many uses for process analytics beyond the ranking approach. Analytic techniques are also used to determine alternatives for process improvement, improvement impact analysis, diagnostic and prescriptive analytics and when used with clustering techniques can provide predictive capability. These techniques are used for analyzing the gap between 'as is' and 'to be' states of processes, assessing impact of changes in enterprise structure and determining points of common process use. Included in process management are analytics for processes that are also part of a typical score-carding effort. It could be balanced scorecard, functional scorecard or discipline score-carding.

## 2. IDENTIFYING PROCESS IMPROVEMENT OPPORTUNITIES:

How can we increase the likelihood of success on process projects? Determining the path of process improvement has always been a questionable effort. There are three core techniques currently available for determining the processes most likely to contribute to business improvement.

Process improvement, one of the more popular business improvement initiatives, has achieved both success and failure. Success has usually been as part of another initiative such as quality improvement six sigma types of projects. Failures have been more prominent in stand-alone process improvement projects. Studies indicate that up to 75 percent of process projects end in failure of some sort. The reasons cited are that the schedules are not met, budgets are exceeded, deployment is not successful, the performance is not met or the scope of improvement is not met.

The approach described here is called the **the risk versus yield approach** that compares the risk with the expected yield of improvement to organize process improvement opportunities

## 3. CONSIDERING PROCESS PERFORMANCE

The goal of any process analysis is to rank a set of processes in some manner to decide where to start and pick where you might get the best yield with the lowest risk. Assessing current process performance is the first step in identifying process improvement opportunities. A reliable method of performance ranking is required to accomplish a process performance assessment.

Measuring process performance comes with a number of issues. If the processes are being replaced by a package then there may be low interest in measurement. There also may be a limited amount of data you can gather about the existing processes. On the other hand there may be a workflow package in use that has built-in measures. Knowing that there are a number of issues with process performance, let's take a simple and basic look at a ranking approach based on performance.

## 4. CONSIDERING PROCESS CONTEXT

In business analysis a process is often analyzed for its internal complexity. A large process with many connections is more complex than a process with few connections. Working with such complexity is well known. There is another kind of complexity that is less known and has a large impact on the success of a process project. That complexity is defined by the number and types of touchpoints in the enterprise. When changing a process, the greater the number of touch points there are, the greater the risk of failure. Touch points means any point within a process that contacts and interacts with the different components (or dimensions) of the business. This would include locations, other processes, organizations, decisions, systems, data bases and so on. In enterprise analysis there are over 25 different categories of components that are of concern to the analyst. Fortunately only six or seven of them are used in day to day analysis work. So, process context in the more general case includes internal process complexity because you can look at the interactions of processes together with the interactions of the process with the rest of the enterprise.

Business processes (actions that are taken to support some purpose by a person or automated procedure) are never executed in a vacuum although some people may believe so. They are executed in context with many assets and enablers of the enterprise. Further, they have constraints or relationships that impact their usage. The enablers have characteristics of their own that may be severely impacted by process change or conversely impact the implementation of the new process. The entire set of influences or factors on a process is called "*its context*".

The context of a process places pressures on the process and may cause it to be analyzed for some improvement action. The degree of influence (the pressure) determines which processes might be a target for action. In addition, the results are often used to identify a set of *requirements*. Requirements, as defined in the dictionary, are things essential to the existence or occurrence of something else and relate information about who, what, where, when, how, and why something is needed. This information must provide sufficient detail so eventually something can be engineered or built. Several strategies such as process replacement, workflow development, automation-via-applications, and so on are approaches used to fulfill those requirements.

## 5. START WITH PROCESS PERFORMANCE – THE YIELD FACTOR

There are seven basic measures that are used for improvement that emphasizes the operation of the process, namely cycle time, wait time (or queue time), transport time (movement between steps or processes), process cycle efficiency (or pure work time), error rate (a quality measure), throughput (an asset use type measure) and finally cost, the more visible measure for management.

One or two process measures are used to determine rank regarding where to apply process improvement funds and efforts. Simple rankings are used where the most costly or largest cycle time is the target of improvement. In some cases two variables are used together in a regression to give a simple 4 – box that points to good candidates. A four box is a logistic regression relating two variables based on a third that is common to both. In this case we can use process name as the common item and cycle time and process cycle efficiency as the two variables since each process name has the two variables.

The chance for a better and more reliable process ranking increases when you use two quantitative factors. Below is a graphic example of a logistic regression or 4 – box using two performance variables (process cycle time and process cycle efficiency) to assess opportunity.

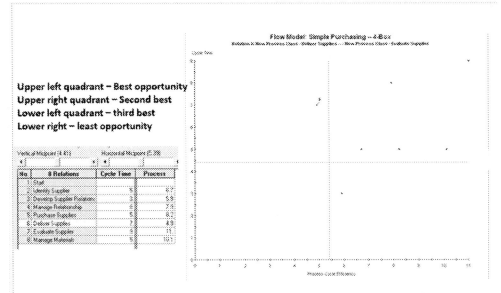

Upper left quadrant – Best opportunity
Upper right quadrant – Second best
Lower left quadrant – third best
Lower right – least opportunity

Example Interpretation of 4 -box: improved process cycle efficiency falls direct to bottom line.

Best yield is reducing cycle time and increasing efficiency which means looking at dots in the upper left quadrant

If you gather performance numbers on more than two of the seven types of attributes (which can be done with workflow packages and ERP types of packages), then you can integrate them in to a single value and get ranking something like below.

The graphic below shows the ranking of a small group of processes to do a simple purchasing task. If you were to rank these based on cycle time alone then the choice for improvement would be the step or process with the longest cycle time. In this case it is Evaluate Supplier. If you were to use 2 attributes the best candidate is Deliver supplies. For four attributes it is Develop Supplier Relationship and for six attributes it is the same but the second candidate changes. Of course this does not take into account the interests of management who may have a totally different perspective.

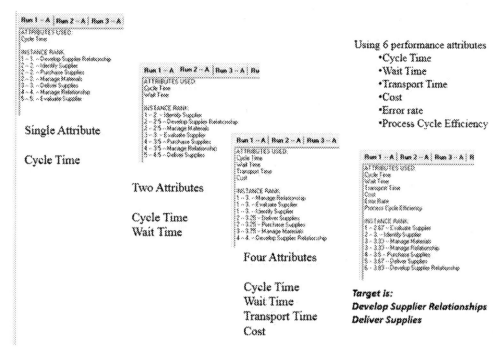

Single Attribute

Cycle Time

Two Attributes

Cycle Time
Wait Time

Four Attributes

Cycle Time
Wait Time
Transport Time
Cost

Using 6 performance attributes
• Cycle Time
• Wait Time
• Transport Time
• Cost
• Error rate
• Process Cycle Efficiency

*Target is:*
**Develop Supplier Relationships**
**Deliver Supplies**

So the first conclusion that is drawn from the process ranking and risk remediation effort is to get a ranking of the best yield opportunity to the least. In theory, start with the best yield and work down to the least. No method is perfect. Of course, there are some other considerations. Here are a few:

- You may want to start with processes in one location or organization or function. In that case you do this ranking within those boundaries
- You may want to use weight factors to give added emphasis to what might be an important attribute. While a good idea, these weight factors get manipulated until the desired process comes out on top
- You may not have hard numeric performance values for all the processes. In this case you divide the processes into two (or more) groups according to the quantity and quality of the numbers.
- You may have to conduct a baseline study of the processes to measure their performance. Since this adds cost to the effort, there is usually resistance. However, return cannot be calculated without a baseline.
- If the evaluations of the attributes are subjective with values like High, Medium and Low then the technique of Sabermetrics is used. Sabermetrics is a method of quantification of things like expert ratings of athletic performance as combined with quantitative values with some correlation. In these efforts you are looking for an indicator of performance (through correlation) or direct cause and effect which is a bit more difficult to achieve.

What we do not know at this point is the degree of risk associated with changing the various processes. A high yield high risk process may represent a good opportunity for failure. This is the purpose of context analysis.

## 6.   ADDING PROCESS CONTEXT – THE RISK FACTOR

Earlier it was mentioned that one goal of process analysis is to rank a set of processes in some manner to decide where to start and pick where you might get the best yield with the lowest risk. Context analysis is an attempt to measure risk of changing a process. The question is: which processes are the most risky to change? Context analysis is a method that provides an answer to that question.

There can be a large number of context categories that are used for context analysis. It is most useful to use five or six categories that are common to most processes. Typically this would include the following:

- Documents
- Technology
- Locations
- Organizations
- Other processes

In many cases, if requirements for systems are the issue, then you might use Applications, IT Infrastructure and Databases along with the above categories. If workflow is a target, you might add policies, procedures, rules and decisions.

Often only one or two categories of context are used in determining the complexity of the relationship between processes and the enterprise. There is a simple technique to relate two categories together. Using multiple context factors improves the assessment of risk and provides a better and more reliable process ranking relative to complexity.

If you gather context relationships on five or six categories then you can integrate them into a single value and get a process ranking something like below. The example below shows a set of five context matrices that are used for ranking. Matrix 4 is the one that relates the target purchasing process set to the overall core processes of the enterprise. That means the purchasing process either supports or connects to the core process.

Model Name: DAC Technology Context [From Dimension: FUNCTIONS - To Dimension: TECHNOLOGY]

Model Name: DAC Location Context [From Dimension: FUNCTIONS - To Dimension: LOCATIONS]

Model Name: DAC Organization Context [From Dimension: FUNCTIONS - To Dimension: ORGANIZATIONS]

Model Name: DAC Process Core Process Context [From Dimension: FUNCTIONS - To Dimension: FUNCTIONS]

Model Name: DAC Document Context [From Dimension: FUNCTIONS - To Dimension: DOCUMENTS]

***Row headings are the processes and the column headings are the context***

In the graphic above, you can see how the ranking of the seven processes changes as more context is added. Using only documents the ranking gives Manage Relationships as the process with the most touch points.

The graphic below uses the small group of purchasing processes used earlier. If the rank were based on only one type of context such as location, technology or documents, then the choice for improvement might be skewed towards that context at the expense of other context factors that may be more significant or have greater impact.

In this case, using just documents connected to the processes the greatest frequency of reference for a process is by the Manage Relationships process. However this is pretty weak by itself because there is not much difference between the least and most referenced process. If the matrix were larger, this factor would most likely improve. If you were to use 2 context factors by adding the organizations that the processes touch, then the best candidate is still Manage Relationships. However, when all five context categories are used the most referenced process is Develop Supplier Relationship and Manage Relationships are both tied for the process with the most connections. Also, notice that there is good discrimination between the lowest and the most referenced.

The significance of the references is that the more touch points there are the greater the complexity with respect to the business and therefore risk related to process change. Larger matrices used in actual analysis are typically 30 to 50 row headings by 30 to 50 column headings. This analysis becomes more significant when dealing with the emerging use of workflow engines as the enablers become more significant. There are files, screens, data groups, rules, documents, policies, procedures, analytic flows and a number of other enablers that become involved with the process.

Included in this set of context matrices is a matrix that covers process to process complexity. Often this matrix is important as it shows all the interconnections between sets of processes or which processes support other processes as an enabler.

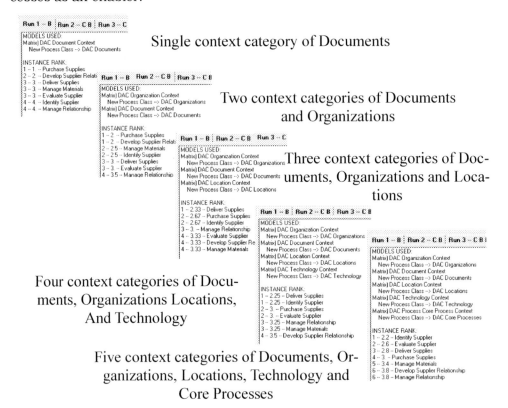

Single context category of Documents

Two context categories of Documents and Organizations

Three context categories of Documents, Organizations and Locations

Four context categories of Documents, Organizations Locations, And Technology

Five context categories of Documents, Organizations, Locations, Technology and Core Processes

So the second conclusion that is drawn from the process ranking and risk remediation effort is to get a ranking of the least risky to the most risky. In theory, start with the least risky and work down to the most. There are some considerations that are needed to make this work well:

- The more accurate the associations the better the context analysis. Here are the extremes:
  - Associations that come from management interviews are OK but not the best. However, they are a good start.
  - Associations that come from fact such as what systems connect to which processes or workflows are much better but their scope is more narrow than the management view and more material is gathered to get the larger view. The material must be summarized and integrated for the more general views.
- The only way to use weight factors is on the final ranking results.
- It may be an advantage to divide the context by major component of the business to focus the eventual improvement effort.

- The most useful approach is to do the higher level associations and then to validate with some detail work. With the validation you can determine the approximate bias and factor that into the analysis.

First, the performance of processes was analyzed for a ranking based on typical attributes such as cycle time, cycle efficiency, wait time and so on. The result is one set of ranking that can be used just focusing on the yield from process change. Then the focus was on the context of processes. This gives a ranking based on the complexity of the interconnection of the processes with the enterprise. This reflects the potential risk involved with the changes. Below these two are combined to get a ranking based on both yield and risk.

## 7. Combining These into the Yield Versus Risk Proposition

So far both yield and complexity (risk) have been analyzed. The real value of this type of analysis is to use the two perspectives together to get a ranking of processes in terms of the greatest yield with the least risk. Of course, management interests will always override these considerations but at least the degree of risk and yield are known for the deviation. Here we bring the two perspectives together.

Process analysis is not like physics where things are precisely known. Often the numbers relating to process execution vary according to the stability of the process. A machine-based process might be very stable while a customer service process might vary considerably. The difference is usually in the variety of inputs and results from the process. Single input and single output are very predictable especially for machine output and assessing quantity and quality of the output. When it comes to variations in input and output, more measure variance exists between outputs. The process then has a variable set of performance parameters that need to be averaged. We assume here that this has been done so there is no need to worry about it here but we need to be aware of the situation if we are to change the process.

Further, management often is changing the structure of the enterprise to respond to some market situation or competitive threat and so the context may also change. The point is, there is no perfection or exactness here only approximation. Even in best practices the results will vary from enterprise to enterprise. The enablers may also change over time or there may be a project in effect that is upgrading or changing a number of enablers that are not obvious. So the context may vary a bit also.

All of the 'variation' is normal in any enterprise that is adapting to its environment. The averaging out of values takes most of this into account. So perfection in measuring is not needed here but consistency is. If there is any bias it should be consistent. The reason is that we are concerned with ranking not absolute values. With this in mind we prepare a yield/risk 4 – box to rank process opportunities.

## 8. Preparing a Risk to Yield 4-Box and Assessing the Result

The initial interest is to go directly to the relationship of the largest composite yield values and compare them or regress them with the largest composite context results. This is a good place to start. Of course you need two values for each point (in this case a each point is a process component) to get a plot. The following two steps are required to get this to work:

1. The yield values are used with a focus on the five performance parameters used to identify candidate process for improvement based

only on performance. The 'Y' or vertical axis is used for this value. The ranking might change a bit with more parameters in consideration but the changes are usually insignificant unless the parameter is heavily weighted.

2. The context or risk values of are used with a focus on a set of four context matrices. The 'X' or horizontal axis is use for these values. These are used to identify the probable maximum complexity of the processes under consideration. The context used here is only partially complete as it does not include the enablers. The enablers would provide another degree of complexity or difficulty to making a change.

Usually four, five or six performance parameters are used to get the yield ranking and four or five context categories to get the risk rank.

If process enablers are added then four or five enablers will give you a ranking based on enabler context. This results in a three dimensional assessment box with eight boxes (2 by 2 by 2) for determining the risk – yield. This is a bit more difficult to work with and certainly not easy to explain quickly to management. A good approach is to use two 4 –boxes, one for the yield – business context and another for yield – enabler context, get a ranking for each and compare the two rankings.

9. INTERPRETING RESULTS OF THE 4-BOX

The 4-box can be interpreted by quadrant using the following approach:

| Quadrant Position: | Description | Business Implication |
|---|---|---|
| Upper Left: | High yield, low complexity | low hanging fruit, low risk |
| Right: | High yield and high complexity | high risk, cause of failure |
| Lower Left: | Low yield and low complexity | learning opportunity |
| Right: | Low yield and high complexity | leave alone |

# This is what the 4 - box would look like

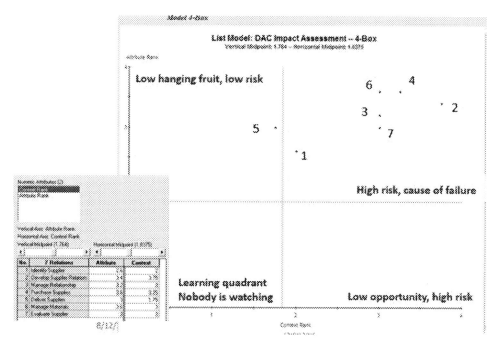

To select which processes, steps or groups on which to work the processes must be ranked. The final ranking can be done based on risk or yield. The guidelines are as follows:

- Minimize risk – Start with the lowest risk, highest yield process and rank according to risk
- Maximize yield – Start with the highest yield and lowest risk process and rank according to yield

Ranking according to risk is placing the sub processes in order of increased risk values. To minimize risk the steps or sub processes would be transformed in the following order:

Notice in the ranking above that the high yield processes are somewhere in the middle of the risk rank. Often these will be chosen as a balance between risk and yield.

**Rank by Risk (lowest first):**
1.  Step 5 – Deliver Supplies (1.75) This is the lowest risk sub process.

2.  Step 1 – Identify Supplier (2.0)

3.  These next three are about equal from complexity perspective, discrimination is by performance:

    a.  Step 6 – Manage materials (3.0) best performance yield (3.6)

    b.  Step 3 – Manage Relationship (3.0) next best (3.2)

    c.  Step 7 – Evaluate Supplier (3.0) least of the three (3.0)

4.  Step 4 – Purchase Supplies (3.25)

5.  Step 2 – Develop Supplier Relations (3.75)

Maximizing yield requires placing the sub processes in order of decreasing yield, highest yield rank to lowest. To maximize yield, the steps or sub-processes would be transformed in this order (Yield value is in parenthesis):

**Rank by Yield (highest first):**
1.  Step 6 – Manage materials (3.6) (higher rank because it is lower risk than Step 4)

2.  Step 4 – Purchase Supplies (3.6)

3.  Step 2 – Develop Supplier Relations (3.4)

4.  Step 3 – Manage Relationship (3.2)

5.  Step 5 – Deliver Supplies (3.0) (higher rank because it is lower risk than Step 7)

6.  Step 7 – Evaluate Supplier (3.0)

7.  Step 1 – Identify Supplier (2.6)

Here the high risk sub-processes are right up there with the yield. The yield is what makes the transformation of those processes attractive to management.

## 10. AN ALTERNATIVE - DOING A STEP-WISE ANALYSIS

Sometimes a step-wise analysis is done to see the change in ranking as the yield and context change. This approach is used to find out which performance parameter and/or which context has the most influence on the results. The result is evaluated by observing the movement of the dots of the 4-box across any of the quadrants. The idea is simple, which parameters or context seems to cause the greatest movement.

The step-wise approach starts with one performance parameter ranking such as cycle time and one (or more) context rankings such as organizations impacted. The performance parameters are added one at a time and the change in ranking (noted by movements of the dots on the 4-box) are evaluated to find the parameter that seems to have the most influence. While a bit more tedious this technique may focus efforts more sharply into certain processes or process groups.

## 11. SUMMARY OF THE RISK – YIELD APPROACH METHOD:

1. Identify the target process, suite of processes or suite of groups of processes of interest
2. Gather four to six performance parameters on the processes (actual values or estimated)
3. Create a composite ranking that represents the yield opportunity part of the method
4. Gather the relationships of the same process suite and categories of the business (locations, technology, organizations, strategies and so on) using simple matrices. four or five of these are sufficient.
5. Create a composite ranking of the context results that represents the risk part of the method
6. Create a 4 –box (regression technique) using yield as the vertical axis and context as the horizontal axis.
7. Draw interpretations of the results

## 12. COMMENTS AND CAUTIONS

A few comments and cautions are in order for using this approach.

- You can do this type of analysis on a set of process steps, a group of processes or on a set of groups of processes. The level of detail depends on the data you have and if it is actual measured numbers or estimated numbers. Both work quite well.
- The example used in this here is very small consisting of seven steps or sub processes. More likely a real suite of processes or steps will be 30 to 50 long and the context categories will have 30 to 40 instances.
- Matrices should have a density of about 33 percent to 66 percent, that is, the number of cells with a relationship should vary from 1/3 to 2/3 to be useful.
- The source of these matrices is often swim lanes used in the development of process flow diagrams in many process modeling tools. Swim lanes identify both connected components of the enterprise (often organizations, locations, or external players) and enablers (often systems, databases machines and so on) that define the context of the processes.
- Without tools, a good and easy way to work with quantity is about 15 to 20 processes (or steps) and about 15 to 20 instances of categories for the context and enabler analysis.
- There are several ways you can calculate a composite ranking for performance parameters or context. Weights can be added though we do not favor using such an approach due to manipulation by interested parties.
- Finally, management interest will always overrule any formal method of ranking.

The idea of a formal way to rank processes based on possible or expected yield of improvement and potential risk were introduced in this section. At the end of the day you want to know in what order to do the work to provide the best yield and the least risk. At least if you need to tackle something with a higher risk than expected, you know the issues since you have risk matrices to identify all the connections or touch points from the processes to the components of the enterprise. The types of rankings described here provide the analyst with a good baseline and starting point for initializing a process project.

# Learning from the Leaders

## Prof. Mark von Rosing, Maria Hove, Henrik von Scheel

### 1. INTRODUCTION

When you take the time to compare your own knowledge to that of others, you become better at learning. This is not a new phenomenon or concept; this is a basic reason why so many organizations want their employees to work together, to collaborate, and/ or to create the circumstances for them to share knowledge. The growing amount of software that supports collaboration to enable effective mutual learning is a confirmation of this trend.

This chapter looks at why it's important to read the BPM case studies in this book, what we can learn from them and how we can take the most of them.

### 2. CASE STUDIES: LEARNING FROM THE WINNERS

Case studies bring interesting, real-world situations[1] that have proven to work. Specifically we can learn their:
- way of thinking
- way of working
- way of modelling
- way of implementation
- way of governance
- way of change

The BPM cases unlock ways of thinking, working, modelling, and sometimes even the ways of implementation and governance, and specify what works, again and again (best practice), and what are unique practices applied by leading organizations (leading practices).

They identify the benefits that may be accrued with the common and repeatable patterns that provide the basis for the ability to apply the same principles and receive the same benefits.

These award-winning stories detail how we can benefit from their experience, inherit their wisdom and knowledge. At the same time, they also share their experiences of what not to do, giving us the unique opportunity to learn from them.

There are positive lessons to be learned from failure. New research suggests that the failure of others might be a better source of learning than our own shortcomings or missteps. Researchers led by Emory University's Professor Diwas KC[2] recently examined the experiences of cardiovascular surgeons to uncover whether success or failure was the better teacher[3] — and, if so, whose

---

[1] Adapted from: Seperich, G.J, M.J. Woolverton, J. G. Beierlein and D. E. Hahn, eds., Cases in Agribusiness Management, Gorsuch Scarisbrick, Publishers, Scottsdale, AZ 1996

[2] http://goizueta.emory.edu/faculty/academic_areas/isom/kc_diwas.html

[3] http://smartblogs.com/leadership/2012/10/10/how-learn-best-others-failure/

failure held better lessons[4]? The team analyzed data from 71 cardiothoracic surgeons over 10 years as they performed over 6,500 minimally invasive coronary artery bypass grafts, a complicated and relatively new procedure at the time of the study. They examined the rates of successful and unsuccessful procedures and the process by which the surgeons were learning and improving their performance. As they analyzed the data, they found something striking: while learning from success is important to identify the right way to execute the work, failure was the best teacher mostly when someone else has failed. Surgeons learned best from their own successes and the failure of others; their own failures were much harder for them to learn from. One possible explanation for this is attribution theory — specifically, self-serving bias and fundamental attribution error. Taken together, these psychological biases predict that individuals more often attribute their success to their own efforts and their failures to outside circumstances, while simultaneously doing the opposite for others — assuming others' failures are caused by their efforts and their success' by outside circumstances.

In the case of the surgeons, their own failures made for difficult learning material, since self-serving bias made it more difficult for them to notice and correct their own faulty actions. The failures of others, however, created a perfect learning laboratory, as they could observe actions similar to theirs but free of the tendency to attribute the outcome to bad luck. Interestingly, as the surgeons became more confident in their own abilities by accumulating successful operations, they also became more likely to reflect on their failures and learn from them.

Good practices and bad practices: The physicist Niels Bohr once defined an expert as "a person who has made all the mistakes that can be made in a very narrow field." Bohr's quip summarizes one of the essential lessons of learning, which is that people learn how to get it right by getting it wrong again and again. This also means that the limitation of our learning is based on all the mistakes we have to do or as just discussed 'failure of others'. Newer learning psychology therefore builds on being able to learn from the good and bad practices of others.

The business marketing word for this is called: **lessons learned**. This is what education is about; it is the wisdom of what works and what does not, obtained through the experience of others. The results carry strong implications for leading organizations. While the recent efforts to view failure more positively are a good start, perhaps leaders need to spend more time reframing individual failures as positive learning experiences.

Seeing the failures in others not only aids learning, but helps to make one's own failures less appear less threatening. However, to see what works, one cannot focus on failures. Indeed, organizations can help increase the learning of their members by taking time to review and reflect upon successes, both their own or those of others. How to learn from their own success? Well, most

---

[4] •KC, Diwas, 2013, "Does Multi-Tasking Improve Performance? Evidence from the Emergency Department" MSOM

•KC, Diwas, Brad Staats and Francesca Gino. 2012. "Learning from Your Failure, But Not My Own," Management Science

•KC, Diwas and Brad Staats. 2012. "Accumulating a Portfolio of Experience: The Effect of Focal and Related Tasks on Surgeon Performance," M&SOM (Published online before print July 13, 2012)

often, when a project or procedure is successful, individuals are simply sent on to new projects without the benefit of a "post-op" review. Establishing a "post-op" protocol for every failure and every success might ensure that experience becomes the best teacher, regardless of whether that experience was a success or a failure.

Learning from others is not a passive process, but one that requires work on our part. Below is a list of lessons learned of how to learn from other success and failures.

3. LESSONS LEARNED - HOW TO LEARN FROM THE CASE STORIES:

Here is how to get the best from these case studies:

- Read the case thoroughly. To understand fully what is happening in a case, it is necessary to read the case carefully and thoroughly. You may want to read the case rather quickly the first time to get an overview of the industry, the company, the people, and the situation. Read the case again more slowly, when there is something that has caught your interest[5].
- What was the purpose: behind every program and or project there are specific drivers, forces, and strategies that shape the purpose of the innovation and/ or the transformation initiatives. Identifying that will help you understand what they did and what is more important why they did it.
- Identify the Expectations: In the end of the day, a project is about fulfilling specific value expectation and or performance expectations, the ability to identify them enables one to understand the benefits and how the project fulfilled them.
- Define the central issue. Many cases will involve several issues, problems, or challenges. Identify the most important problems or pain point, and separate them from the more trivial business issues.
- Top Down or bottom up: it is vital to know if the project followed a top down and thereby the goal chain approach or a bottom up and thereby situational problem chain approach. The key to appreciating a case is understanding not only the why and the what, but the how.
- The solution: What was the solution, how did they solve the problem or the goal? Identify all the relevant alternatives.
- Measurements and scorecards: how did they measure success and what were their scorecards/reports.

The above suggestions are summarized in figure 1, where it is vital to remember that learning is a practice; what has succeeded and can be repeated.

---

[5] Adapted from: Seperich, G.J, M.J. Woolverton, J. G. Beierlein and D. E. Hahn, eds., Cases in Agribusiness Management, Gorsuch Scarisbrick, Publishers, Scottsdale, AZ 1996

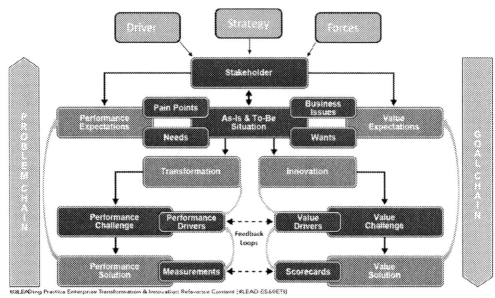

**Figure 1 - A conceptual model to break a case down and see in which areas it can be applied**

### 4. EXAMPLES OF WHAT TO LEARN FROM THE CASE STORIES:

Now that you know how to get the most out of reading the award winning case studies, let's review some of the case studies in this book:

### Example: Bank Dhofar, Sultan of Oman

Industry: Finance-Banking

It is one of the fastest growing banks in the Sultanate of Oman, with a strong presence in corporate banking, consumer banking, treasury banking and project finance. The bank's central issue is that they were realized that to facilitate and manage the growth of its retail assets, it needed to enhance its operational capacity, productivity, and ability to scale-up operations

Leading practice in terms of good patterns:
- Forces for change identified and therefore the solution can be tracked against it.
- Strategy was identified and clear
- Value expectations and value drivers defined
- Considered the End2end flow, not only parts
- Process automation in two full areas (Retail Loan and Credit Card)
- Process innovation and transformation aspects are detailed
- Elimination of paper based processes
- Removal of manual calculations
- Eradication of manual service in terms of automating them
- Roll out plan specified
- Decision making was though into the process
- Measures of before and after are quantified
- Best Practices and Learning Points are stated
- Steps done are described and repeatable

Learning from bad practices, mistakes or missing points:
- The solution still used programming in terms of Java; Java script; Dot net and SQL to customize the BPM solution, today BPM automation should as a rule of thumb deliver solutions with minimal programing / scripting.
- The way the loan process architecture is descried is reactive ("if the customer appears again to apply for the loan" BPM solutions need to be able to reconsider the flows based on social media, knowledge workers, customer or service flow. Just automating the way it was done before is not a recommended way of execution.
- While decision making was thought into the process in terms of after the data entry fields are captured properly and documents are verified, the branch initiator takes a decision, the automated report of data entry was not specified. Possible creating new manual steps and thereby work

### Example: Prince Sultan Military Medical City

Industry: Healthcare and Medical

Prince Sultan Military Medical City (PSMMC) is a military hospital and is considered as one of the most advanced medical centers in the Middle East. With a capacity of more than 1,400 beds and 12,000 employees, there naturally will be a build in complexity. In order to address patient safety issues a BPM system was introduced to streamline and manage the improved processes of various departments associated with Patient Affairs.

Leading practice in terms of good patterns:
- Key issues and pain points where identified
- Performance expectations and performance drivers are defined
- Business Competencies where linked to the processes
- Business and IT aspects where considered
- Mobile devices where considered automating the process beyond applications
- Role oriented process modelling was considered
- Key reports where identified
- Measurement metrics where defined
- Process analytics where build into the decision making process
- Evidence-based concepts where build into the process
- Best Practices and Learning Points are stated
- BPM was used to streamline process
- BPM was used to monitor and control the activities of Patient Affairs

Learning from bad practices, mistakes or missing points:
- While there could be specified missing aspects, due to the nature of case descriptions, the aspects might still be done in the project, just not specified in the case. For example:
  - The challenge of identifying the Right Patient and provide the right treatment was specified, but how it was solved was not detailed.
  - The challenge of or prevent identity theft of eligible Patients was specified, but how it was solved was not detailed.

- Difference between process flow and the information flow was not specified, disabling the ability to rethink the information and service flow.
- The case focuses strongly on the description of the BPM system, while a BPM system is very important, the tool alone will not solve the problems.

### SBB - Swiss Railroad

Industry: Transportation and Logistics

The challenges and complexity of rail network operation and all the possible incidents with the roles involved have to be efficiently managed and controlled. It is a complex mixture of processes and organizations

Leading practice in terms of good patterns:
- Forces for change where identified and therefore the solution can be tracked against it.
- Issues and Pain points where classified.
- Performance expectations and performance drivers defined
- The link between performance issues and value impact where quantified.
- Contradictory system requirements where recognized
- Innovation & transformation aspects where stated
- Self-learning processes was implemented
- Preventative measures where build into the planning and operations. Moving the organization from reactive to a proactive way of working.
- Agile approach was used
- Steps done are described and repeatable

Learning from bad practices, mistakes or missing points:
- While it has good use of traditional Agile techniques to show rapid execution, the agile principles applied to BPM were not specified.
- A lot of emphasis and focus on the methodology versus opposed to result and value focused.
- While heat maps where used for role mapping, the solution of how the role-oriented process modelling was done, was not applied

These examples illustrate that the art of learning from others is not a passive process, but one that requires work on our part. It's important to read and understand the case, identify the purpose, the expectations, define the central issue, pinpoint the approach and determine the solution as well as spot the possible measurements and scorecards. By exposing what are good practices applied by leading organizations (leading practices); they also expose what not to do, giving anyone that understands the lessons the unique opportunity to learn from the (often expensive) failures of others.

### 5. CONCLUSION

These award-winning cases present a rich fountain of documented way of thinking, working, modelling, implementation, and governance. They show what works repeatedly (best practice), and what are unique practices applied by leading organizations (leading practices); they also expose what not to do, giving anyone that understands the lessons the unique opportunity to learn from the (often expensive) failures of others. They can identify the benefits with the common and repeatable patterns that provide the basis for the ability to apply the same principles and receive the same benefits.

# Section 2

# Using BPM

# Bank Dhofar

## Award: Banking and Financial Services: Loan Origination
## Nominated by Newgen Software Technologies Limited, India

## 1. OVERVIEW

Established in January 1990, Bank Dhofar commenced operations with two branches, in Muscat and Salalah. Today it is one of the fastest growing Banks in the Sultanate of Oman, with a strong presence in Corporate Banking, Consumer Banking, Treasury Banking and Project Finance. The bank realized that to facilitate and manage the growth of its retail assets, it needed to enhance its operational capacity, productivity, and ability to scale-up operations. Automation of key business processes was identified as a key imperative. The bank decided to automate two of its key business processes, Retail Loan Origination (covering Home Loan & Personal Loan), and Credit Card Processing.

The Loan Origination process is highly regulated and data-intensive, requiring input and feedback at multiple steps throughout the loan cycle. The bank realized that there was a strong need for a solution that could effectively digitize and handle the effective flow of the documents from across the process life-cycle. Further, to keep up with the demands of the ever-increasing customer-base, the bank needed a solution for end-to-end automation and centralization of its credit card processing and approval systems.

After evaluating a host of solutions, Bank Dhofar decided to go with a solution comprising a proven Business Process Management (BPM) platform, an Enterprise Content Management (ECM) platform, and a Scanning and Digitization suite, for end-to-end automation of its Retail Loan Origination and Credit Card Approval processes. The solution offered enhanced business flexibility, better credit risk management, and rules-based processing, resulting in improved business performance for the bank.

Below is a brief overview of the processes automated:
- Loan Eligibility – Built on a proven BPM platform, the process performs loan calculations. When a new customer approaches a branch of the bank, to avail Housing/Personal Loan, the Loan Officer logs in to the Loan Origination system to initiate the Loan Eligibility process by entering the relevant customer details. The system performs some calculations based on the entered information and informs whether the customer is eligible for the required loan or not. Once eligibility is confirmed, the Loan Officer fills in the complete customer details and routes the application for necessary approvals. Upon necessary approvals the application is sent for creation of account (Operative account, Marginal account, Loan Account) and disbursal.
- Credit Card – The Credit Card Process is designed based on the assumption that the person applying is an existing customer of the bank. Using the scanning tool the branch user scans the completed application form along with supporting documents, enters the CIF ID in the text field, maps the documents to the corresponding document type, and exports to the BPM solution. This automatically creates a

work item in the BPM solution and all the document and data are made available to the system, which checks the application for eligibility. If the customer is eligible for the service, the branch user fetches the complete information of the customer from Core System and routes the work-item for approval. Once the application is approved, it is sent to the Card Operations team for Card Creation and Account Opening.

The document digitization and scanning tool along with multiple image servers and a centralized document management system, made it possible to make all the business decisions on electronic documents available anytime-anywhere on the web. The electronic documents archived in the document management server are accessible to users as per their access rights.

The BPM platform defined the entire process flow for the Retail Loan and Credit Card processes. It also defined the document image flow from the branch offices to the back-office (Central Processing Center) for all the processes.

As a result of the implementation the turnaround time for Retail Loan Approval was reduced from 7days to 1 day (86% reduction). The turnaround time for Credit Card approval process was reduced from 5 days to 1 (80% reduction).

Direct and indirect benefits accrued to the bank include:
- Reduction in Operational Costs, Travel, and Communication Expenses,
- Reduction in process turnaround times
- Improved customer satisfaction as a result of faster loan disbursals and credit card approvals
- Better performance monitoring using audit trails and ability to drill down to granular details
- Reduced operational costs for document capture, retrieval, and processing
- Parallel processing of loan application documents
- Anytime anywhere rights-based access to necessary documents, enabling faster decision-making

## 1. BUSINESS CONTEXT

Bank Dhofar was aggressively looking at expanding its business both vertically and horizontally. To facilitate its growth agenda the bank wanted to automate key retail processes and decrease the process cycle times, while enhancing operational efficiencies. Bank Dhofar wanted to develop a Central Processing Center (CPC) and several Regional Processing Centers (RPCs) for complete back-office process automation, which was an integral part of the bank's growth strategy. The bank realized that to achieve all these objectives they needed a BPM platform to underpin their operations, which would not only bring complete automation and process visibility but also ensure adherence to regulatory compliances, enable continuous process improvement, and help improve quality of customer services. The bank decided to start with the automation of two key processes - Credit Card Process and Loan Eligibility Process.

Before the implementation, all the physical documents were processed manually. Everything work-step from filling of the details, and processing of the request for approval, to opening of accounts, was manual. Even the eligibility for the loan was checked manually.

Key issues that the bank was looking at resolving as a result of the implementation include:

- Providing visibility to employees for all work items pertaining to them, to help in streamlining their activities in an efficient way
- Providing easy access from desktops to all documents and processing status of cases
- Establishing best-in-class operations and productivity standards through analysis of time and motion data coming out of the workflow database, rather than using traditional averages that could be skewed by idle time, low skilled staff, and poor practices
- Skill-based dynamic work allocation and tracking
- Faster exception resolution
- Higher process efficiency
- Tracking the status of applications (at CPC/RPC)
- All the documents were physically managed and transported to RPC/ CPC site from the branches pan-India for processing
- Reducing turn-around-time
- The bank did not have a comprehensive audit trailing facility
- All the loan calculations were done manually. A loan calculator was provided to do the calculations
- Manual hand-offs of documents made it difficult to track and manage the right versions of documents
- Escalation and exception management process was manual and error-prone
- Manual processing of all customer requests, received via multiple channels

Post implementation all customer requests and work-items are processed in the central offices resulting in leaner branch offices. The branch offices capture the customer documents and some key customer details, using the Distributed Capture tool. The system performs a duplication and blacklist check, and then sends the customer requests to the centralized back-office for Loan Approval or Credit Card Approval. This allowed the branch staff to concentrate on customer-facing activities. Further, the simplicity of operations made it easier for the bank to roll out new branches in quick time.

## 2. THE KEY INNOVATIONS

### 3.1 Business

The solution offered some innovative features and capabilities that helped the bank achieve operational efficiencies. Some of the innovative tools are detailed below:

- Loan Calculator – The Loan Calculator is an application within the Loan Eligibility process to perform loan calculations based on a customer's credit history, income, and other details. A prospective customer submits a request for a new Housing/Personal Loan through Bank Dhofar's designated branches. The Loan Officer logs into the Loan Eligibility process and enters the necessary customer details (Salary, D.OB etc) in the relevant fields. He then clicks the 'Check Eligibility' button to perform necessary calculations. The system carries out the calculations as per Bank Dhofar's policies and the results are displayed to the Loan Officer.

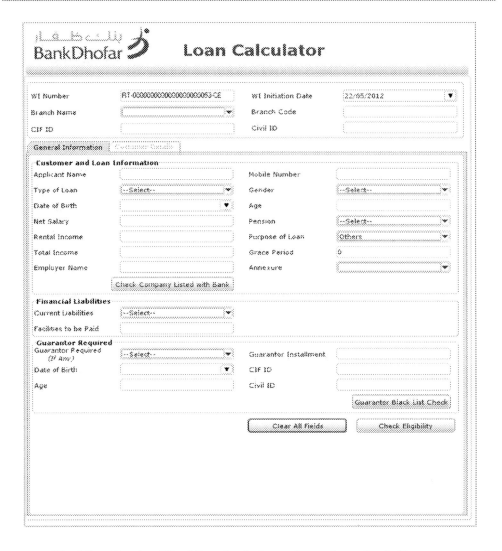

- **Blacklist Check** - Blacklist check is performed to check if a customer is blacklisted. To Perform Blacklist check, the user clicks on the Blacklist button on the form and the acknowledgement (Yes/No), is successfully populated in BPM system. Blacklist check can also be done for the Guarantor provided by the customer.
- **Fetch Customer Details** - This operation is used to fetch the customer's details from Finacle (Core Banking System). For fetching the customer's details, user needs to press an action button - "Fetch Customer details". At this work step, the system automatically checks existing customer database and updates CIF (Customer Information).
- **MIS** - Below mentioned custom reports are made available in the Personal Loan process apart from the inbuilt product reports.
  - **Branch Initiation Report**: It is generated on daily basis and provides details about the total number of cases initiated by any branch. It also provides details on the loan ticket number associated with customers.

- Daily Loan Booked by Branches: It provides details about the Loan booked by branches on daily basis.
- Summary Report for Approved Applications: It provides details about the Loan applications approved by branches on daily basis.
- Summary Report for Rejected Application: It provides details about the Loan applications rejected by branches on daily basis including rejection code and reason for rejection.
- Daily Summary Report For Pending Application: It provides details about pending applications such as at which stage the application is pending and since how many hours

### 3.2 Case Handling

The design of the Loan Origination System process is based on the Pro-Agile Approach. It is a blend of both prototyping and agile methodology. It makes early visibility of functionality in less number of iterations without any scope creep. It is very simple to understand and use. The Pro-Agile approach follows the following workflow:

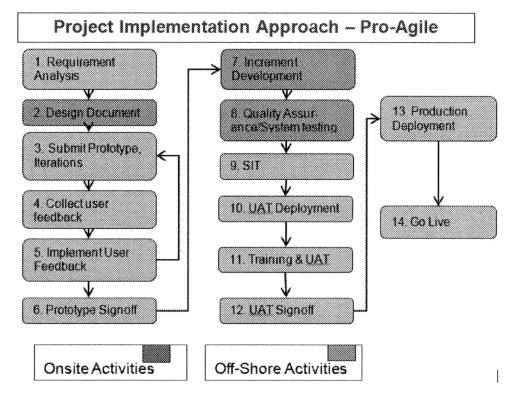

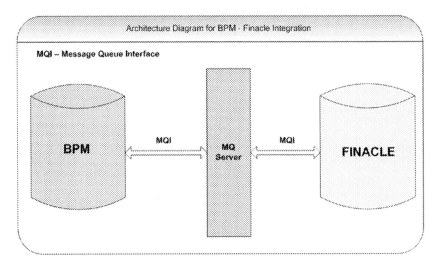

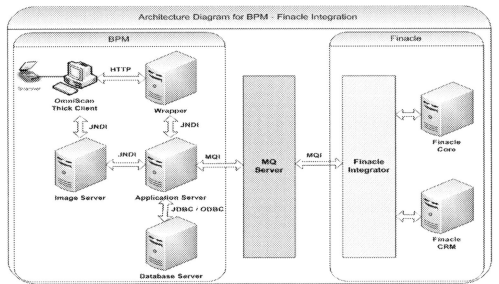

### Architectural Diagram
### Components Used:
- Business Process Management Tool
- Enterprise Document Management System
- Digitization and Automatic Data Capturing Tool
- Business Activity Monitor- a graphics based process analysis tool for business processes.

Bank Dhofar implemented the BPM-based solution to automate two key processes i.e. Credit Card Approval and Loan Processing.

### Credit Card ->Credit Card Process:
The main objective of automating this process was to enable electronic flow and archival of the application form and documents submitted by the customers, and accelerate Credit Card application approval process.

Brief Description:
- Work introduction begins from the scanning engine where the completed Application Form and relevant documents of the customer are scanned and the work-item/application is introduced into the workflow
- Once the work-item has been initiated in the workflow, the user starts with the processing of the work-item/application by referring to the scanned/attached documents
- The Branch initiator enters the CIF ID in the Proposal form and automatically the details of the customer stored in Finacle are displayed in the proposal form in the relevant fields
- The Branch Initiator performs the Blacklist Checks, CBO Caution list Check, and Customer Rejected Check
- The Branch Initiator captures the details required for the system to calculate the DBR & proposed credit limit of the card based on the information provided by the customer
- After the data entry fields are captured properly and documents are verified, the branch initiator takes one of the below mentioned decision:
  - Submit -- Will send the proposal form to the Branch Manager for approval
  - Discard -- If the application does not fulfill the Terms & Conditions
  - Finacle Exception -- If the application comes up with the Finacle Exception

### Retail Loan Origination

**Loan Eligibility Process** -Data Entry users enter the data of the applicant i.e. Name, Date of Birth, Salary, and Type of loan i.e. Home Loan and Personal Loan. All the validations based on the bank policy are incorporated in this process based on the type of Loan (i.e. Housing Loan and Personal Loan). The validations can also be configured. Once eligibility criteria is cleared, completed loan application is then forwarded for further processing i.e. approval and Loan Account opening. Once the loan is approved the pre-printed template report is taken. The typical reports are bond reports, sanction order, etc.

**Loan Calculator-** The Loan Calculator is an application within the Loan Eligibility process to perform loan calculations. A prospective customer submits a request for a new Housing/Personal Loan through Bank Dhofar's designated branches. The Loan Officer logs into the Loan Eligibility process and enters the customer details (Salary, D.OB etc) in the relevant fields. He then clicks the 'Check Eligibility' button to perform necessary calculations. The system carries out the calculations as per Bank Dhofar's policies and the results are displayed to the Loan Officer.

**Detailed Description of Loan Eligibility Process**: If a customer comes to apply for a Personal Loan and he is also eligible for a Housing Loan, the system displays results for both the Housing Loan & Personal Loan while carrying out calculations. Once the filled customer application is approved by the Loan Eligibility process, it is routed to the respective processes i.e. Housing Loan or Personal Loan or both based on the Loan Type selected by the customer.
- **Scenario 1** - If customer agrees to loan:
  Loan officer clicks on the 'Apply for Loan' button if customer agrees

to take the loan. A new tab is opened where the Loan officer captures the complete details of the customer. An option is provided to recalculate the Loan if there are any changes in the details given by the user at Loan calculation stage & actual details given while initiating the work item (as per the documents ). Another option is provided to the Loan officer to initiate the work item either in Housing Loan or Personal Loan or both the processes. Loan officer selects the appropriate option and clicks on the submit application button. Work items are created automatically in the corresponding processes (Housing Loan/ Personal Loan) depending on the option selected by the Loan Officer.

- **Scenario 2:** If customer doesn't agree to take loan
  Loan officer clicks on 'Discard' button, all details entered by the Loan officer are saved in the system and the work-item moves to exit queue. Records saved in the BPM database and can be used in future to generate leads.
- **Scenario 3:** If customer agrees but doesn't want to apply on same day
  In this case the Loan officer can click on the save button and details are saved in the system. When the customer comes to apply for the loan again (with actual documents), the Loan officer can search for the work item (based on CIFID or customer name) and initiate the work item in PL/HL process as per the customer's request.

### Detailed Description of the Loan Approval Process (Home/Personal)
- The Housing Loan/Personal Loan officer receives the cases from all the branches in a common pool
- All the cases are then filtered branch-wise by applying the proper filter. These filters are configurable as per the bank's requirement and can be changed in future.
- The officer then assesses the cases submitted by all the branches and also reads the decision and comments of the branch manager and accordingly takes a decision.
- When the officer takes and submits his decision the cases are forwarded to the CCU for further review.
- If the Loan officer rejects any case, an auto email is triggered to the branch manager and the case is discarded from the system.
- The officer can also send the case back to the initiating branch for rework if required. If he takes the decision to send back the cases for rework, they are sent to the Loan officer (initiating branch) from where the cases were initiated.
- Loan summary sheet is generated and is automatically attached with the case in the predefined format shared by the bank
- Once the Loan is approved by the approving authority, it is sent to the branch officer for generation of the offer letter which is signed by the customer and scanned and attached with the application, and sent to the CAD (Disbursement) department.
- When the application is received by the CAD department, they perform below mentioned tasks through the BPM tool-
  - Open SB/OD Account, Loan Account

- Update Insurance Details
- Disbursement of the loan

### 3.3 Organization & Social

- The end-to-end automation of the previously manual processes re-sulted improved employee productivity and satisfaction.
- Elimination of manual hand-offs resulted in drastic reduction in calculation and other processing errors
- Centralized processing of applications at the back-office resulted in freeing the branch staff to engage in business development and other customer-facing activities
- Anytime-anywhere access rights-based access to relevant infor-mation helped in better and faster decision-making

## 3. HURDLES OVERCOME

### 4.1 Management

Ever-changing requirements of the bank as the implementation progressed.

### 4.2 Business

For the success of this project in-depth knowledge of Retail Banking opera-tions and patience was the key. Understanding the requirement from the Busi-ness Users' perspective and delivering a solution in such a short span was the key to success in this project.

### 4.3 Organization Adoption

Acceptance of the new system by the bank staff required few training & infor-mation sessions to explain the need and benefits of the new system.

## 4. BENEFITS

The project was a landmark decision for Bank Dhofar, which facilitated its aggres-sive growth plans. The solution solved the business concerns of the bank and be-came a game changer for them as it brought about complete Business Transfor-mation for the bank.

### All the processes were rolled out in 2 months across 63 branches.

Some of the key benefits accrued to Bank Dhofar include:

- Vertical and horizontal business growth
- Easy audit and tracking
- Report Generation
- Faster process cycle times
- Process and performance metrics for process visibility
- Reduction in operational costs
- Improved customer interaction resulted in higher customer satis-faction
- Real-time exception handling between the branch offices and the Central office, such as invalid documents, documents not attached, credit card not issued, Loan Guarantor paper issues, etc.
- No data redundancy
- More flexibility in the business process as process route works au-tomatically as per the type of work - debit card requests, internet banking request etc., and the amount associated
- Total time taken for loan processing was reduced from 7 days to 1 day

- More accuracy while producing legal documents like Sanction Order, Bond etc.
- Physical document movement was minimized
- Reference to existing loan is made easier, as it can be referenced from the system rather than the physical documents

The performance improvements of the bank were observed in the following areas:

### Improved Process Cycle Time

The BPM platform significantly reduced the number of steps (Almost 50% reduction) involved in both the processes. Digitization made sure that there was no physical document movement across departments and locations. This contributed to achieving faster process cycle times and lower operational costs as there was no extra expense in courier or transportation cost. Since, all documents were digitized there was no chance of documents being misplaced or damaged in any process.

### Higher Process Efficiency

All the external processes were seamlessly integrated and run automatically with existing banking processes. Now, the entire process requires minimal manual intervention. The system performs automatic data entry by using unique automatic data fill technique. The system automatically checks for duplicate customer entries and prevents user from doing so. The double data entry method also reduces data entry errors. All the physical documents are converted into digitized documents which transverse across departments and locations. The system also generates electronic data captured forms for the Loan Process and Credit Card Process, which includes KYC Process. The BPM solution supports automatic bulk upload of the general excel file to Flexcube. The process related data in XLS files are automatically uploaded in the core banking system without any manual intervention.

### Skill-based Dynamic Work Allocation and Tracking

Work allocation and tracking of tasks had been a major challenge for the bank. The BPM solution provided a work distribution console that eliminated the bottlenecks in the job allocation process and ensured and equal distribution of tasks. Work is distributed as per the employee's skill set and furthermore the solution supports complete audit trail of all the tasks and activities for monitoring purposes.

### Faster Exception Resolution

The bank had an exception management process which was manual, time-consuming, and error-prone. The BPM solution provided an exception management mechanism which requires minimal manual intervention. Whenever and wherever an exception occurs an alert message is sent to the employee as well as the concerned business manager. Different activities such as document validation, KYC verification, document re-scan, loan eligibility check, credit card limit, etc. are triggered automatically when an exception is raised. Parallel triggering of necessary activities helps resolve the exception and results in a faster exception resolution.

### Improved Customer Experience

The mandated cropping is performed using the scanning tool. All customer signatures are cropped and archived separately with other necessary documents. The customer requests for credit card /home loan /personal loan are now processed automatically and the system ensures that the SLAs are maintained by giving automatic alerts or message to the users. The system automatically generates proposals for credit limit based on the rules and regulations of the bank. It sends automatic alert messages to the users once the credit limit or loan is approved, or rejected. The BPM platform supports auto-processing of e-Alerts, SMS alerts, customer queries, and other banking requests.

### Secure Banking Process to Prevent Fraudulent Activities

The BPM solution automatically performs a blacklist check at the time of data entry and prompts users if the customer is blacklisted. The solution is seamlessly integrated with the credit scoring and KYC process to prevent forgery and fraudulent activities. Customer signatures are cropped and archived separately for future reference and online signature verification.

### 5.1 Cost Savings / Time Reductions

| Area | Benefits | Measure |
|---|---|---|
| Process Cycle Times / Customer Satisfaction | • Faster Customer On-boarding<br>• Quick Customer Service Delivery | • Reduction of process TATs by 80%<br>• Improved Customer Satisfaction |
| Agility & Responsiveness | • Faster change management adaptability<br>• Lower time for new process roll-out | • Reduction from months to weeks / weeks to days |
| Compliance & Quality | • SLA Adherence within departments | • Increased to 99% |
| | • Customers audit-ability and adherence to regulations and compliance | • Increased to 100% |
| Operational Efficiencies | • Productivity | • Increase by 80% |
| | • First Time Right | • Increase by 90% |
| | • Process TAT | • Increase by 80% |
| Costs | • Resource Reduction; Reduced operational expenses | • Reduced by 50% |

### 5.2 Increased Revenues

The implementation resulted in faster loan disbursals, allowing the bank to grow lending revenues and sustain profitability.

### 5.3 Quality Improvements

- Better process monitoring and tracking
- Better and more informed credit decisions
- Improved customer service levels
- Elimination of errors due to manual processing of applications
- 100% process visibility

## 5. BEST PRACTICES, LEARNING POINTS AND PITFALLS

### 6.1 Best Practices and Learning Points

✓ *Ensure representation from all relevant departments during process study and planning, including the bank's IT department*

 ✓ *Integration requirements should be kept in mind during initial planning phase*
 ✓ *Use prototype approach to finalize specifications*
 ✓ *Involve business users in the process design phase not just management*
 ✓ *Follow a methodology to keep track of interim process change requests*

### 6.2 Pitfalls

 ✗ *Attempt to establish perfect specification of a process without prototyping*

## 6. COMPETITIVE ADVANTAGES

- By implementing the solution, the bank provided a competitive advantage to its sales force allowing them to focus on customer facing revenue generating activities
- Ability to scale-up of operations facilitated the bank's horizontal as well as vertical growth plans
- Enhanced process visibility, monitoring, and real-time tracking of applications ensured improved "First time Right" rates

## 7. TECHNOLOGY

The solution comprised of a robust Business Process Management platform, an Enterprise Content Management platform, and a Distributed Scanning Engine. The BPM platform enabled end-to-end automation of the key processes, while ensuring real-time process monitoring and tracking. The Scanning tool enabled multi-channel distributed capture, to facilitate process initiation at branches and further processing at the Central back-office. The ECM platform helped in electronic archival, retrieval, and movement of documents, eliminating manual-handoffs, speeding-up the process, and eliminating human errors.

The design of the Loan Origination System process is based on the Pro-Agile Approach. It is a blend of both prototyping and agile methodology. It makes early visibility of functionality in less number of iterations without any scope creep.

## 8. THE TECHNOLOGY AND SERVICE PROVIDERS

**Primary Vendor:** Newgen Software Technologies Limited

**Trademarked Products from Newgen's Portfolio:** OmniDocs™, OmniFlow™, and OmniScan™

# HCL IBS, United Kingdom

## Banking and Financial Services, Back Office Optimization
## Nominated by Corporate Modelling, UK

### 1. EXECUTIVE SUMMARY / ABSTRACT

HCL IBS is an outsourcer carrying out policy administration and affiliated services in the UK closed book Life Assurance and Pensions market place. We deliver those services to demanding commercial SLAs, cheaper than the insurance companies with whom we contract and we have to make a profit!

Our client contracts are on a "per policy" basis so revenue from those contracts reduces year on year in line with the attrition of each book of business. HCL IBS also have to meet stringent and emerging UK regulatory requirements.

In 2009, as a response to this challenge we began a journey to deliver immediate reductions in operations costs (c.30%) and ongoing ability to control costs whilst improving people productivity. The Operational Excellence ("OpEx") project was initiated to design, build and implement a Transaction Management Solution. The design was to be owned by the business, supported by IT and relevant professionals. The overriding principle was to develop a model that embraced end to end transaction processing where work could move seamlessly through each process step from start to finish – a factory floor approach! Supported by philosophies of "one and done (where a single interaction completes all or part of a process), "no case ownership" and queue management.

After a year's hard work we created an environment enabling our business leaders, to manage throughput of work, assess and improve their team's productivity and utilization, assess and remedy any skills shortages real time and manage their SLAs and KPIs in line with evolving client and regulatory demands.

We have benefited from more than a 15% increase in the number of transactions processed per person (FTE). This has been a key enabler to delivering more for less. Within the first year, we also realized a progressive reduction in overall operating costs of c. 15%. These savings have enhanced our competitive standing and reputation allowing us to profile new opportunities to gain market share. In addition, upcoming releases and implementation of improved and additional workflow functionality will cause further savings putting us well on track for our targeted 30% reductions.

### 2. OVERVIEW

HCL has more than 95000 employees providing integrated services covering BPO operations, software development, testing and infrastructure support services for more than 100 customers globally. The financial services vertical contributes more than 25% of HCL's revenues and employs 13000 people.

HCL IBS Ltd, a UK subsidiary of HCL and part of the financial services vertical, is a provider of outsourced life assurance, pensions and investment administration. We manage and service closed life and pensions books for leading financial organizations and are responsible for complete end-to-end processing and associated services. We are also directly regulated by the FCA.

Our presence in the UK closed book life and pensions business is significant and we, in the main, adopt a platform based approach servicing over 1 million closed book policies with a diverse range of features and benefits.

Insurance companies outsource their policy administration (and other functions for three reasons – to achieve reduced and certain cost, to ensure improved productivity and to pass on operational risk. HCL IBS must meet these requirements whilst working in a heavily regulated environment and ensuring that our clients customers continue to receive a great service.

Being a "closed book specialist", our revenue (which is contracted with each client to be on a per policy basis) reduces in line with the reduction in numbers of policies in force. This reducing revenue streams has also been significantly impacted by customers' financial awareness, volatile economic markets and the adoption of increased regulation. Together, these have increased operating costs which are borne by us, the outsourcer.

HCL IBS were initially able to counteract the ongoing reduction in income on the aforementioned contracts through BPR, Six Sigma, KAIZEN and other initiatives. However, the benefit of these faded over time and this combined with varying levels of platform functionality, a reliance on manual workarounds and a vast range (c.4000) of different product types all reducing in number meant that we needed something more substantial that would change attitudes and behaviors across the breadth of our organization and enable the delivery of sustainable large scale change. It was felt that, especially given the ongoing changing face of UK regulation, that a robust and flexible solution owned by business users for the business would ensure a level of engagement most likely to refocus hearts and minds, creating a common goal and shared vision of the future.

Nobody can change a culture, but we wanted to create an environment where the desired culture would emerge Our approach was to document the principles, philosophies and outcomes that we wanted in place and having done this we invited a number of workflow/MI suppliers to tender. The contract was awarded to Corporate Modeling a company already providing BPMN based modeling, process analysis and workflow technology to the market. They also understood our approach and our desire to put an in embracing Transaction Management Solution in place.

To achieve the required model and to achieve the necessary increases in productivity, utilization and throughput, we had to start from the ground. We had to redefine people's roles and align them to the new principles and philosophies. We had to ensure that performance management measured the correct behaviors and were also suitably aligned. Most importantly we had to design and build supporting workflow and MI tools that would allow us to run the "factory" the way we wanted.

Identifying what we wanted led us to the following approach:
- Enable straight through processing; analyzing and challenging existing breaks in each process (hand offs)
- One and done; try to have one person at one interaction complete the work in a single step. Work allocated to the right person who is competent administering the same activities on a regular basis.
- Encourage a more suitable culture; get everyone onboard with the concept of "QPP":
- Queue - processing by distinct queues to aid throughput.
- People - skills and resource management.
- Performance - qualitative, quantitative work ethic and recognition and reward scheme.
- Create our own USP a roadmap built on a factory model. Fast, efficient, compliant and low cost.

- To create a more compelling new business model where OpEx encourages prospects to move to a seamless processing model and enables HCL to price competitively without necessarily being platform dependent.
- MI delivered that is simple but critically relevant, accurate and timely.
- Rapid deployment – targeted implementation in 4-6 months sitting alongside in place platforms therefore not necessitating migrations.
- Empower our users through business ownership of initiation, development and implementation of process change and improvement through productive dialogue with other stakeholders (i.e. IT and compliance).
- Measure everything; if you can't measure it you can't justify change

The project highlighted a number of challenges. As soon as the OpEx principles and philosophies had been agreed, operations staff were empowered to draft a more detailed operating environment. The dialogue with both the chosen vendor and with internal stakeholders was critical to ensure that the solution and supporting technologies were aligned to what the business wanted – rather than being sold something that was off the shelf! We wrote a request for tender that stated the strategic goals as well as the underlying principles such as:

- No impact or critical dependency on existing systems as this would slow delivery and take longer to test.
- Minimal IT involvement after initial set up and configuration.
- Needed no specialist training to operate.
- Needed end-user reporting and analysis as soon as we knew what it was we needed.
- Management sees health of business in minutes.

A shortlist of vendors were given the opportunity to show us their BPMN based products but only one; Corporate Modeling, understood what we were trying to do and were willing to change and enhance their existing workflow and MI solution to meet our needs and to help crystallize our vision into a tangible solution that would reduce our costs and manage/mitigate key business risks.

After a year's hard work, we had created our vision of Operational Excellence. The resultant program delivered a new way of working, an opportunity to achieve a leaner more efficient workforce and the ability to analyze and continually improve our organization and we have not stopped there. We have turned into an organization which is continually learning and improving and works in partnership with IT to deliver change. We are, we believe, the epitome of the Agile Business Process Company.

## 3. Business Context

HCL IBS is a mid-sized company providing business process outsourcing solutions. Operating out of four sites in two countries, we needed a new philosophy and approach designed by operational managers for operational managers.

With the implementation of the OpEx platform we have evidenced a cultural and behavioral shift. OpEx has made it possible to deliver claims earlier, contribute to improved servicing and complaint resolution, streamline multiple touch points, reduce operating costs and increase client and customer satisfaction.

The human element realized its potential through performance management. Our staff were provided new job profiles and with improved management information we were able to actively support personal development plans relevant to our business needs and reward-based outcomes. Clear learning tools, supporting controls and governance help encourage a positive working environment and this makes a world of difference.

A fully engaged workforce allowed us to deliver the project in a timely implementation period with positive responses pre and post launch enabling further benefits.

## 4. The Key Innovations

Key innovations from the OpEx project included:
- a whole new mechanism for defining business processes, allowing users to define processes as linear and removing the complexities of BPMN notation, replacing this with data-driven parameters that can be controlled by the team-leaders and the workforce users.
- a new way of managing the team based workforce, using daily one-to-one meetings and a rigorous continuous daily assessment of productivity, utilization, time management, skills and competency, activities and work ethic - to do this we had to split processes away from case management therefore moving to an environment with no case ownership.
- a unique fully integrated quality assurance toolkit as part of the core workflow architecture, providing open and closed QA, peer review, checklists across all our processes.
- a new integrated complaint categorization toolkit including automated regulatory report generation.

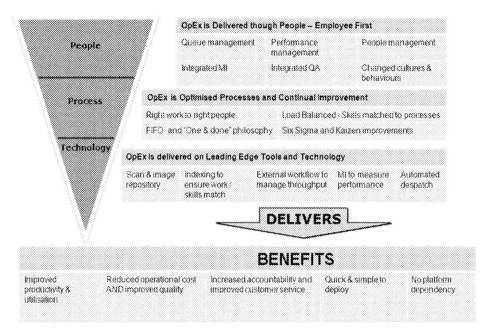

Figure 1 – OpEx overview: About the people, the processes and the technology

### 4.1 Business

OpEx provided HCL IBS with a new way to optimize its working practices, many of which were a legacy of manual processes, a plethora of product types and process steps that are abundant in the financial services. The project has resulted in a huge demonstrable increase in productivity, utilization and throughput, resulting in increased service quality for our clients and their customers at a lower cost to ourselves.

The solution is user friendly and easy to understand. In addition, the business now has a common platform capturing key business metrics necessary for achieving its service level agreements internally, to the clients and to the regulatory bodies.

The platform delivered a multi-sited queue management capability, clear responsibility for task based processing, uniform metrics and clear benchmarking capabilities and is able to manage high-volume processing and continues to aid the elimination of inefficiencies and non value add, costly activities.

Through data analysis, we are able to continually meet the changing regulatory and economic world, and most importantly grow our business.

### 4.2 Process

The original HCL IBS model was heavily built on an organizational tree structure, hindered by client centric processes and a dependency on key persons. Our model was somewhat dictated by contractual obligation and grandfathered employee agreements. Our old administration system workflow was based on the ability to 'choose' cases to be processed from an ordered workflow queue and the user then being able to 'own' this case through to completion. It did not consider prioritization, effort, resource or competence, and required line leadership to manually collate and distribute work types. The concepts of get next, one and done and no case ownership did not exist.

OpEx is intelligent and works in conjunction with our staff. It is built on the basis of FIFO (first in first out) processing requiring staff to select the next available price of work. With the introduction of business rules as evidenced in the slide below, the work is ordered into queue based structures built and owned within the operation.

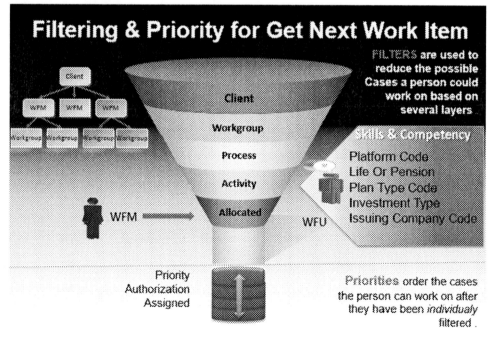

Figure 2 - OpEx has data-driven filtering, ordering and skill definition in its work allocation

OpEx incorporates contractually agreed KPIs, skills and competencies of the person, product specifications and a host of other attributes. It actively uses this information when capturing a new work item to then push it to the workforce user who has skills to process the work. If for any reason they can't perform the work, they can refer the case to their superior or a specialist process team all managed by data setup.

The work is captured in queues and is grouped under owners who actively manage the clearance of their daily target. They are able to access all resource, managed capacity planning and update competence in real-time.

The organization is defined in an organizational chart painter and then the processes' and activities' ownerships are assigned to one or more organizational chart department. Similarly, roles and responsibilities are also painted and used to define permissions, reporting authority, MIS templates and many other features.

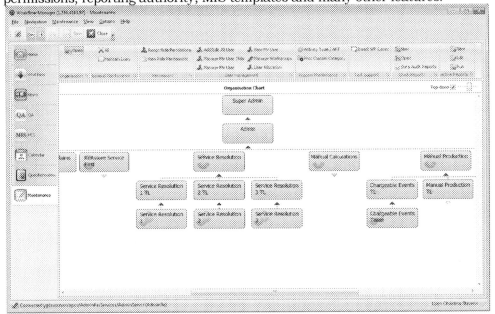

***Figure 3 - OpEx allows users to paint their operational organization and process allocations as well as change these real-time through simple "drag and drop" functionality.***

As stated above OpEx is based on a *"get next"* philosophy where the system knows what's best for the workforce user and what's best for the company. Team leaders can adjust priorities if needed based on emerging business requirements as well as who has access to which queues of work associated with the process activity. This ensures the right work is allocated to the right person all the time. Generally, the system works on a FIFO basis as this relates best to a queue driven process mentality. OpEx supports multiple role definitions, such as:

- WFU: a workforce user
- WFTL: a workforce team leader, who manages a team of WFUs
- WFM: a workforce manager who manages a team of WFTLs

All have real-time dashboards showing outstanding work, completed work and estimates for the resource required to complete the work governed by the prevailing service delivery model. Key business metrics include performance management reporting (average and actual handling times for an activity and class of case which are part of the continual improvement process), quality (right first time), straight-through processing and customer satisfaction. OpEx statistics are used as part of the business case for changes in underlying systems, processes and procedures.

- OpEx uses properties of the case payload as skill identifiers. In our case we hold:
- Relevant platforms (our back-end systems)
- Life or pension: a class of policy
- Plan type: the type of policy
- Investment type: how the insurance plan is dealing with assets
- Issuing company: who issued the policy with the client group

These are held against the payload, as well as against the workforce users who need to be skilled and authorized in these as well as authorized for the process and activity.

Processes are developed with activity based steps to enable the delivery of an end-to-end model. The process is built within a BPM tool and loaded to OpEx. This was delivered by the business and was built with a clear understanding of procedural requirements, business interactions and all touch points.

OpEx simplifies the traditional BPMN models by using a data-driven approach while BPMN is used under the hood. The user-interface is primarily straight-through linear process modeling.

**BPMN**                  **OPEX STP**

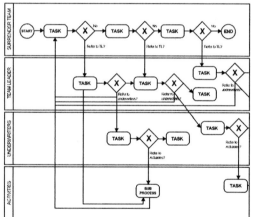

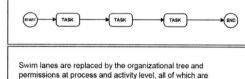

Swim lanes are replaced by the organizational tree and permissions at process and activity level, all of which are data-driven.

Decision gateways are replaced by rules engines and manual referral options to send cases to other swim lanes based on values or manual selection, aka a referral.

As a result of these and some other data-driven features, the complexities of routing can be reduced to a critical linear path and data-driven properties for variations to the straight through process. OpEx is a BPMN engine that can execute the process defined in either of these visual styles. The STP appeals to business users, and BPMN to IT users.

OpEx reports and dashboards are *user-aware* and adjust to show the information on the processes, activities and WFU's relevant to the individual's role. OpEx reports support multiple formats including:

- Calculation sheets: similar to a spreadsheet, these calculate using real-time data, driven by end-user defined parameters and formula
- Quick reporting: end-user reporting wizard to extract key datasets for analysis
- Advanced reporting: as above, but allows end-users to create traditional reports with headers, footers, charts etc.
- Charting: a set of manager or MIS charts that can be created into dashboards by the end-users or administrators.

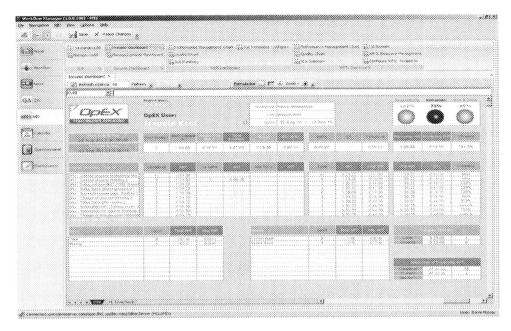

*Figure 4 - OpEx has real-time sophisticated end-user reporting*

### 4.3 Organization & Social

OpEx has been transformational. As we rolled out the new methodology and philosophy the whole company's attitude to work and quality has been enhanced. Rather than having a few bespoke centers of excellence, we have succeeded in raising the bar across the board.

OpEx was conceptualized by champions and built by staff at the grassroots of the business. The champions lived and breathed all aspects throughout the delivery phase and their passion is now evidenced though our posters, ongoing learning and development, and a passion for continuous improvement.

The appetite for information to enhance our business model is limitless and through well-considered and controlled delivery, we continue to reap the benefits alongside our clients and their customers.

### 5. Hurdles Overcome

### 5.1 Management

The main issues the management had to resolve were concerns from employees that the change was too radical. We were planning to replace archaic and embedded operating cultures and behaviors. This combined with the complexity of bringing together a multi-platform legacy system, sites and clients into our holistic OpEx vision did prove too much for some.

We addressed employee concerns by introducing development days and feedback sessions that encouraged buy-in, generated enthusiasm and a willingness to change ensured the transformation was successful. We adopted an open environment and listened throughout the project.

Values were addressed by gaining senior HCL management (C level) sponsorship to our vision.

Operations management were encouraged to invest time in the principles of our model and through new real-time information engaged staff each morning, held daily team huddles and shared regular targets achievements. All management displayed the right behaviors, lead by example and supported continued improvement in the operating model.

OpEx was a defining moment in our leadership approach. The direct move away from management that was built on experience in process was replaced by inspirational leadership based on people, performance and targets.

### 5.2 Business

The major challenge from a business perspective was gaining approval for the financial investment in the vision. It required a leap of faith by those approving the necessary expenditure as we were moving the operational element of the business to a completely different model and replacing one which had been in place for many years.

However, once approval had been given the journey from OpEx conception to pilot in a year demonstrated how our business as a whole adopted the new work approach. Everyone involved in the project were passionate as understood the expected outcome, they had a clear vision and this dedication ensured we were able to overcome each issue and launch to production on time.

The successful implementation has reduced our operating costs associated with policy administration, duplication and hand offs considerably within a twelve month period. That value continues to be evidenced through year on year cost savings therefore justifying the leap of faith!

### 5.3 Organization Adoption

OpEx was trialed on one of our customer accounts. It was a success and we rolled the system out across all client portfolios within the operation. An unexpected outcome from OpEx highlighted internal dependencies which are now being added to the OpEx platform to ensure we have complete visibility of our universe – such functions include Compliance, Actuarial and Finance.

## 6. Benefits

### 6.1 Cost Savings / Time Reductions

We have benefited from more than a 20% increase in the number of transactions processed per person (FTE). This has been a key enabler to delivering more for less.

The improved throughput of work together with an increase in "right first time" processing means fewer delays - a major source of customer dissatisfaction and complaints. As a consequence, we have halved the number of complaints received, strengthening client relations and enhancing our position in the BPO market.

Within the first 18 months, we realized a progressive reduction in overall operating costs of c.15%. These saving have enhanced our competitive standing and reputation allowing us to profile new opportunities to gain market share.

### 6.2 Increased Revenues

As a business process outsourcer in the closed book marketplace our revenue on existing contracts reduces over time. As such, our revenue has not increased as a consequence of OpEx, however the cost reductions we have achieved have increased profitability and are now allowing us to compete more effectively for new business with market leading pricing models which we could not have previously done without both the system and the metrics to back up the complex bid processes we undertake.

### 6.3 Quality Improvements

OpEx is built to deliver quality assurance controls through various internal mechanisms.

Peer review – developed and available to all required processes. It is dynamic within the linear model using competence and resource alignment to ensure correct allocation of work with no manual intervention. We capture peer review volumes, effort and outcomes each available to engage root cause and process improvement initiatives in addition to process and performance management.

Key improvements include:

- reduction in offshore rework
- improved learning and development plans for staff that meet business priorities
- OpEx's trend analysis provides actual data for changed business cases.

Checklists – defined "pop-up" screens within each process and activity. These capture user-agreed activities and approvals necessary to drive the straight through processing. We have developed these further to accommodate procedural and audit controls.

Key improvements include:

- reduction in internal and external audit findings
- accountability enforcement
- improved learning opportunities
- less time to achieve competence on multi-platforms and products.

Independent Quality Assurance built in the toolkit routes all activities to the quality system for open (captures right-first-time and potential customer detriment information) and closed QA (actual customer detriment) allowing in process QA to be carried out efficiently.

Real-time error recording, action setting and closure is all managed between the administrator, assessor and line leader.

The system flexibility is able to support all our clients' demands, including QA capture by user, process and volume. M.I. is captured real-time, daily and month end.

Key improvements include:

- ability to capture and analyze a customer's journey.
- actions and outcomes traced and evidenced.
- improved staff interaction with quality associates.
- personal/unique staff development plans.
- increased end to end handling times.
- client satisfaction, including re-engineering control questions and a cyclic approach enforcing actions in month two and three.

## 7. Best Practices, Learning Points and Pitfalls

### 7.1 Best Practices and Learning Points

- ✓ *Keep processes linear and track any hand-offs*
- ✓ *Integrate all business functions to ensure accountability*
- ✓ *Map internal and external key performance measures*
- ✓ *Show everyone real-time data*
- ✓ *Use peer statistics to motivate laggards*
- ✓ *Use real team leaders as system set up and administrators*
- ✓ *Assign users to busy teams daily from less busy teams*

✓ Capture business re-engineering opportunities in the project
✓ Do not be afraid to change the business model; allow it to evolve as this is more likely to deliver the most effective and efficient outcome
✓ Business owns solution working collaboratively with other stakeholders.

### 7.2 Pitfalls

× Don't underestimate the true number of process steps (some may not be apparent in legacy world)
× Don't use existing or pre-built MIS. Ensure business requirements understood and develop accordingly
× Don't underestimate the size of the project.

## 8. COMPETITIVE ADVANTAGES

HCL IBS has now become one of the most efficient companies in the marketplace at BPO for the insurance industry. We have stepped ahead of our competitors with our original advanced back-end administration systems augmented by the OpEx solution - so far ahead that we have cemented a commercial relationship with Corporate Modeling to actively support the marketing of OpEx to other life and pensions administration specialists whilst progressing further functional enhancements that will continue to push current boundaries, enhancing the value proposition.

## 9. TECHNOLOGY

The OpEx solution has two "click once" deployed user interfaces - one for the administrators and one for the managers. Both interfaces have many *applets* that can be enabled or disabled by job–role - this is administrated by the operational managers. While the manager system is designed to look like a traditional application, the administrator screen is designed and implemented like a mobile phone.

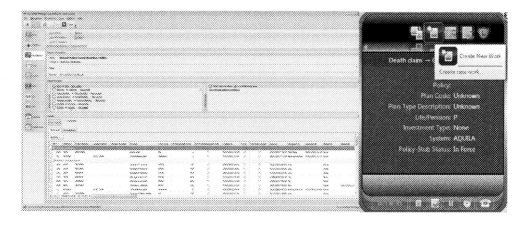

**Figure 5 - an OpEx manager interface with quick reports and administrator with a work item**

OpEx was developed with Microsoft.Net web services providing the application logic. The solution runs on an SQL Server Cluster providing high availability and disaster recover capability.

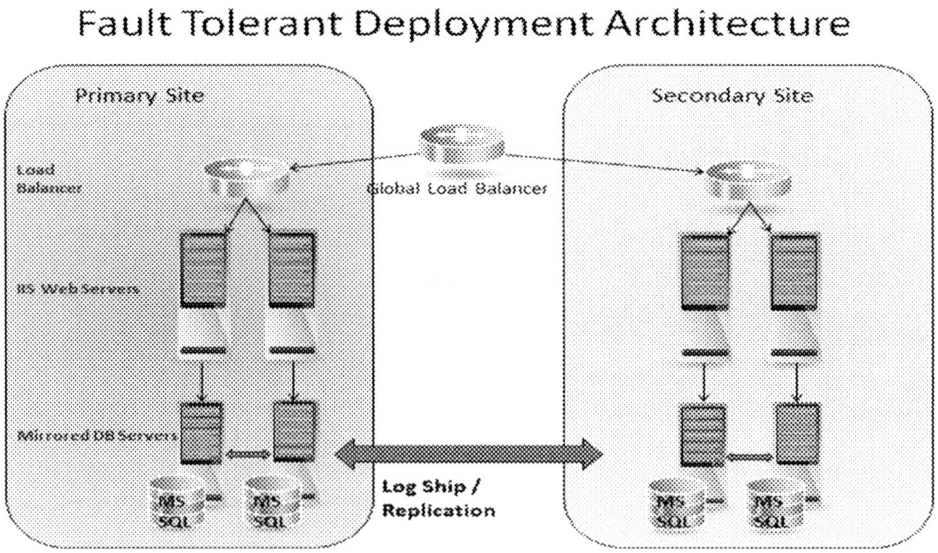

# Fault Tolerant Deployment Architecture

*Figure 6 - OpEx has high availability and disaster recovery*

A browser-based solution is in development and all servers are VMware virtual machines. The offshore clients use Citrix terminal server.

## 10. THE TECHNOLOGY AND SERVICE PROVIDERS

OpEx was devised and implemented by HCL IBS and Corporate Modelling Services Ltd.

# HML, UK

## Finalist: Financial Services
## Nominated by IBM, UK

## 1. ABSTRACT

HML responds faster to customer communications, streamlining workflows for incoming correspondence with IBM Business Process Manager. When your business depends on your clients' trust, you need to make sure that you meet their expectations, not just most of the time, but all the time.

As a leading provider of outsourced mortgage, savings and loan administration services for the financial services sector, HML understands this better than most.

To ensure that it is serving customers effectively, HML works to strict service level agreements (SLAs), which are agreed individually with each client. The company constantly looks to improve its performance in this area. HML receives up to 30,000 letters, 50,000 emails and 5,000 faxes from customers or a diverse range of third parties each month. Each item of correspondence will initiate one of 80 corresponding processes, depending on the type of request received.

We wanted to automate as much of the correspondence handling process as possible. By helping our consultants spend less time on low-level admin and data entry, they can focus on the most important aspect of their job, which is providing first-class customer service.

**The need:** To meet client requirements for its mortgage administration services, HML needs to process huge volumes of correspondence which can trigger a number of differing processes with a high level of content variation within strict SLAs which requires an agile approach to workflow management. Additional challenges to be overcome arise from managing multiple clients, multiple sites and legal jurisdictions.

**The solution:** HML uses IBM® Business Process Manager to orchestrate an end-to-end process for incoming correspondence and provide automation, workload management and performance monitoring.

**The benefit:** Customer correspondence is now processed in an efficient manner allowing for improved response times. Saved £400,000 from reduced manual processing and £150,000 from consolidating processing onto a single platform. Flexible solution enables new functionality to be developed quickly, with no need to invest in additional software.

## 2. OVERVIEW

### *Managing complex service level agreements*

To ensure that it is serving customers effectively, HML works to strict service level agreements (SLAs), which are agreed individually with each client. The company constantly looks to improve its performance in this area.

Our ability to meet SLAs often depends on the efficiency of our internal workflows. A few years ago we adopted IBM Business Process Manager software to enhance efficiency in our collections management processes, and based on that success, we decided to extend the solution to support our incoming correspondence processes too.

### Processing huge volumes of correspondence

HML receives up to 30,000 letters, 50,000 emails and 5,000 faxes from customers or a diverse range of third parties each month. Each item of correspondence will initiate one of 80 corresponding processes, depending on the type of request received.

We wanted to automate as much of the correspondence handling process as possible. If we could help our consultants spend less time on low-level admin and data entry, they would be able to focus on the most important aspect of their job, which is providing first-class customer service.

### Enhancing workflows

Now, when a new item of correspondence arrives at HML, it is scanned and read by optical character recognition (OCR) software. The scanned image is automatically tagged with metadata such as the relevant account number and document type, and IBM Business Process Manager starts a corresponding workflow. The item is then automatically placed in the appropriate queue, and assigned to the next available consultant for processing.

The new system allocates work to consultants fairly and makes sure every request is handled in a timely way. If a particular case is more complicated or difficult, consultants can escalate it to their supervisors for assistance – but one way or another, the job gets done. There's no scope for ignoring difficult problems or putting them to the back of the queue.

### Improved management information

The IBM Business Process Manager solution also improves the level of oversight for managers, by providing real-time analysis of workload and SLA performance.

Previously, our managers had to count the number of items in each queue manually, several times a day, just to make sure that we were getting through the work within each SLA. Now, they get a dynamic scorecard that shows exactly how their team is performing on all their tasks – so if one queue is ahead of schedule and another is lagging behind, they can quickly divert resources to make sure that service levels are maintained.

### Simpler communication

Communication within and between teams has also been streamlined. Instead of sending internal emails to each other to ask for information or help, they can now use a new workflow to add work requests to their colleagues' job queues. This dramatically improves traceability, because once a request is in the system, it can be monitored and tracked through to completion.

We have recently extended the work request process so that our clients can use it too. It's a much safer and more controlled way of handling work requests. Once they're in the system, we know they will be dealt with – whereas if they're stuck in someone's email inbox, it's more difficult to guarantee appropriate action.

### Flexible SLA management

Over the past 12 months, HML has migrated all of its clients over to the new correspondence management process, and has implemented all the individual SLAs to ensure that each client receives the right level of service. Using the new system HML can quickly and effectively board new clients taking into account their own post management SLA's and also for specialised cases which are identified such as customer complaints.

IBM Business Process Manager is excellent for managing large numbers of SLAs, because it's easy to build a core process and then add specific rules and variations for different clients. If requirements change – either for a single SLA or globally – we can update the system very quickly because we have a central point of control.

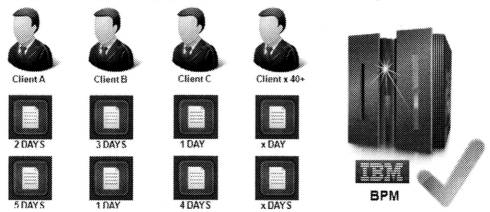

**Business Context**

Post from customers was received and sorted into department order in HML's mail-room. It was then scanned using Tower scanning software. From here the image was passed to operational teams via Staffware who would then indexed each item. To index the item the consultant would have to read the document to find the customer account number, search the database and check the customer and client details matched. The next step was to determine what type of post/request the customer was making by looking for key words, phrases and information. For example if the customer was asking for the title deeds to their property. The consultant would then save the item into the corresponding work tray i.e. 'deeds requests'. The manager of the team would then ask consultants to work on work trays depending on number of items and date. The manager had to manually count work items to determine workloads, in some instances up to three times a day to report SLA's. This would then be accessed by a consultant working the tray. There was no restriction as to which item could be worked and when and lead to come 'cherry picking'. Once a work item was completed it was closed and a record was held against the customer account.

Similarly requests taken over the phone from a customer were emailed into the Staffware queues and then had to follow the indexing process.

## 3.  THE KEY INNOVATIONS

### 4.1 Business

Strong collaboration between Operational and IT team members was absolutely key to ensuring a successful delivery.

### 4.2 Process

Before: Post, Fax & Email

Incoming post, Fax & Email from customers. Consultant scans post and fax and emails external emails to Staffware. The post, fax and email is then indexed by finding the customer account number, validating the client and determining what it is. The item is then routed to a queue waiting to be worked. Managers have to manually count and collate figures for reporting. Consultants manually record work completed.

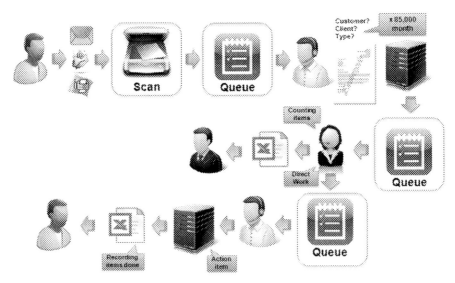

After: Post, Fax & Email

- Post is scanned and passes through OCR which determines customer de-tails, client and what the request is. The image is passed to the image store, a task is created in IBM BPM and a record is created on the customer ac-count.
- Managers have visibility of workloads and SLA's and can set consultant work filters to direct them to the required task type. Consultants log into the BPM portal and click 'get next task' which presents work in priority order. Client reporting is automated as is consultant productivity. This system cannot ex-ist as individual components but has to be integrated to provide a robust method of managing inbound correspondence.

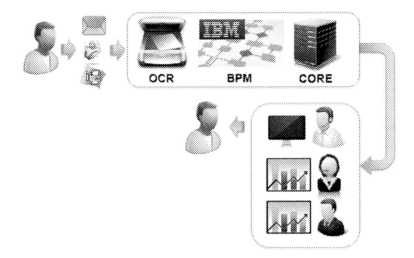

Before

Customer requests taken over the phone. Internally created requests. Consultant creates request and has to copy customer details onto email then sends email to Staffware. The email is then indexed as per post and sits in a queue waiting to be worked. Managers have to manually count and collate figures for reporting. Consultants manually record work completed.

After

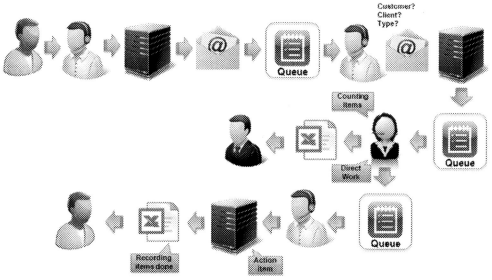

Customer requests taken over the phone. Task created in BPM. Task is then worked alongside post, email & fax in line with SLA's.

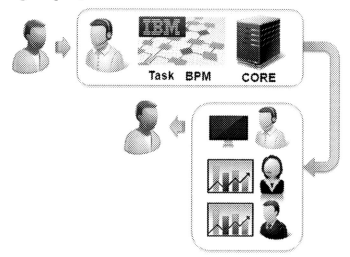

### 4.3 Organization

- Management of work is simplified, controlled and automated where possible.
- Managers now have full visibility of workloads using real time dashboard reporting which give an instant view of key data such as SLA reporting. Allocation of resources is easy and controlled. No work items are missed, consultants are accountable and the playing field has been levelled by removing the opportunity to cherry pick work.

## 4. HURDLES OVERCOME

### Management

We found that some areas of business management had become very comfortable with how they legacy system worked and often found themselves describing current system 'features' when specifying requirements for the new system. Always asking 'why' a certain process was completed, what is the problem, what were the benefits, does it ever fail and what would success look like. The challenges helped create and focus on the key goals and objectives. Agile tools and techniques helped massively along the way.

### Business

A key hurdle was the perception that everything had to be done at once rather than a more staged approach. Encouraging the senior user group to embrace uncertainty and prioritize what needs to be done now and what can wait. Challenging requirements that were based on today's limitations was also key to driving out an efficient process/system. Process mapping and demonstrations gave the user group visibility of the system all the way through. We got sign off to smaller portions as we went rather than a huge set of requirements.

### Organisation Adoption

By promoting the success of previous projects with BPM at their heart we had a much easier path to organisational acceptance of the technology to be used. We did however have a legacy system that was 10 years old and very familiar to a lot of users.

## 5. BENEFITS

### 6.1 Cost Savings

HML has realised benefits totalling £400,000 from the reduction in manual processing workload that has resulted from automating various aspects of the correspondence management process. In addition, HML has achieved annual savings of £150,000 by consolidating correspondence processing onto the IBM Business Process Manager platform.

- All productivity savings were determined by analysing actual and projected volumes and time saved per item.
- Process efficiencies derived from:
- Reduction in manual indexing and routing of post items
- Reduction in manual indexing of archive items
- Elimination of indexing of internally generated email
- Reduction in time spent creating internal email
- Reduction in time spent indexing external emails and faxes
- Auto populating customer details in the legacy system
- Enhanced automated reporting
- Scanning enhancements

£150,000 saved by adding the correspondence component to existing BPM estate. Additionally the cost to run and maintain a separate infrastructure for correspondence is removed.

### 6.2 Time Reductions

Post can be processed straight through from scan to user in a matter of minutes rather than hours. Having items quickly available has also assisted our contact centre handling calls from customers.

### 6.3 Increased Revenues

HML's Clients benefit from a number of features:

- Customer post, Fax and Emails can be dealt with quicker
- Elimination of manual intervention ensures greater accuracy and compliance with client SLA's
- IBM BPM allows far greater flexibility to adapt to changing business requirements. One change can be applied to many clients.

### 6.4 Productivity Improvements

The company has also seen an improvement in average response times to customer queries. The project has been a huge success in itself, and has also proved the value of our business process management strategy. When we first implemented IBM Business Process Manager, we invested significant effort in integrating the software with our core systems. Since the integration work had already been done, this current project was much quicker and easier to implement – and we expect future projects to be similarly straightforward.

The ability to build sophisticated business processes with no major development effort and no further investment in software is a huge advantage for our business in terms of both cost-efficiency

## 6. BEST PRACTICES, LEARNING POINTS AND PITFALLS

### 7.1 Best Practices and Learning Points

- ✓ Agile delivery
- ✓ Demonstrations
- ✓ Collaborative
- ✓ Process visibility
- ✓ Close integration with the operational and IT teams
- ✓ Top down buy in
- ✓ Staged migration from legacy systems
- ✓ Phased business roll out
- ✓ Take every opportunity to simplify
- ✓ Challenge the status quo
- ✓ Look for what can be delivered now and then evolve
- ✓ Incremental delivery is key
- ✓ Prioritise based on customer need
- ✓ Measure the baseline process
  - o Speed – How long does the process take
  - o Cost – What is the cost of the process
  - o Experience – What value does the process bring
- ✓ Involve everyone the process touches
- ✓ Set Expectations
  - o Speed – What time improvements are expected?
  - o Cost – What cost reductions will be made?
  - o Experience – How will the user experience change?
- ✓ Ownership is important for collaboration purposes
- ✓ Close partnership with your BPM provider and 3rd party resource providers.
- ✓ Transformation
- ✓ Changing the cultural aspects of how we work, e.g.
- ✓ Collaborative working and emphasis on face-to-face communication
- ✓ Cross-functional, co-located and empowered teams
- ✓ Making continuous improvement and learning a way of life

- ✓ *Learning to accept and embracing uncertainty and change*
- ✓ *Adoption*
- ✓ *Learning and Using new working practices, tools, techniques, e.g.*
- ✓ *Incremental and Iterative development, typically fortnightly cycles*
- ✓ *Visual Management and techniques such as Kanban*
- ✓ *Regular 'customer' demonstrations*
- ✓ *Removing variation in repetitive processes through automation*

### 7.2 Pitfalls

- ✗ *Don't rush in to a build*
- ✗ *Don't prioritise based on what you think is right, it has to be the team*
- ✗ *Know your baseline to enable clear measurement of improvements.*

## 7. COMPETITIVE ADVANTAGES

The correspondence system has allowed HML to showcase what can be achieved through close collaboration between business and IT functions to deliver a class leading product. HML can offer a streamlined correspondence processing solution that can be tailored to client needs. Regulatory requirements can be dealt with quickly and efficiently. HML have real time top down reporting capability for all correspondence, allowing far greater oversight.

## 8. TECHNOLOGY

The key elements of the solution are;
- IBM BPM. This has been used to automate the delivery of work items
- HML's Core System. This is the legacy system which maintains the customer account detail
- Eflow OCR. This handles the scanning and recognition of post items

## 9. THE TECHNOLOGY AND SERVICE PROVIDERS

HML uses IBM® Business Process Manager to orchestrate an end-to-end process for incoming correspondence and provide automation, workload management and performance monitoring.

# Liberty University, USA

## Finalist: Education
## Nominated by BizFlow, USA

## 1. ABSTRACT

Liberty University is the largest private, nonprofit university in the United States. It has grown more than 1000% since 2003 and 100% since 2010. In order to both enable and support such growth, Liberty has invested heavily in technology infrastructure and automation. Liberty uses BPM to continually improve process efficiencies, user effectiveness, and overall customer services with students and staff.

In this paper, Liberty describes how it started with BPM and BPM Suites and where it has implemented BPM beginning with Student Financial Aid. To date, Liberty has reduced Verification record processing 42% from 12 minutes per record to 7 minutes per record while increasing the number of records processed by 25% (13,826 to 18,349 records). More than 10 other processes have been fully automated.

## 2. OVERVIEW

Liberty University is the largest private, nonprofit university in the nation, the largest university in Virginia, and the largest Christian university in the world. Nestled in the Blue Ridge Mountains on more than 7,000 beautiful acres in Lynchburg, VA, Liberty offers over 300 programs from the certificate to the doctoral level, and is home to more than 100,000 residential and online students. Since 1971, the mission of Liberty University has been to develop Christ-centered men and women with the values, knowledge, and skills essential for impacting tomorrow's world. With a unique heritage and an ever-expanding influence, Liberty remains steadfast in its commitment of *Training Champions for Christ*.

Liberty currently has 12,600 residential and more than 90,000 online students, a growth of 1000% since 2003 and 100% since 2010. It offers 206 residential and 166 online programs of study. About 26% of the residential and 65% of the online programs are post-graduate. The university is a member o the Big South Conference and holder of 18 conference titles in the last two years. With net assets of $1B Liberty is in position to grow significantly more.

In order to support and enable the past rapid and great potential for future growth in both on campus and online student populations, Liberty executive leadership decided to invest in business process automation. The objective was to move from paperless – scanning incoming documents to route through electronic means – to full workflow automation in the context of everyday student and staff interactions. The result has enabled Liberty to cut per record processing in specific areas by 42% and do double the amount of more work with the team already in place.

## 3. BUSINESS CONTEXT

In 2013, Liberty University has more than 100,000 residential and online students, up from 64,610 in 2011. This phenomenal growth has been enabled through a $400M investment in its physical facilities and online curriculum as well as a great reputation for teaching and installing Christian values. Growth will continue as the mission of the university is to significantly increase its residential community students and expand online education to a truly global student body with both English and Spanish daily instruction.

Since the inception of Liberty University, executive leadership understood that the best way to achieve such growth was to compliment a dynamic university experience with highly efficient and effective business operations and customer services. Staff has looked for every opportunity to be more efficient and effective in the way they engage with students and parents.

By 2010, Liberty had already invested in going "paperless." For example, paper forms received via mail and other channels for student aid were scanned to create electronic files that could be routed for review and approval. However, internal teams realized that electronic paper was not enough to produce efficiencies needed to support dynamic growth. It was a good first step but fell short of real automation. Users still had to spend time reviewing, entering, and fixing data in the submitted forms. Teams also found that students often submitted the wrong forms resulting in rework and frustration.

Led by the Office of Financial Aid, Liberty decided to invest in full process automation. This area is the tip of the spear for student on-boarding. A good customer experience can make all the difference in a student's decision to matriculate. Liberty University is a full participant in Federal student aid programs. With Liberty's support, students can apply for government loans and grants that cover tuition and living expenses. Administering these programs requires the capability of processing a number of varied forms and applications.

Through collaboration between the Information Technology (IT) team and the Office of Financial Aid, the university selected the Federal Verification process (the review and validation of data received from FAFSA) for the first project. IT had already several years experience designing websites, portals, and scanning and routing documents. They felt that building electronic forms would be straight forward, but wanted a tool to speed up this process. Additionally, routing data and images required a more flexible approach that a typical code based solution. For this reason, IT considered Business Process Management Suites (BPMS) as a platform for automation.

Complete the Four Steps for Financial Aid

Liberty has condensed the financial aid process into four easy steps. Follow these steps to ensure that you receive all sources of aid that you need.

STEP 1: Complete your FAFSA at www.fafsa.ed.gov with your federal financial aid PIN from www.pin.fafsa.ed.gov with Liberty's school code (010392). You must complete the FAFSA to be considered for financial aid at Liberty.

STEP 2: Apply for grants, scholarships, outside aid, and work study. For more information on these aid options, visit www.liberty.edu/financialaid. Virginia residents should also apply for the Virginia Tuition Assistance Grant at www.liberty.edu/vtag.

STEP 3: Learn about and apply for federal and private loans at www.liberty.edu/loans.

STEP 4: Log in to ASIST and complete Financial Check-In (FCI) once you have submitted all requested documents and your financial aid is ready.

In their review of BPM platforms, Liberty felt that it was important to be able to separate the form from the process engine so that internal users (i.e., staff, faculty), customers (i.e., applicants, students), and external people (i.e., parents, employers) could all access and participate important student workflows. Also, the team wanted to leverage current systems such as Banner to both serve as a place to start the process and a way to provide data to the process.

## 4. THE KEY INNOVATIONS

### 4.1 Business

Liberty uses Ellucian Banner for its student information system. As the system of record, Banner contains data (i.e., names, class schedules, roles) about students, faculty and staff. Banner also provides functionality for students to register online and conduct specific, out-of-the-box workflows. These workflows are defined and structured.

Liberty also has a website where students and others access forms. Workflow participants would download forms and send documents via mail or attachment.

The Liberty team decided to leverage the existing Banner self service application as the main user interface. They would add BPM as a layer of process management and forms development in order to support non-out-of-the-box and/or ad-hoc processes.

### 4.2 Process

Through integration among Banner, BizFlow BPM, and imaging system software application Xtender, students can access electronic forms in the context of their specific needs. Forms can be auto-populated from the Banner SIS. When all data has been submitted, Banner triggers the Verification process in BizFlow and starts routing work to add/update student records as well as to identify good/bad data. After many system-based verification and routing activities, Liberty staff compares information from students with data from the Government. Based on rules, the solution creates Flags (color codes) showing differences/deltas.

The process ensures that students are filling out the correct forms. With integration, forms are auto-populated and validated before routing, cutting down data entry time as well as wasted approval steps. Internal staff can review, add, and change data as needed in order to approve or reject requests.

The Verification process has 35 unique activities. There are multiple integrations with Banner. Using a combination of integration techniques (e.g., SQL activities, database stored procedures, Banner UI functionality, and written code) data is shared. Liberty also uses BizFlow's feature for publishing process as a web service that Banner then uses to trigger processes.

### Verification Process (First Set of Activities)

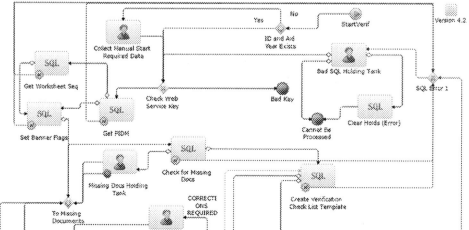

Liberty's approach to development falls between waterfall and agile. There are lots of customer interactions: paper walk-throughs, whiteboard sessions, mock-ups, interviews, sticky notes. Highly collaborative. Build, show, change, etc. Users are always involved. Everyone is given a voice and agrees to the big picture. The objective is no surprises. The team then carves the project into phased deliveries.

Liberty makes changes on request and has a formal review at the beginning of the processing cycle for the next school year. In the review, leadership and other stakeholders decide both how to integrate changes to improve the process based on the data collected in the prior cycle and to facilitate the changes required by the Federal Department of Education.

Publishing the process as a web-service is clearly strategic. Most of the other integration is at the database level.

### 4.3 Organization

Prior to BPM, users would look at scanned images and compare them with known data in Banner. Using a paper check list placed next to their computer, they would note discrepancies. Then they would manually collate and scan the checklists into EDMS and routed to QC for review.

Since moving to BPM, the vast majority of items are combined into a single screen. Team members see data submitted by students side by side with data from Banner. Discrepancies are automatically highlighted for fast reviews. Routing to Quality Control is also automatically done through specific business rules in the process. As a result, Liberty reduced Verification record processing 42% from 12 minutes per record to 7 minutes per record. Cutting turnaround time enabled Liberty's same 10 Verification Processors to support a processing volume 25% greater today (13,826 to 18,349 records). Liberty can promise to return verifications within 2 business days while other universities have timeframes of 4-6 weeks.

As noted above, Liberty is a very large school. Its business is related to volume processing. It has to be efficient for self-sustainment and growth. The university wants to turn around work faster and cleaner. Through process transformation, the school has faster turn around and visibility as differentiators.

Another example of change is with the Withdrawal application. The process was originally routed to each Verifier no matter whether they had a specific role in the review and approval. This activity caused waste as verifiers would open items that didn't pertain to them. Using BPM, Liberty now only deliveries work to required participants. Through intelligent routing waste was eliminated and common mistakes identified to process greater volumes of work automatically. Liberty also added a set of checks to select the percentage of work items most likely to be incorrect to send to QC. So rather than taking a random sample of 10%, QC received work that was most likely to need correction.

Prior to BPM, the scholarship applicationforms were filled out, routed manually for approval, and then manually keyed into Banner. With a new award program, LUO Advantage, designed from the ground up to take advantages of electronic processing, Liberty melded new business processes and new technology to allow for faster turnarounds and the removal manual intervention. Now students fill out forms online which the system approves based on business rules and automatically enters data to create awards. There is no manual intervention. Similar scholarship processes take 10 minutes per record. Liberty's processing time is practically zero.

## 5. HURDLES OVERCOME

The primary challenge faced at Liberty was transitioning from "as-is" to "to-be" processes. Everyone knew the big picture. The Federal verification process is fairly standardized across Higher Ed institutions, and many staff members had been working at Liberty for years. But during the business process re-engineering exercise, the team learned that exception handling was not well documented.

In the past, someone just took an issue to their supervisor. For Web-based solutions all options need to be identified upfront in order to be added to the solution. For example, FAFSA rules require universities to handle students from Micronesia differently than other countries. This exception was not understood or captured in the beginning so Liberty had to add it in a later release. Liberty ended up refining the process as it identified new exceptions.

Another challenge faced with all new solutions is user acceptance. Bringing on board of new technology is always a transition. Users (e.g., staff) need to feel comfortable. Business analysts and developers tried to engage users early and often to get feedback, mollify concerns, and look for opportunities to turn issues into resolutions. Through continual collaboration users were more ready to accept solutions and make suggestions for improvement.

## 6. BENEFITS

The efforts toward business transformation have really paid dividends for Liberty University. See below a summary.

- The timetable to the initial Verification process was the following:
    o May 2011 – Conducted market analysis and vendor reviews
    o June 2011 – Issued RFP
    o September 2011 – Selected vendor
    o January 2012 – Started implementation
    o March 2012 – Went live with Verification process
    o April 2012 to August 2013 – Roll out one new process per month
- Team members (2 ½ FTEs):
    o ½ Business Analyst
    o ½ Developer
    o ½ Subject Matter Expert
    o ¼ Project Manager
    o ¼ System Administrator
- Processes Automated
    o Financial Aid processes automated to date: Federal Verification
    o Endowment Scholarship Application
    o Federal Direct Student Loan Change Form
    o LUO Advantage Discount Form
    o LUO Advantage Discount Spouse Validation Form
    o Professional Judgment Request Form
    o Satisfactory Academic Progress Appeal Form
    o TEACH Grant Application
    o VTAG (Virginia Tuition Assistance Grant Application)
    o High School Certification (graduated from HS, when, where)
    o Household Size Verification
    o Satisfactory Academic Progress Appeal
    o Cost of Attendance Adjustment Form

- o Medical School Application
- o Student Community Service Registration and Verification
- Benefits:
  - o Reduced Verification record processing 42% from 12 minutes per record to 7 minutes per record
  - o Maintained the number of Verification Processors at 10 while the number of records increased by 25% (13,826 to 18,349 records)
  - o Removed 2 FTEs from imaging group that were assigned to the Verification process
  - o Reduced corrections (i.e., typos, blank fields) from 10% of forms submitted to <1% of forms processed forms resulting in faster turnaround time and minimal rework by students
  - o Reduced Quality Control review turnaround time 50% from 4 weeks to 2 weeks

Liberty has processed 58,000 Verifications since going live (24 months). In 2013, students at Liberty receive an estimated $775M in federal aid loans and grants (USA Today), up from $284M in 2008-09. Process automation contributed to this growth.

Liberty is doing more for more people. And they are handling much deeper and broader areas of business operations. For example, more students mean more facilities, dorms, parking places, food dispensaries, computers purchased, athletic games played, etc. Investment in IT and process automation contributes to both sustainability and growth.

## 7. BEST PRACTICES, LEARNING POINTS AND PITFALLS

From the beginning, Liberty employees asked themselves how they can do things better, faster, and cheaper. As a result, they are willing to try new things and be innovative. They take lessons learned and apply them elsewhere.

### Best Practices

✓ *Collaboration – Ask lots of questions. Every member of the team will have some insight into process flows, bottlenecks, workarounds, and potential improvement. Get their input early and often to expose potential problems before development begins.*

✓ *Project Management – Solutions become real when they are being used. It is OK to roll out solution in phases. What users cannot use cannot be tried and tested. Get feedback now and apply lessons learned to phased deliveries. If you have to, start small and grow. Do not bite off more than you can chew.*

✓ *Standards and Templates – Look for opportunities to standardize flows and business rules especially in processes with similar characteristics. Using templates you can accelerate design and development of similar processes.*

### Pitfalls

✗ *Terminology – Removing paper doesn't mean you have gone "paperless." Make sure to capture data as well as routing data along with documents enables true workflow automation.*

## 8. COMPETITIVE ADVANTAGES

Using BPM, Liberty University is more efficient and effective. As a result, it provides faster turnaround time, which equates to better customer service and student experience. It can do more with less. According to USA Today[1] the online division accounts for 61% of the university's revenue but just 44% of expenses. What Liberty saves in operational costs can be invested in new curriculum, new teachers, and new amenities, which all contribute to a more dynamic and attractive student experience.

## 9. TECHNOLOGY

The solution combined features from two off the shelf solutions: BizFlow Plus BPM suite and Ellucian Banner student information system. Both products utilize an Oracle database behind the scenes and allow for significant customization and development inside of their frameworks, allowing for robust solutions to be created quickly and effectively.

In the Banner SIS it is very easy to create targeted, custom facing text inside of the product's the web interface by building algorithmic rules based on the data Banner contains for the logged-in user. This functionality allowed for the rapid creation of a dynamic forms library with a seamless transition from the SIS interface to the BizFlow interface for Liberty's customers. This was all completed through configuration, not code customization, speeding implementation, but also removing concerns about code maintenance in future versions of the product.

Similarly the out-of-the-box feature of BizFlow to publish start activities as a web service allowed Liberty to facilitate the launch of the process from Banner processes with a very small amount of code. The triggering of workflows in this manner allows for the existing logic in Banner to drive the processes, rather than being duplicated. Once again, this made implementation quicker and the system more easily maintained in the future.

Another distinctive feature of BizFlow that was key to this implementation is that the Bizflow forms are extremely flexible, allowing not only interaction with the Bizflow engine, but also interaction with 3rd party web services and databases. This functionality allowed for authentication for students and parents to be managed by the SIS rather than the BPM product, which only can be used by employees of the University. Additionally, the data generated can be stored in the SIS in processes like verification where information from several sources needs to be gathered before there is value in beginning the workflow for reviews.

## 10. THE TECHNOLOGY AND SERVICE PROVIDERS

| Team Member | Role | Website |
|---|---|---|
| Liberty University Information Technology | Project Management, Development, Business Analysis | www.liberty.edu |
| BizFlow Corp. | BizFlow Plus BPM Suite training and support | www.bizflow.com |
| Ellucian | Banner training and support | www.ellucian.com |

---

[1] USA Today http://www.usatoday.com/story/news/nation/2013/09/14/liberty-university/2764789/

# Prince Sultan Military Medical City, Saudi Arabia

## Finalist: Healthcare and Medical

## Nominated by Bizagi, UK

EXECUTIVE SUMMARY/ABSTRACT

Prince Sultan Military Medical City (PSMMC) formerly known as The Riyadh Military Hospital (RMH) is located in Riyadh City and considered as one of the most advanced medical centres in the Middle East. PSMMC is the Medical Services Department (MSD) for the Ministry of Defense (MOD). The hospital now has a capacity of more than 1,400 beds and employs over 12,000 staff.

Key challenges faced by the hospital were related to patient safety. These included identifying the right patient, providing the right treatment to the right patient and preventing identification fraud and misuse of medical services by patients.

Existing legacy system used by the Patient Affairs department (as explained below) could not address these challenges. A BPM system was introduced to streamline and manage the improved processes of various departments associated with Patient Affairs.

PSMMC has already had a positive experience with the BPM and Bizagi system after the Family and Community Department, Al-Wazarat Health Centre (WHC), was automated with over 70 processes last year. The system delivered end-to-end patient care for over 2,000 outpatients.

The success of the first BPM initiative encouraged the PSMMC management team to consider the same BPM solution for this much larger initiative which required the end-to end automation of a 1400 bed hospital, serving the big part of the city.

Key drivers for both projects was to deliver a highly intuitive system that medical professionals can use daily and easily and that helps to improve patients care and reduce costs.

## 1. OVERVIEW

Many hospitals around the world are aware of the significant operational and administrative efficiencies delivered by the Hospital Information System (HIS). Apart from time savings, reduced paperwork and increased focus on patients, HIS also provides two additional benefits: laying the groundwork for improved quality of care, and qualification for disease-specific treatment recognition programs, which may eventually lead to increased reimbursements. One may document clinical outcomes on paper, but HIS makes it easy to track data, identify trends and target specific areas for improvement.

PSMMC started using BPM in conjunction with HIS at one of its Primary Family and Community Health Care centres, WHC. After a very successful implementation of BPM in that centre, the ICT department of PSMMC proposed the use of BPM to streamline, monitor and control the activities of Patient Affairs department of PSMMC. Thus the Project "Patient Affairs Management System" (PAMS) was initiated.

PAMS is one of the sub-module for e-Medserve HIS. The project was led by a team, with advanced BPM implementation experience and deep technical knowledge gained by implementing the WHC project.

There are nine departments within Patient Affairs:

- Registration
- Patient Relation
- Appointment and Reception
- Medical coordination
- General Admission
- Obstetrics and Gynecology
- Medical Records
- Medical Reports
- Mortuary
- Translation

The key objectives of the PAMS project were as follows:

- Cleanse and validate the patient data fetched from the legacy HIS system with the help of the integration layer provided by the BPM system
- Introduce advance verification devices and Smart Medical Cards which will help PSMMC to meet their Patient Safety objectives
- Effective fraud detection with biometric verification, which prevents ineligible patients from receiving medical treatments
- Controlled Monitoring of day-to-day activities of Registration Office of the Patient Affairs
- Key reports and metrics generation for Patient Affairs Management regarding the number of new patient registration and other patient related activities

The key challenges faced were as follows:

- Identify the Right Patient and provide the Right treatment
- Prevent identity theft of eligible Patients
- Address the challenge arising from the fact that in the local Saudi culture, it was challenging to request women to identify themselves by uncovering their face
- Ensure seamless integration of BPM system with the existing HIS (Legacy System)
- Deliver integration of BPM system with Ministry of Interior's National Information Center for registering new patients
- Clean and enhance the validity of the patient data coming from the Legacy system

All these challenges were addressed successfully with the help of the BPM system implemented with Bizagi BPM suite.

## 2. BUSINESS CONTEXT

When an unregistered patient visits PSMMC they need to visit the Patient Registration Department to get registered and receive the Patient Medical Card. This is very essential for the patients to receive all the medical service benefits.

Prior to the implementation of the BPM system, the patients were registered via the Hospital Legacy System which does not have a proper validation option leading to fraud and misinformation of patients, restricting PSMMC in adhering to the JCI's Patient Safety Standards.

The HIS system used by the Patients Affairs Department was based legacy system (mainly Mainframes). The system was very rigid and had many drawbacks. Auditing clerk's activities and running complex validations on screens was difficult to accomplish. Due to this, the system was prone to user input errors and mistakes, which corrupted the patient data on the system.

So the first phase of the project focused on improving and automating the **Patient Registration** process taking into account that the **Patient Security** is a key component of it i.e. ensuring that each patient is correctly identified when registers for treatments.

Security and correct identification is a huge problem in Saudi Arabia as nearly all women come dressed in their religious clothing including the veil that covers big parts of the face, so the identification is impaired. The traditional identification approach based on the medical identify cards proved ineffective as many citizens borrow medical cards from relatives and as the identity is difficult to confirm when the face is covered, some patients in the past were treated with wrong medications based on the card information. This could have proved fatal.

## 3. THE KEY INNOVATIONS

In addition to streamlining and automating the Registration Process, a very important innovation was the introduction of the advanced verification devices with biometric verification and Smart Medical Cards that contained the identification data. This technological innovation delivered effective fraud detection which helped to identify patients properly, prevented ineligible patients from receiving medical treatments while providing the right care to the right patient.

### Business

Migrating from the legacy platform to a new process oriented Patient Affairs Management System was a huge leap for PSMMC Patient Affairs. PAMS BPMS project streamlined and automated the activities of the department. A robust process for registering patients were established with clearly defined roles and responsibilities for the clerks and managers of the department. With the powerful process analytics tool, it was possible for the management to audit the activities performed by the clerks, analyze the trends and foresee the requirements of the Medical city in ways never done before.

### Case Handling

Multiple processes were defined and implemented to cater to the needs of all the departments of the Patient Affairs.

**Registration Process**: The Registration process is the key process to enroll the patients at PSMMC. The registration process used to be a fairly simple task which involved entering patient data into the legacy system and printing a card for the patient to identify them at the medical facilities for treatment purpose.

This task was made more reliable and robust with the new BPMS system. Apart from entering demographic data related to patients, the new BPMS system allows the patient demographic data to be embedded in the patient card (on a chip).

As an add-on, a Palm sensor was introduced in the new BPMS system to capture the palm information of the patient for identification purpose. This was a great achievement that met the goals of the Patient Safety at PSMMC.

The Palm data is also stored on the chip of the Patient Card. Palm Identification devices and Smart Card readers were introduced at various locations (nursing stations and point of care), to rightly verify the patient and to provide the right care to the right patient.

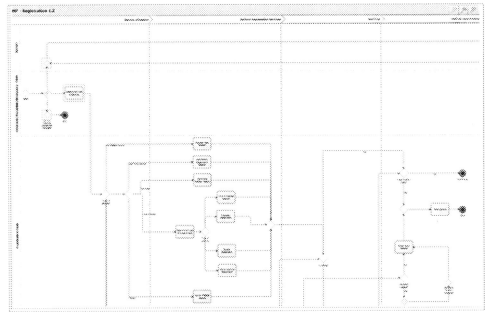

***Figure 1 – Patient Registration Process***

The Registration process incorporates various registration services namely – New Patient Registration, Patient family member Registration, Amending Patient details etc.

The process starts by searching for the right patient as the first activity of the process. On successful searching of a patient, various registration services appear on the screen for the user to choose from. The process takes various paths in the process flow based on the services selected by the clerk.

This automated step-by-step approach in the process (modeled to cover all the scenarios) helps the clerk not to miss any steps related to the patient registration.

Cases can be divided into two sections, a Medical Card Exchange and cases related to New Registration at the Registration Office. The key case related innovations include:

- Creation of **8 new cases for card exchange, per hour**, per work station during peak hours
- 10 work stations were established around the hospital for Exchanging the Medical Card (old card with the new one). This enabled PSMMC to handle **400 to 600 cases per day** related to Card Exchange
- On average there are over **600 Registration case created each month**

In terms of business process innovations, they were:

- A total of **13 Main Processes** were automated
- A total of **18 Structural Sub-Processes** were created
- A total of **120 Sub-Processes & Electronic Requests** were automated

- A total of 50 WHC Printed-Letter Templates were created

### Organization & Social

From an organization perspective, this was a huge success. A process oriented work culture was introduced and adopted at the Patient Affairs department. There was more clarity on the tasks that was assigned to the Clerks. Continuous improvement and optimization of Registration processes was possible now with the help of Bizagi BPMS suite.

The implementation of a BPM process ensured that there were clearly defined roles and responsibilities, so the registration process speed has improved which boosted morale and job satisfaction within all teams involved.

All stakeholders are more efficient and productive, as they handle less paperwork, all steps are archived in a structured manner and there is more control and visibility over the whole operation, which leads to increased compliance with healthcare auditory policies.

As new processes were more structured and transparent, it became easier to follow the agreed workflows and deliver improved quality of service.

## 4. HURDLES OVERCOME

### 4.2 Management

The major challenge that Patient Affairs management had to overcome was a very weak processes and data consistency delivered by the HIS legacy system. There was hardly any knowledge of BPM or process automation within the management team. This understanding needed to be built from scratch. Having a management that clearly understands the benefits of BPM, makes the design and implementation considerably easier. Strong management sponsorship is key to the success of any BPM project.

### 4.2 Business/Technology

There was a high dependency on the patient data which was maintained in the legacy system. The Patients Affairs Department had to undertake a huge paradigm shift in technology when moving from the legacy system to BPM.

Due to this, there was a high complexity in the integration layer with the Bizagi BPMS suite. Complexity involved integration of Bizagi BPMS suite with the existing legacy systems at PSMMC. The Patient data is constantly accessed across various ICT applications in PSMMC for verifying the identity and eligibility of the patients. Synchronization of Patient data fetched from Bizagi BPMS with the centralized repository was made possible with the help of the integration layer and web services layer provided by Bizagi.

There were hurdles in optimizing the Business Activity Monitoring (BAM) and the accuracy of Process analytics due to the unclosed and pending process tasks started by the end users. This was resolved by taking advantage of the Bizagi SOA layer. SOA layer was used to detect and monitor pending process instances and analyze its state before performing the transfer to the process instance creator or process rollback.

### 4.3 Organization Adoption

There were many challenges faced by the PSMMC's team during the implementation of Patient Affairs Management System. A lot of credit goes to Bizagi for supporting the implementation by providing advice and sharing Best Practice.

The end users were more accustomed to working on the legacy system as they were using it for years. The concept of process oriented approach and BPM was new to the team and the knowledge transfer delivered through training and informal meetings had its own challenges (both technical & cultural).

## 5. BENEFITS

The BPM approach for implementing PAMS delivered various benefits to the hospital, users and patients. It enabled the PAMS management to manage their departments more efficiently and effectively.

Specific benefits of e-Medserve HIS using BPMS platform include:

- *Treatments delivered on-time* by the Emergency Department which ensures higher patient safety and reduction of undesired outcomes
- *Reduced errors and costs* associated with manual administration of medication in the pharmacy and nursing units
- *Delivery of evidence-based error reporting processes* that provide a better understanding of where errors occur and how much they cost
- *Clinical alerting applications* to notify clinicians of abnormal results and to interrupt medication administration more rapidly until results are analyzed
- *Clinical decision support reporting analysis* to help physician and clinical decision makers understand data and affect clinical protocols
- *Disease Management processes* that help proactively manage chronically ill patients, thus slowing the progress to more serious stages of disease
- *Computerized Physician Order Entry* (CPOE) - preparedness, application readiness, and implementation support to address physician order entry tasks

### 5.1 Cost Savings / Time Reductions

Together with the aim of improving customer service and patient care, there was the need for reducing costs. Cost reductions are observed from the reduction of manual activities and paperwork as well as optimization of resources and reallocation of activities and people.

The Patient affairs department at PSMMC was dependent on accessing the Legacy system daily to do their job and to maintain the patient data. The legacy system were not able to provide correct and accountable data due to its current state.

With the help of reports provided by Bizagi's BAM and Process Analytics, Patient Affairs department were able to save cost, stop malpractice and speed up their overall processes and procedures.

An important process at PSMMC Patient Affairs department was the Audit Process. Audit process were used to audit and monitor each and every data change done by the department employees. Before BPM, the procedure was to validate each and every data entry in the system based on the printed report, provided every day. This caused a huge waste of time and paper.

A significant improvement was achieved with the BPM system by introducing document scanning and processing within the system. This helped to reduce employee time as they no longer depended on the printed reports and needed to perform manual verifications.

The process and sub-process cycles have experienced a significant reduction in time. The effective interaction and coordinated work between different areas as well as between healthcare providers and other personnel has helped Patient Affairs to deliver a faster and high-quality patient-care service. Effective communication, rapid data entry, and coordination from one party to another have been the key factors in achieving time reductions.

Other cycle time reductions were observed in: decreased patient waiting times, faster completion of procedures, shorter treatment times and quicker activity planning.

The following describes the quantifiable costs savings and time reductions that resulted from this project:

- The registration process has been optimized and *reduced from 15 to 6 minutes, an improvement of 50%*
- The normal new patient registration cases were *increased from 100 to 150 (50% increase)*

### 5.2 Increased Revenues

The main objective of this project was to streamline and automate the Registration Process and improve the patients' security. These objectives have certainly been met and because new levels of efficiency have been reached, there have been indirect increased revenues. Specific revenue numbers are confidential.

### 5.3 Quality Improvements

Well-defined and controlled business process was implemented at the Patient Affairs department of PSMMC. Earlier systems were prone to human errors and were not capable of restricting users from performing unauthorized tasks. All this factors contributed to lower quality and lower productivity of the employees.

These issues were addressed successfully in the new BPM system. User data entry is controlled and validated, based on the registration service type selected by the user. Roles and responsibilities are well defined, based on business process activities to restrict unauthorized patient data manipulation. A proper and well defined sub process is in place for auditing the activities performed by the staff. This increased the accountability and quality of service at the Patient Affairs.

Changes made during the process improvement phase (introduction of patient verification activity) reduced the serious incidents and patient complaints which contributed to the patient safety.

PSMMC has to comply with lengthy government policies and procedures. New standardized processes, transparency, better control and easy access to all related information provided by the BPM system helps to deliver traceability and auditability at any stage required.

Use of Bizagi e-Medserve HIS substantially improved the quality of data gathered, facilitated precise prescription writing and helped to capture important information regarding the patients' health. Because the entire patient's data resides in one electronic clinical data repository, the system can alert providers of important patient care issues based on widely accepted evidence based clinical guidelines.

The most obvious example is prescription drug interaction warnings. But the system does also recognize more subtle care issues, such as a diabetic patient's need for an annual eye exam, and a foot examination on each visit. The system actively assists physicians and nurses by highlighting issues which have an overall effect on the quality of care offered to patients.

The Patient Affairs department were successfully able to track the stock levels of all consumable items (like Patient Cards) and order them on time thus avoiding shortages and patients' dissatisfaction.

Key quantifiable quality related improvements:

- *Human Errors have decreased to 80%*
- Most of the registration steps are automated, reducing staff intervention and time taken. *Staff productivity has increased by 60%* as early as two months after Go Live date.

## 6.  BEST PRACTICES, LEARNING POINTS AND PITFALLS

### 7.1 Best Practices and Learning Points

✓ *Integration with Legacy system are always a big challenge, so a well prepared approach is advised to face the worst case scenarios*

✓ *It is a good practice to initiate a comprehensive change management program involving all stakeholders and senior management in the very early phases of the project to encourage adoption and knowledge transfer*

✓ *Learn your BPMS first before the design phase; understand its strength and limitations well as this will help to avoid delays in the project delivery*

✓ *Encouraging end users to visualize and simulate the process activities from their perspective at an early stage will help with the training and cultural acceptance after project Go Live*

✓ *Consider project development and Go Live delivered in phases*

✓ *Ensure the involvement, endorsement and feedback from all stakeholders from the very beginning of the BPM initiative*

### 7.2 Pitfalls

× *Define clear and realistic expectation for the end users*

× *Without proper feasibility study, do not commit*

× *Avoid solving problems during advanced stages of the project or late feedback from stakeholders. Try to look at all possible scenarios during the definition and design phase*

## 7.  COMPETITIVE ADVANTAGES

Staying ahead of industry standards has now become a necessity, especially in industries like healthcare where service levels will always be looked at with detail by patients and regulatory entities.

PSMMC has gone one step forward. With the determination of providing the best standard of healthcare services for its patients, PSMMC has definitely achieved a competitive advantage over other health institutions that haven´t recognized yet the value that agile and transparent processes, efficiency and reduction of manual tasks can bring for their patients.

Thanks to Bizagi e-Medserve HIS, PSMMC has become eligible for quality recognition programs, leading to pay-for-performance (P4P). There are several programs in which hospitals and physicians can qualify for recognition as high- quality care providers. To qualify, they must submit a large volume of sample data showing that they meet established treatment performance thresholds.

The new BPM system has not only dramatically improved efficiency throughout the hospital, but has also improved clinical care and treatment as per established evidence based treatment guidelines. As more P4P programs are rolled out, Bizagi e-

Medserve HIS will become the standard solution for gathering, tracking and delivering required data across all the military hospitals.

The implementation has helped to approach the sensitive hospital processes with ease and to redesign work flows, implement best practices, and adopt technologies that integrate resources and standardize operations in support of specified improvements in clinical, operational, and economic objectives under a BPMS methodology layer.

The BPM system has empowered the PSMMC to achieve the following:

- Deliver Patient-centric solution
- Become Clinician lead
- Evidence based
- Take advantage of Integrated applications
- Utilize tightly controlled Work flows
- Actively embark on the Process Improvement Program

The Patient Affairs department in PSMMC successfully improved its quality of service, many folds with the implementation of PAMS. Many priorities were achieved, like Patient Safety, Unification of Patient Medical records, Paperless work environment etc. It was a huge step forward for the employees, to migrate from Legacy system to completely new BPM based information system.

The BPM based information system have enabled PSMMC to take lead in unifying the Medical Records of Patients, at all military medical facilities in Saudi Arabia by correction and verification procedures within the business processes. A BPM team at ICT is established to continuously monitor and optimize the processes related to the Patient Affairs, and also constantly works with the Patient Affairs to improve their processes, policies and procedures.

For all these reasons the PSMMC gained a significant competitive advantage and has become a flagship hospital in Saudi Arabia, often used as an example for delivering the highest quality patients' care.

## 8. TECHNOLOGY

Patient Affairs Management System (PAMS) project is a light house project for the ICT department of PSMMC. PAMS project was implemented and maintained by the ICT department, with previous successful BPM experience at Al-Wazarat Health Center.

Bizagi BPM suite was the obvious vendor choice because of its ease of use, simulation capabilities and an open platform. The Bizagi premier technical support services were praised for providing expert advice and for addressing various implementation challenges.

The chosen architecture, based on Bizagi system, was in line with the requirement of the Patient Affairs Management System project at PSMMC.

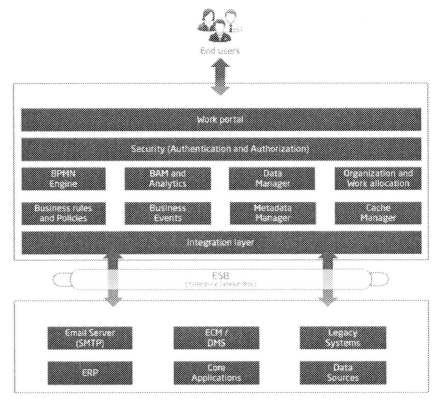

*Figure 2 – Bizagi Architecture*

Complex issues were addressed with the help of custom components that were built to take advantage of the BPMS integration and SOA layer. A lot was achieved with this approach, without opting out for expensive and complex integration and SOA products.

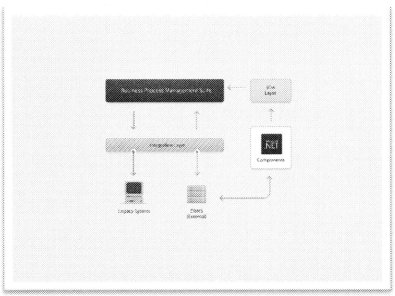

*Figure 3 – Patient Affairs Management Simplified Architecture*

The diagram above explains a simplified architecture of the Patient Affairs Management System project. The BPMS layer and the .Net components were used to meet the Patient Safety requirements at PSMMC. Smart Card Encoding devices and Human Identification devices (Palm Sensors) were integrated into these layers, enabling PSMMC to meet their patient safety concerns.

## 9. THE TECHNOLOGY AND SERVICE PROVIDERS

Bizagi integrated BPM Suite (http://www.bizagi.com)_enabled PSMMC to manage their complete patient registration process cycle.

As Bizagi Process Modeler can be downloaded for free from the Bizagi website, many users at PSMMC where able to familiarize themselves with the system prior to embarking on the project. As Bizagi website also offers a comprehensive self-service program that includes e-learning, training courses and videos, the learning curve was significantly shortened.

Bizagi Process Modeler is an intuitive drag and drop application which can also be used to generate process documentation. PSMMC used Bizagi BPM Suite to automate their registration processes, turning their process models into executable applications. With Bizagi it is very easy to move from process modeling to execution, without the need for technical knowledge a tool most commonly used by Business Analyst.

Bizagi BPM offers a complete solution which includes design and implementation of the process workflow and automation of processes. As Bizagi is an integrated BPM Suite, PSMMC was able to manage the complete process life cycle without any other additional or external tools. Bizagi's flexibility and capability of integrating and automating several processes at the same time, thereby creating a robust system can be easily adapted to business growth as more and more processes are automated.

Bizagi is a modern business collaboration tool for faster process automation. Bizagi's built-in functionalities, ease of use and flexibility makes it the ideal BPM solution to obtain faster results. In Bizagi, most of the common and reoccurring requirements in process automation have been pre-built. These include:

- Control and visibility
- Alarms and notifications
- Performance analysis and reporting
- Auditing and traceability
- Workload routing and balancing
- Mobility
- Open Integration APIs
- Corporate features (multi-tenancy, BPMN process engine, multiple language support, time-zones, long lasting process transactions, enterprise data model, among others)

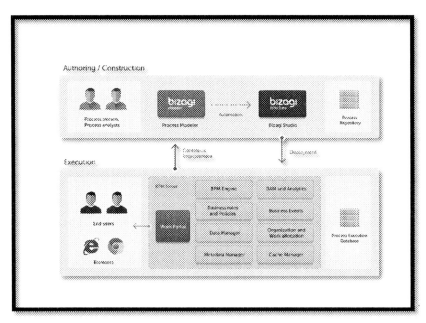

***Figure 4: Bizagi's System Architecture***

Bizagi is available in multiple editions to support the varying needs of organizations. The corporate editions are appropriate for mission critical and core business processes, satisfying the most demanding complexity and scalability needs in larger organizations. Corporate editions (Enterprise .NET and Enterprise JEE) are similar in functionality, the only difference is the deployment platform.

# PSCU, United States

## Award: Banking and Financial Services, Service Request Management
## Nominated by OpenText, Canada

EXECUTIVE SUMMARY / ABSTRACT

PSCU is one of the largest credit union services organizations in the U.S., representing close to 700 credit unions. PSCU implemented OpenText Assure in 90 days, enabling them to realize significant cost savings, improve customer service and satisfaction, and increase efficiencies, The Assure application factory provides out-of-box, industry best practice components to ensure a quick time-to-value and continuous process improvement. PSCU Customer Service Agents use the Assure Work Center to manage requests and resolve issues very quickly. The PSCU customers at the credit unions use the self-service portal to log requests and monitor the status of requests in real-time.

The BPM CoE team was instrumental in delivering a successful solution in such a short time frame. This team combined BPM and Six Sigma specialists to bridge the gap between IT and the business and build trust and collaboration, which was a huge advantage. After implementation, PSCU was able to increase customer satisfaction levels as was noted in recent customer surveys, and by using the out-of-the-box reporting tools, they can now identify trends, predict issues, and proactively identify new service needs. PSCU now responds faster and more efficiently to customer requests, process double the amount of requests with the same amount of staff, and has eliminated 90% of the paper in the process, saving them over $300,000 annually. This is a competitive advantage that PSCU is able to offer free-of-charge to the credit unions.

According to Dan Rosen, Director of the Center for Process Excellence, "This solution sets PSCU far ahead of the competition, and is very strategic to the entire organization."

## 1. OVERVIEW

Operating in a highly competitive industry, PSCU must deliver consistent, superior service to credit unions. PSCU's Center of Process Excellence, a team consisting of process improvement and Business Process Management (BPM) technology expertise, identified several areas of service delivery where inefficient manual processes could be changed and automated to dramatically improve customer satisfaction and productivity. With OpenText Assure, PSCU has transformed its services into a leading differentiator for its business.

## 2. BUSINESS CONTEXT

PSCU provides traditional and online financial services to credit unions and their customers, including industry-leading credit, debit, ATM, and pre-paid card servicing to more than 14 million card holders; innovative bill payment solutions to over one million online subscribers; and e-commerce solutions including mobile banking. Operating in a highly competitive industry, PSCU must deliver consistent, superior service to credit unions.

Prior to implementing OpenText Assure, PSCU had a very manual, paper-based process for handling customer requests. Because of this manual process, customer service representatives had to do traditional "swivel seat" integration between their various systems. They lacked a single view of their customer due to these application silos, which led to inconsistent customer service and a failure to meet service level goals.

PSCU also lacked visibility into a very fragmented customer service process. A customer service rep could not accurately tell the customer where their request was in the process or what the current status was. After conducting a customer service survey, PSCU realized that their customer service was in need of improvement and much homework was done to identify where the process broke down and how they could gather and report on additional customer service metrics.

The project was sponsored and paid for by the business and business executives were heavily involved throughout the project lifecycle. The IT organization created a BPM CoE team and this team worked closely with a Six Sigma team throughout the project to make sure that they were capturing and measuring the right customer service metrics. From day one, the primary goal was to understand the customer or credit union that was contacting PSCU and guarantee that customer received a positive, intimate, personal experience.

## 3. THE KEY INNOVATIONS

After assessing three major vendors based on expertise, product, and pricing, PSCU selected OpenText Assure which provides a portfolio of out-of-the-box best practice processes, including request management, incident management, and case management. This platform includes a work center to improve productivity, advanced reporting and analytics for business insight, and change tools for process improvement. Rosen explains, "We needed to be able to grow with a solution that was flexible, adaptable, and priced right. OpenText fit the bill perfectly."

Having conducted a complete assessment of existing systems and requirements, the PSCU team set an aggressive schedule to deploy the customer service solution, dubbed "TIMS" (Total Inquiry Management System). TIMS would serve both internal PSCU agents and external customers, and PSCU planned to launch the new system within 90 days. During the first phase of the project, the primary objective was to improve usability and request delivery through the automated inquiry and request routing capabilities.

With the final phase deployed, credit unions can now log into a personalized customer portal to submit a request to PSCU. The solution's smart routing procedures allow the request to be sent automatically to the proper team based on the request type. The internal team then works from their personalized agent portal to resolve the request. The automated tracking functionality ensures that each request is addressed and resolved on a timely basis. The credit unions are empowered through the self-service customer portal to view the status of their submitted requests, search for and export their current requests, and provide or request additional information on previously submitted ticket.

PSCU and its customers now have complete visibility into credit union requests from creation to resolution. Rosen explains, "The credit unions now have immediate access to see the progress of inquiries and requests within our system. We have empowered our customers with a portal that was so easy to use, no training was required. The feedback from our customers since implementing TIMS has been overwhelmingly positive."

### 3.1 Business

In the past, PSCU's process for handling service requests and issues from credit unions included numerous manual and paper-intensive steps. The manual nature of most of these steps made tracking of both the overall process as well as individual steps extremely difficult. This lack of visibility and inability to identify the responsible party at any one point within the process negatively impacted the overall service delivery. Credit unions submitted requests that routed to PSCU account management specialists; however, there was no single source of the truth for reporting on and identifying the status of these requests.

PSCU knew that improving overall customer satisfaction would require a different approach that moved away from a manual, paper-based environment. It was clear that PSCU and the credit unions needed real-time visibility into the status of requests, as well as reporting capabilities. Reports on historical trends would provide valuable insight to improve the performance of overall operations.

Daniel Rosen, Director of the Center for Process Excellence, summarizes the requirements; "We needed a solution that would provide more visibility, easier reporting, and faster response time to customer demands." The decision was made to implement a customer service platform and portal for all credit union requests, which would allow PSCU to track requests, assign ownership, manage accountability and service-level agreements, and ensure proper resolution of each item.

The deployment has dramatically increased PSCU's ability to respond to and track incoming requests. "Last year, we responded to hundreds of thousands of requests from credit unions. This year, we're on track to resolve more than double the request volumes without increasing head count. We are now able to tackle requests faster and more efficiently," says Rosen.

Feedback has been overwhelmingly positive, according to Danielle Hollis, PSCU BPM Developer. "All the PSCU service departments are impressed with how streamlined the OpenText Assure experience has been," she says. "Now we have visibility to every request and inquiry electronically. We have eliminated 90 percent of the paper within the process and our service agents could not be happier."

Further, using the solution's reporting tools, PSCU is now able to identify trends, predict potential issues, and proactively identify new service needs. "For example, the Assure solution enabled PSCU to see that 18 percent of customer requests were related to report generation. Since that finding, we've been able to automate responses to those requests and reduce our work queue by 30 percent," Rosen adds.

### 3.2 Case Handling

For PSCU, the next phase of implementation addressed a critical issue for credit unions and their customers—fraud management. Similar to the process of handling requests, the process of managing a case of suspected fraud on a credit card was a manual, paper-based effort that required—per month—more than 300 reams of paper, 15,000 folders, 12 ink cartridges, and shredding of 150,000 sheets of paper. Some of the most challenging cases could take up to 120 days to resolve.

Using the case management tools, PSCU now offers a fraud management solution to its credit unions, with a comprehensive electronic repository for case documents and information, an automated fraud reporting process, and full visibility into the status of a case. When a fraud case is created via the portal's fraud reporting function, a PSCU fraud agent sees it automatically on his or her to-do list, with all the relevant background information. In addition, credit unions now have real-time access to the case and the related documentation without having to call PSCU or wait for records to be provided.

The PSCU fraud team has happily embraced the new electronic system. After a few hours of training, the team was able to go live the next day without support. "It is so intuitive," says Rosen. "We eliminated their need for paper—and 30 days after launching the solution, the file folders were gone."

With an expected 150,000 – 170,000 fraud cases in the next year, PSCU anticipates significant savings simply via the reduction of paper documents used to manage cases.

As a side benefit, Assure has reduced the risks associated with relying on paper files physically stored on the premises. PSCU can now meet its Business Continuity Planning (BCP) requirements, with redundant copies of all fraud cases. With its Eastern U.S. operation located in Florida, hurricanes and severe weather make BCP-readiness a necessity.

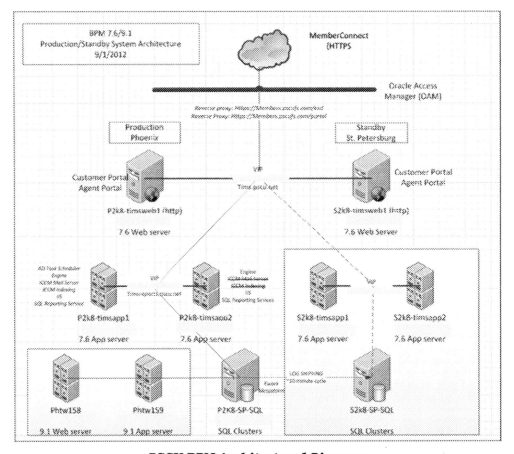

*PSCU BPM Architectural Diagram*

### 3.3 Organization & Social

A key factor in PSCU's success has been the collaboration of its technical and business teams within its Center for Process Excellence. Recently, PSCU's team of technical BPM developers joined the Process Innovation and Excellence group, a team of Six Sigma–certified productivity specialists. Combining the forces of these two teams has bridged the gap between IT and the business, building trust and collaboration. Rosen comments, "The benefit of combining BPM and Process Improvement teams delivers a huge advantage." The CoE team was also instrumental in supporting the integration efforts with all of their back-end systems to eliminate that swivel chair approach to data entry.

PSCU's customers are extremely happy and are actively engaging with PSCU. At one time they were frustrated with the process, but now they ask to be involved in defining the process and contributing to the success of the roll-out. The simplicity of the system makes it a lot easier to do business with PSCU and now their customer service ratings are improving.

PSCU employees are also very happy with the system due to its simplicity and the integration with back-end systems. They too were actively involved in defining the requirements and ensuring that the product met their needs.

PSCU executives are also very happy with the implementation and they realize that Assure is strategically important to how they deliver services and make money. Continued evolution and deployment of customer-facing initiatives is their number one corporate priority and it is this team that is delivering on these priorities.

## 4. HURDLES OVERCOME

### 4.1 Management
- Change Management and ability to keep pace with the agility and speed of BPM development
- Ability to look outside the box when developing new solutions and avoid replicating poor processes
- Commitment, empowerment and availability
- Establishing communication channels
- Changing organizational framework (changing stakeholder, etc.)
- Building the right team

### 4.2 Business
- Similar to management, ability to think openly and avoid replicating poor processes
- Commitment, empowerment and availability
- Managing distractions from competing projects and deliverables
- Being adaptable to iterative development and deployment versus a waterfall approach to project management and development
- Huge change management component due to culture

### 4.3 Organization Adoption
- Adoption of process transparency
- Integrating with existing change control process
- Partnering with the business
- Appointing process stewards
- Initial resistance to change and question the "why"
- Lack of incentive to change behavior and adopt to new processes

## 5. BENEFITS

### 5.1 Cost Savings / Time Reductions
$300,000 in savings annually in the cost of paper and ink to support a manual fraud management process, 30% cycle time reduction and improved satisfaction score by almost 100% from 42% to 82%

### 5.2 Increased Revenues

Capacity to increase revenue by 10% due to BPM automation/workflow

### 5.3 Quality Improvements

Improved BCP readiness and mitigated risk exposure to the organization. Reduced potential defect rates by 15% and now has the ability to manage inventory and improve adherence to chargeback regulations.

## 6. BEST PRACTICES, LEARNING POINTS AND PITFALLS

### 6.1 Best Practices and Learning Points

- ✓ *Build the right team – build a team with the right skills and experience. Augment staff with vendor consultants where gaps exist.*
- ✓ *Partner with your vendor*
- ✓ *Development a BPM Roadmap*
- ✓ *Engage the business early on in any process improvement initiative program*
- ✓ *Plan to re-plan – have a plan but remain flexible*
- ✓ *Build a quality business case*
- ✓ *Identify small scope initiatives (quick wins) at first and build iteratively on those deliverables before moving to complex projects*
- ✓ *Hold daily scrums to keep team and business on task – hold sprint status playback to demonstrate progress and elicit feedback early and often*
- ✓ *Establish clear communication channels*
- ✓ *Utilize best practices and established methodologies – Agile, Business Analysis, SDLC/ Project Management, Six Sigma, BPM, Architecture, etc.*

### 6.2 Pitfalls

- ✗ *BPM is extremely fast and flexible which drives the business to developing BPM solutions without understanding the business problem.*
- ✗ *BPM is extremely fast and flexible which drives the business and IT to try to use BPM for solutions that aren't true processes.*
- ✗ *Managing Demand – without a solid governance and prioritization process the BPM backlog can get unmanageable.*

## 7. COMPETITIVE ADVANTAGES

PSCU has been able to improve customer service without increasing costs which is something their competitors have not been able to do. The executives at PSCU credit BPM for this competitive advantage and their improved market readiness, which is why all priority 1 projects are now being run by the BPM CoE group. Due to the success of this first project, Assure will be enabling approximately 70 – 80% of the projects moving forward. The team has been extremely successful on their ability to deliver on their promises from a time and scope perspective.

## 8. TECHNOLOGY

OpenText Assure was the BPM and Case Management solution used by PSCU.

Other internal applications with which TIMS application interacts:

1. **SQL Server Reporting Service** – develop and deploy web-based TIMS reports
2. **Sharepoint**: All ticket attachments are stored in a Sharepoint folder created for each ticket/request
3. **Exchange**: TIMS sends out various status emails at each ticket stage/action. TIMS also received inbound email to servicedesk@pscu.com and
   a. Associates it with an existing ticket and updates the ticket

  b. Appears in "Inbound Email" queue in Agent Portal for each Team's action

4. **Lawson**: Uses a custom employee view to
  a. Populate SECUR employee fields
  b. Facilitates a synchronization process where we automatically add/delete BPM users based on ACTIVE or TERMED status in Lawson

5. **PRIME**: ETL feeds of various PRIME tables with Credit Union and Card Program Info are nightly ETL'ed to our MS SQL server. We use these to constrict our TIMS Accounts and Contacts tables, as well as do lookups.

6. **Oracle**: Custom code in Fraud BPM process to decode Credit Card numbers

7. **Billing**: Fraud BPM "pushes" records to Billing app for transaction charges

## 9. THE TECHNOLOGY AND SERVICE PROVIDERS

OpenText™ Assure – www.opentext.com

Implementation was done with the help of the OpenText Professional Services Organization.

# Refinery of the Pacific, Ecuador

## Finalist: Manufacturing
## Nominated by AuraPortal (AURA), USA

## 1. EXECUTIVE SUMMARY / ABSTRACT

Refinery of the Pacific Eloy Alfaro is a mixed economy institution created to build, operate and sustain a complex 300 MDB refinery, through a strategic alliance between PDVSA and Petroecuador. This alliance contemplates the implementation of process units with profound conversion technology, required for the production of gasoline, distillates, LPG and chemical bases.

Refinery of the Pacific has successfully implemented BPM Methodology supported on a Business Process Management suite (BPMS) for the operational and administrative management of its processes on a corporate level.

This Case Study is based on the first process to be implemented; the Public Procurement Management process. This is a complex process made up of eight sub processes for each type of procurement, which include the intervention of several departments: Administration, Management, Finance, Accounts, Technical Commission and Internal Control.

Some noteworthy areas of the project include:

1. The **total automation** of the entire **document lifecycle** (Capture and Creation, Storage, Flow, Access and Elimination) integrated in the processes.

2. The **implementation methodology**, based on the strategy of **direct implementation** on the BPMS. This methodology is possible thanks to the fact that the suite selected **does not require a single line of programming**, not for the creation of the processes nor for their subsequent optimization for Continuous Improvement. This has greatly increased agility and responsiveness and has drastically reduced times and costs.

The results were immediately apparent. The implementation of BPM methodology has led to an effective automation of Refinery of the Pacific's processes and a drastic reduction in human error.

## 2. OVERVIEW

In addition to the specific issues of the sector's common processes, being a mixed economy institution with public capital, Refinery of the Pacific is accountable to many entities and organisms, which permanently make requests for information.

A process orientation (BPM) was required, so it was decided to undertake a Project for the implementation of a Business Process Management strategy on a Corporate Level, for the operational and administrative management of all processes.

It was clear that automating the processes with a BPM tool would improve the service and reduce response times.

Thus it was decided that the use of technology was required, and a BPMS was chosen to improve process execution and the measurement and analysis of results to enable Continuous Improvement.

The implemented BPM suite has led to the effective automation of Refinery of the Pacific's processes and a drastic reduction in human errors. Furthermore, the implementation has been very simple thanks to the suite's flexibility and its easy-to-make changes (even in real-time), due to the fact that it requires no programming whatsoever to model the processes, regardless of their complexity.

Although it has been a corporate project, one of the most important processes has been selected for this Case Study, named Public Procurement Management, related to the acquisition of goods and services.

Any changes requested by users have been implemented very quickly, and to date not a single line of programming code has been required. Even now that it is in production, some requested changes have been made in real-time. The ability to change something, test it and put it into execution immediately is an enormous advantage.

With the use of the BPMS, an improved process organization and execution has been achieved. The benefits of automating the processes with the BPM suite are starting to show and maximum control of the tasks performed has already been achieved. Bottlenecks are found and localized immediately.

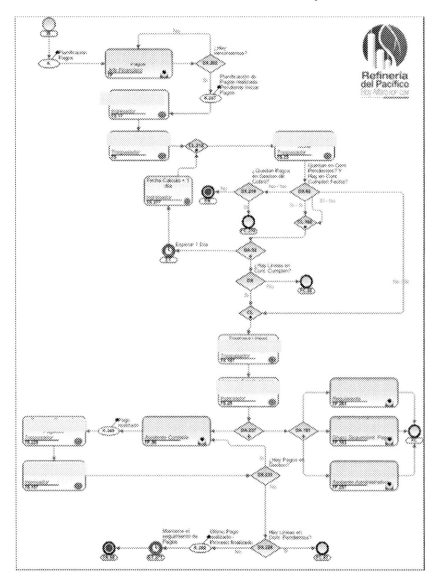

## 3. BUSINESS CONTEXT

In the phase that Refinery of the Pacific founds itself in, one of the most important processes was related to the Acquisition of Goods and Services. This is a complex process made up of 8 subprocesses, which include the intervention of different individuals with their respective positions: Secretaries, Analysts, Assistants, Bosses, Managers, etc., representing in total 75 different Roles corresponding to the following departments: Administration, Management, Finance, Accounts, Technical Commission and Internal Control. Thus, the manual coordination of the activities involved in this process became more and more complex as the procurement increased.

It soon became apparent that the identification and prior analysis of the strategic processes that were carried out was not leading anywhere, as it was practically impossible to know and take into account all the possibilities and combinations that could occur without the help of the appropriate tools.

The impossibility of ensuring compliance with the outlined methods on a theoretical level also became apparent, because, based on experience, good intentions to perform an action are often forgotten in the day to day, and a fair part of the project ends up being left uncompleted when those good intentions get forgotten.

Thus it was decided to undertake a BPMS project based on the **direct introduction** of the **theoretical** performance of the processes and their metrics in the **BPM Suite**, so that the system itself could take charge of automating the processes as much as possible, controlling their compliance and providing the necessary analysis for their Continuous Improvement.

## 4. THE KEY INNOVATIONS

### 4.1 Business

Procurement is now managed efficiently through:
- The standardization and rationalization of the processes
- The control of each of the performed activities
- The notable improvement of the relationship with suppliers
- The gradual decrease in execution times
- The expansion and improvement of the different forms of supply

The consumption of material resources (paper) has also been reduced thanks to the fact that all documentation is filed digitally.

The most effective BPMS features applied to the Public Procurement Management process are the following:

1. With regards to the user management
   - The Corporate Platform which offers an environment for the Information, Communication and Collaboration between staff of the different company departments, work groups, etc.
   - The Communication Channels: Message Boards, Surveys, online Forums and Debates, shared Agendas, etc.
   - The Work Table of each user which incorporates all the necessary elements to manage, organize and control the work to be performed: Process Tasks and Open Tasks (free workflow tasks that are not assigned to a default diagram; they can be used for non-repetitive activities). It can include Ranges, Priorities, Dead Lines, multiple Searches, Viewers, Ordinations, Alerts, etc.

2. With regards to the process management

- **Time controls** for the duration of the entire process, for each subprocess, for each task and between any desired time span. This can be measured in days, hours or minutes (calendar or business depending on working schedules) with alerts, alarms, deviation notifications, etc.
- **Groups of fields and containers** that make it possible to handle purchase items in the processes jointly but simultaneously broken down into their own elements to be treated as appropriate, either as individual elements or in batches (in "grid" format) that meet certain conditions.
- **System Tasks** that substitute Personal Tasks in such that they perform tasks that would otherwise be performed by people, but **in no time**, **without cost** and **without** the possible human **errors**, thus their **effectiveness is maximum**. They are created very simply and quickly by business users.
- Others such as automatic **Notifications**, **Management of Payments** on reaching maturity, control of **Rejections**, the use of **Rules** depending on amounts, or **Prefixes** with Prefilters.

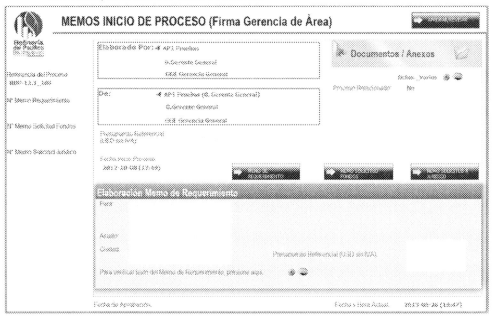

3. With regards to the document management

- **Document Management** totally **integrated** in the Process: archives, approvals, versioning, digital signature, subscriptions for notifications of change, searches by content, discussions, surveillance, tracing for audits, content publication, etc.
- As the document handling is performed within the purchase context, all the actions to be performed with documents will have been included on designing the process, thus **automating** the entire **lifecycle**: creation, capture, security, storage, conversion, search, localization, reading, modification, printing, interpretation, analysis, monitoring, mailing, linking, elimination management and other more complex actions with all types of document.

- Creation and automatic placement of **Libraries** that have been **designed** and **configured** to adapt to the requirements of the users.
- Capture or **automatic creation** of documents with labeling for their subsequent search and classification in libraries.
- **Intelligent Virtual File**. Already captured or created documents are **automatically** lodged inside the **Processes** (electronic file) and/or in the corresponding **Libraries**.
- Management of the **Counters** for Document types.
- **Digital signatures** in automatic documents (Signatures in PDF and guaranteed signatures depending on document types).
- Public Document **Queries** with customizable Filters on the set of treated libraries. Furthermore, and the most interesting is that, as the queries are commonly performed in the purchasing activities, **most of the documents do not need to be searched for**, because they are already available to the task performer to be consulted, modified, approved or eliminated **without even leaving the task**.

### 4.2 Case Handling

Prior to the AuraPortal implementation this was treated entirely manually, but given the amount of documents and initial processes being generated, the implementation of the system became increasingly urgent, in order to gain control of these processes and documents.

Information security was a priority; the security of the libraries and their queries performed by users. For this purpose Groups and Roles were created with permissions to query, edit, add and/or eliminate in each of the existing libraries in the application. Additionally, the queries of processes that manage documents also have access security.

The documents, document types, counters by type, suppliers, types of contract and modes. Some are maintained from the corresponding areas and others are updated automatically from processes, as is the case with the counters.

The system allows the cases to be defined, organized logically so that the users are capable of accessing them and executing them. The options to be managed in each case are selected through Start Messages. This has allowed increased flexibility when managing the processes and cases.

### 4.3 Organization & Social

Now the working atmosphere is very friendly. Each user receives their assigned tasks on a work table that incorporates all the necessary elements to **manage**, **organize** and **control** the work to be performed: Ranges, Priorities, Deadlines, multiple Searches, Planning by different criteria, Viewers, Ordinations, Alerts, etc.

On entering a task, the performer will find some forms that contain all the data and documents necessary to perform their task without having to leave it, although this data is in fact located in other application files. Thus, the effectiveness is maximal. The performer does not need to leave the task to look for information; the information comes to the performer.

Furthermore, using **DAD** (Dynamically Activated Divisions) technology –which is exclusive to the BPM suite purchased and recognized by Gartner as an innovative feature—as the performer performs the task the system makes the necessary Fields appear in the forms automatically, or even entire Divisions, according to the actions performed or the automatisms that the application allows: conditional fields, divisions and pages, calculated fields, calculation and business rules, automatic document creation (based on the information in the form), action buttons, link buttons, etc.

This way, the work to be carried out by the users is substantially **simplified** and **optimized** regardless of its complexity.

## 5. HURDLES OVERCOME

### 5.1 Management

From the beginning it was requested that the BPM manufacturer be involved in the implementation, in coordination with the local representative. Two teams were formed, one for each process to be implemented. Each team consisted of a representative from the manufacturer, the local supplier and the company itself, along with a general project coordinator from the manufacturer and from Refinery of the Pacific.

The initial implementation time was forecast to take three months, which was the result of a prior analysis of the processes to be implemented. However, once the implementation process was initiated and the processes were analyzed in more detail, it became apparent that the Public Procurement process required several controls that made it more complex. Thus a new implementation time was agreed upon, this time of four months to implement the project.

Basically, the methodology that has been followed can be summarized in three steps:

1. **Analysis and creation of the process Diagrams**. Several meetings took place for this between the different areas involved, taking note of the agreements. Most importantly, this step was **performed directly on the BPMS**, using the objects of the BPMN notation: Subprocesses, Tasks, Events, Gateways, KPIs, etc.

2. **Assignation of attributes to each of these objects**. In other words, the definition of the behavior of each of the diagram objects: the Personal Tasks (performers; instructions; creation of forms and their divisions, fields, buttons, libraries and documents; chronometrics; process rules; conditions; intelligent options; automatic document creation, etc.), the System Tasks that perform actions automatically (without human intervention), Gateway behavior, etc.

3. **Real Simulation**. The modeled and defined processes were then **put into execution** immediately to perform **simulations** with real users, using fictitious data.

**NOTE**. The **Real Simulation** (also called TESTING) is based on the preparation of the process to then be executed as though in real-time, but in a simulation environment to not affect the processes that are running daily in the organization. This simulation allows 100% verification that what has been modeled executes correctly.

This improvement cycle is repeated several times, allowing the implementation of any improvements requested by the uses.

### 5.2 Business

- Organizing, facilitating and limiting access to document queries in libraries, which in themselves can be located easily, quickly and securely. Defining the necessary metadata structure to ease the search and location of the required documents.

- Defining counters, by Area and Type, for all the documents generated automatically, following the corresponding sequences in each one. Additionally the storage of these documents in their corresponding libraries, optimized to the maximum by means of a filing system in independent disk drives (File System) in order to avoid overloading the institution's databases.
- Managing the Payments and checking for pending due dates on a daily basis to take the appropriate action.
- Primarily the need for all departments to work together in an organized fashion, avoiding at all costs any unrelated, disorganized or isolated work.
- The need to have all the information in one unique system in the organization (Documents, Tasks, Processes, Users, Roles, etc.) which can be shared between the different areas quickly, precisely and securely.
- The need to avoid the loss of information and ensure that the information is controlled and organized at all times.
- Having control over work times to achieve objectives.
- The possibility of having sufficient information available to the management through dashboards to aid the decision-making.
- The implementation of a full security system which prevents unauthorized persons from viewing processes or documents that do not concern them.

## 6. BENEFITS

### 6.1 Cost Savings / Time Reductions

As Refinery of the Pacific was in the initial construction phase and the implementation of the product and the process coincided with the start of the activities, there was no real work comparative with previously existing mechanisms. But given the vast amount of information generated in the handled documents and the treatment it receives as the process passes through the different institutional departments by means of tasks, any system other than a BPM or a document manager would have implied a severe lack of organization, the possible loss of documents, a lack of security control and significant difficulties in getting the information to the right people in the different departments involved. Given that the process contemplates the generation and inclusion of documents, the departments and people involved for the approval, review or rejection, automatic document generation, signed approval by the different managers and the security for the involved departments to view the documents, any system that was not a BPM and did not include a document manager would have meant an increase in cost and significantly higher execution times for the Refinery. Not to mention the consequent vulnerability of the information, the possible loss of documents, an increased amount of paper on the desks and the consequent disorganization. This is not the case with AuraPortal, which includes everything in one,BPM with a powerful document manager.

### 6.2 Increased Revenues

Top-line growth: As explained in the previous point (6.1) there are certain guidelines for the institution's Public Procurement process which involves several company departments, depending on the amount and the type of process. To achieve this, the tasks to the different departments and people are employed in an orderly manner by monitoring performance and execution times, using alerts to notify the higher bodies responsible for taking appropriate corrective measures of any deviation that may occur. It is understood that in this way any possible deviations are controlled and the execution times of the tasks and processes are delimited. Thus, the control of the processes has an exponential involvement in increasing revenue and in the continuous improvement of the processes, to obtain productive results that are increasingly accurate and optimal.

### 6.3 Quality Improvements

When designing the process, both the internal and enforceable regulations that applied in each case were taking into account, including the tasks to be performed to ensure their compliance. The corresponding Rules, both textual (instructions in the tasks performed by users) and automatic (executed by the system without human intervention) were also used.

Thus, the technical instructions and the regulation specifications are not dependant on the memory that needs to apply them, nor are they only on paper for consultation; they actually form part of the process. The natural result of using this system is the scrupulous **compliance** with the regulations. The system itself induces compliance, as it marks the steps to follow.

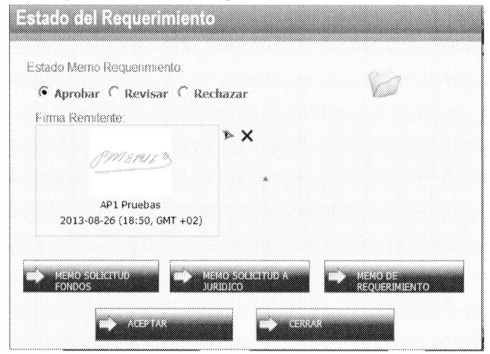

## 7. BEST PRACTICES, LEARNING POINTS AND PITFALLS

### 7.1 Best Practices and Learning Points

- ✓ *Time control in the tasks and processes, with notifications and alerts if times are exceeded.*
- ✓ *Document control in the processes and supervision of the security to view these documents from the libraries where they are stored.*
- ✓ *Important document coding system with counters by type of document and the area involved. The association of metadata or labels to the documents to make them easier to locate through filters.*
- ✓ *Consultation of documents associated to the process via queries with parameters or from the libraries themselves.*
- ✓ *Management of the Payments associated to a procurement process and the follow-up and warning of the forthcoming due dates.*

✓ *The possibility to return a process to the review stage, from and to different points of the procurement process, eliminating generated documents and established signatures.*

✓ *Control of all the comments made by the different areas with follow-up throughout the entire process, available for consultation by any person involved in the process.*

✓ *The application of Rules to determine the type of purchase based on amounts. Although there may be different types of contract per amount, Prefilters are applied depending on the type of contract. This way the process and its established logic determine the departments that it must pass through.*

### 7.2 Pitfalls

✗ *The theory is not the same as the practice. Months can be spent thinking about how to design the "perfect" process, but when you put it into execution you discover that it doesn't work. The reason for this is that it is virtually impossible to know and consider all the endless combinations and possible outcomes.*

✗ *In a diagram everything seems perfect but when you look at the processes in execution, the users contribute much more. Hence the importance of having a BPM that allows for changes to be made quickly, easily and without any programming.*

*In our case, the initial implementation time was forecast to take three months. However, once the Public Procurement Process was initiated it became apparent that it required several controls that made it more complex. Thus a new implementation time was agreed upon, this time of four months to implement the project.*

## 8. COMPETITIVE ADVANTAGES

- The fact that NO programming is required is one of the most important product features, as it allows complex actions to be performed in the processes just by establishing conditions or applying varied system tasks that are only required to know their operative.
- The easy to learn tool and the possibility of obtaining results almost immediately.
- The product is designed specifically to be implemented by company departments, not necessarily the IT department, as is the case with other BPM from the competition.
- The possibility to implement the process logic externally, by means of the AuraPortal named Own Families which are 100% customizable. This way it is possible to link this defined logic with the process operative, so changes that have a direct impact on the process operation can actually be made externally.
- The integration of the customer's other products in the system, which means that there is no need to rely on or acquire third-party products, with the aim of reducing costs to the greatest extent possible.

These five points largely summarize the main advantages that AuraPortal offers over other BPM software and that have been applied directly to the Macro-Public Procurement Process developed in the Refinery of the Pacific project.

## 9. TECHNOLOGY

The infrastructure was built jointly by the staff of the Refinery's involved departments. Given how easy it is to build processes and design tasks in AuraPortal, **with**

**no need for any programming**, the consultant provided the product knowledge and the team of people from the different Refinery departments provided the corresponding know-how about the functioning of their departments. This way, the users themselves built the process autonomously with only the supervision of the consultant, which meant that all work carried out was validated daily. Thanks to this, the Refinery itself is now capable of building its other processes, following the guidelines and knowledge acquired in the initial construction of the Macro-Procurement Process. Therefore, all knowledge of the process requirements is held within the actual process, by the employees of the involved departments and consequently the organization.

**There is no need to rely directly on the IT Department for the construction of the process**, only on their collaboration as an additional department.

- **Short development and testing period** estimated to take around 4 months. After this, the process passed to production mode where all the involved departments worked with it 100%.
- **Easy to make changes** to the process, implemented directly by the Refinery staff and supervised by AURA consultants, that have become necessary over the two year period since its construction, to improve and optimize different operational aspects.
- **The application's ease of use** in both the design and production. All options are highly intuitive.

## 10. THE TECHNOLOGY AND SERVICE PROVIDERS

**Microsoft**     Products linked directly with AuraPortal (Word, Excel and Outlook) as well as SQL Server (Database storage) and SharePoint (integrated with AuraPortal).

**www.microsoft.com**

**AuraPortal**     Created in 2002 and present in 40 countries with more than 300 customers. Its decision centers are located in Europe (Spain and Holland) and it has an executive delegation in USA (Florida).

**www.auraportal.com**

# Right of Way, Department of Transport of Abu Dhabi, UAE

## Award: Public Sector Planning and Permitting

## Nominated by DoT, United Arab Emirates

### 1. Executive Summary / Abstract

The Department of Transport (DoT), in line with the overall strategy for the government of Abu Dhabi, has identified the need to improve customer care as a key objective. They consider their customers one of their greatest assets. One of the key drivers for this project was the improvement of customer care through the identification and implementation of a leading NOC application and approvals procedure to create clear impact on both internal and external customers.

All contractors, consultants and developers in the emirate of Abu Dhabi of the United Arab Emirates are required to obtain No Objection Certificates (NOCs) from the DOT for any intended construction within the Emirates' Rights of Way.

An NOC is an approval, stipulating their conditions, granted by the ADDOT indicating that their requirements have been adequately addressed and that they have no objection for the intended work to proceed. A Right of Way (ROW) is defined as being the road corridor from property boundary to property boundary.

Prior to the implementation of the project, the previous process lacked clarity, consistency and often involved considerable delays.

The DoT began their project in late 2010 with a view to developing a ROW section and Online NOC System to launch in 2011.

As outlined in this document the main objective was to significantly improve the application process required to obtain the Departments approval for third parties to undertake work within the Rights of Way. This was achieved through the development of the online NOC System as a single contact point for receiving NOC applications and to facilitate the expediting the issuing of consolidated NOCs on behalf of the DOT.

The system is based on work flow processes, integrated with GIS and is available to registered users via web access in English or Arabic, the first multi-lingual online NOC application process system in the Middle East. Processes and business rules contained within the system ensure that all tasks required in assessing applications are identified, directed to and completed by relevant individuals within stipulated timeframes.

The system has been operational since late 2011 and continues to be enhanced by the project team.

### 2. Overview

The Abu Dhabi Department of Transport (DoT) has recently concluded a project, the objective of which was the establishment of a Right of Way (ROW) Section and the provision of an online No Objection Certificate (NOC) System as a single contact point for receiving NOC applications for any work to be undertaken within Abu Dhabi's Rights of Way and to facilitate and expedite the issuing of consolidated NOCs on behalf of DoT.

The purpose of the project was to define clear procedures for obtaining DoT NOC's so as to eliminate NOC applications being made on an ad-hoc basis and to ensure consistency with regard to NOC types and application requirements as well as to ensure that all affected DoT Divisions are consulted in the process.

The project was undertaken by the Abu Dhabi Department of Transport with the support of global consulting firm Aurecon, the UK & Middle East based legal firm Trowers & Hamlins and South African-based Business Process Management (BPM) provider FlowCentric.

The project was initiated with an information gathering phase which included comprehensive interaction with stakeholders within the DoT and external to it. It included research of best practice in ROW Management both regionally and internationally.

The international study included desk top studies of 14 cities throughout the USA, Canada, Australia, Europe, Hong Kong and Singapore. The study focused on issues relating to online NOC systems, organisational structures, NOC processes and the legal framework in which these cities operated with regard to the Management of ROW's. Based on the finding of the desk top study, benchmark study tours to four cities, New York, Vancouver, Sydney and Singapore, were undertaken.

The systems and processes which were previously practiced within the DoT were studied and mapped. These were then analysed to identify challenges and areas for improvement with the aim of streamlining the processes and increasing efficiency. New, clearly defined processes were developed and together with the established international best practice formed the basis upon which the organisational structure for the ROW Section and the online NOC system was developed.

The new online NOC system represents the single point of contact for NOC applications which is available to registered users via web access. Figure 1 below provides a schematic representation of the NOC application process.

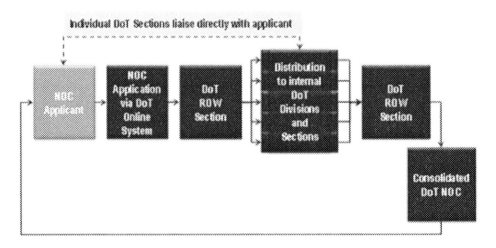

***Figure 1: NOC Application Process***

## 3.  BUSINESS CONTEXT

Prior to the project implementation the DoT had no formal section responsible for the management of their Right of Way or the processing of NOCs. There was also no clearly defined single process in place for Authorities, Contractors or Consultants to apply for NOCs. This meant that submission and processing of NOC applications were generally highly ad-hoc with no real control on the outcome of the process.

In the initial stages of the project the Process Mapping team conducted a series of interviews to develop an "as is" process map outlining the current process for obtaining an NOC from the DoT. Feedback from these interviews indicated that, due to the lack of a formal process, the following key issues existed:

- There was no clear information available to applicants as to with whom they should lodge their application;
- Once an application was received the processing of that application was often handled differently by individuals based on their own interpretation of what should be required of the applicant;
- The section who received the application would often only consider the impacts of the work from their perspective, not necessarily sharing the application with other DoT sections who may or may not have been impacted by the proposed works. They would then issue an NOC to the applicant on behalf of their Section who would then believe they had fulfilled their obligation to the DoT in getting that approval;
- There was no timeframe on the application process which often resulted in lengthy turnaround times for approval and significant delays to work;
- Frustration with the process, particularly from other government authorities or service providers, often resulted in potential applicants ignoring it altogether and going ahead with the work without approval;
- There was a lack of willingness with the DoT to provide approvals as accountability was unclear;
- There was no clear process for the pricing of NOC applications nor the collection of associated monies often resulting in no fees being charge at all;
- There was no overarching control over the process to ensure that it was adding value to the both the DoT and its customers.

The impact of the lack of clarity in the existing process was often resulting in significant delays in approvals processing but also compromising the DoT's assets with approval for work often being granted without proper consideration from all impacted stakeholders from within the DoT.

The driving motivation for the project was therefore to address the issues raised above by creating firstly a ROW section within the DoT to take ownership for all approvals and secondly to implement a web based system to facilitate the processing of applications.

## 4. THE KEY INNOVATIONS

### 4.1 Business

The core objective of the project was to implement a structured system that would benefit not only the DOT but also the variety of stakeholders reliant on the DOT for the provision of NOCs.

The online system is basically the front end outcome of the various project components and represents a significant improvement in the way in which the DOT interacts with its stakeholders within the permitting environment.

Prior to the project implementation much of the feedback received by the DOT in relation to the issuance of NOCs was focused on core problems such as:

- a lack of consistency in processing between and within sections;
- significant delays in approval processing timings;

- variable documentation requirements resulting in rework and time delays.

After the project completion and with the system implemented the above key issues were addressed. Clarity and consistency was bought into the permitting process providing both the processor and the applicant a more efficient and timely means by which to provide or gain an NOC approval.

### 4.2 Case Handling

Prior to the project implementation the DoT had no formal section responsible for the management of their Right of Way or the processing of NOCs. There was also no clearly defined single process in place for Authorities, Contractors or Consultants to apply for NOCs. This meant that submission and processing of NOC applications were generally highly ad-hoc with no real control on the outcome of the process. The key issues arising out of the scenario were elaborated upon in Section 2.

While development of the ROW Section and the Online NOC System are the rcognisable outcomes of the project, these represented the final two of six interdependent project components as illustrated in the diagram below and elaborated upon thereafter.

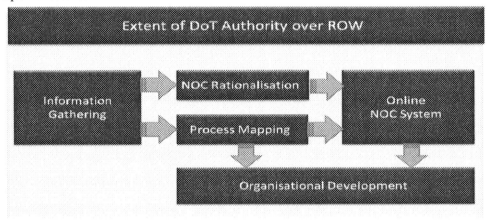

### Extent of DoT Authority Over Row

From the beginning of the project it was clear that inconsistencies existed within the current legislative environment both internal and external to the DoT which could hinder the ability of the DoT to achieve its project related goals. For this component it was important of the project team to study and understand the current applicable legal structure in place and determine the necessary amendments or improvements required to be implemented either within the DoT itself or in the context of the wider Emirate of Abu Dhabi government structure.

This process including looking at all documents from the DoT's own Charter through to the legislation governing ownership of the ROW throughout the Emirate. Once a clear understanding was developed the project team needed to identify and establish a variety of both legal and non-legal documents which could then be taken to the Executive Council (Abu Dhabi Government) for implementation to empower the DoT as the primary responsible party for the applicable ROW corridors within the Emirate.

### Information Gathering

Whilst the team were establishing the above information it was also important to glean as much general information relating to the project from as many sources as possible. As such, this component was always seen as a critical step in ensuring the long term sustainability of the project outcome as it involved not only interaction with all internal DoT stakeholders but also with the wider external stakeholder which not only included Contractors and Consultants who may use the system but also other government authorities and service providers who have a vested interest in the outcome of the project.

The stakeholder interaction was done in a series of workshops focused on sharing and collecting information relevant to the project as well as through a series of Assessment Questionnaire aimed at gathering information on the perception of the existing processes.

Furthermore, studies were undertaken to establish best practice benchmarks both regionally and internationally with trips to Dubai, New York, Vancouver, Sydney and Singapore undertaken to visit local authorities and service providers to gain insight into different systems around the world.

### NOC Rationalisation

The critical part of this component of work was to develop an understanding for all the different types of NOCs required by the various sections within the DOT in order to rationalize them into a series of standard NOCs that could be included in the automated online system.

The types of NOC's previously issued by the DoT were therefore identified, analysed and then rationalised to ensure consistency and clarity with regard to identifying NOC's relevant to work within the Abu Dhabi Rights of Way with regard to both the scope of work (Work Type NOC's) and the project stage (Stage Type NOC's). In the end, seven Work Type NOC's were identified and, for clarity, these were further expanded upon as Work Sub

Types. In total, 34 Work Sub Types were defined from which an applicant may select the most appropriate.

**Stage Type NOCs** which were applications made at various stages of a project as shown below:

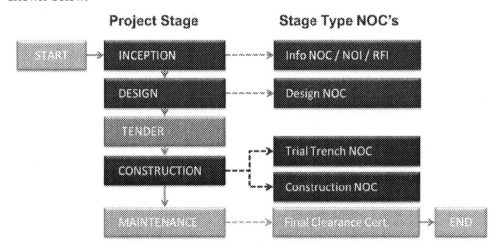

**Work Type NOCs** which represented applications made for different types of work as shown below:

| Type | Sub Type | NOC STAGE TYPE | | | | | |
|---|---|---|---|---|---|---|---|
| | | NOI/RFI | Design | Trial Trench | Construction | Final Clearance | Non Stage Specific |
| **Roads and Access** | New Roads & Structures, Road Improvements | ✓ | ✓ | ✓ | ✓ | ✓ | - |
| | Access to plots | ✓ | ✓ | ✓ | ✓ | ✓ | - |
| | Parking within ROW | ✓ | ✓ | ✓ | ✓ | ✓ | - |
| | Diversions / Temporary Roads | ✓ | ✓ | ✓ | ✓ | ✓ | - |
| **Road furniture, Signage & Landscaping** | Traffic Signs (incl. electronic) | ✓ | ✓ | ✓ | ✓ | ✓ | - |
| | Temp Signboards | - | - | - | - | - | ✓ |
| | Advertising Signs | ✓ | ✓ | ✓ | ✓ | ✓ | - |
| | Landscaping | ✓ | ✓ | ✓ | ✓ | ✓ | - |
| **Utility Infrastructure** | New & improvements to existing installations | ✓ | ✓ | ✓ | ✓ | ✓ | - |
| | House Connections | ✓ | - | ✓ | ✓ | ✓ | - |
| | Diversion / Removal of utility infrastructure | ✓ | ✓ | ✓ | ✓ | ✓ | - |
| | Routine Maintenance | - | ✓ | ✓ | ✓ | ✓ | - |
| | Emergency Maintenance/Rehabilitation | - | - | - | - | - | ✓ |
| **Building Related** | Basement Extension | - | - | - | - | - | ✓ |
| | Shoring Works | - | - | - | - | - | ✓ |
| | Temp Hoarding / Fencing | - | - | - | - | - | ✓ |

The rationalization process saw the number of NOC types drop from 60 to 34 with an increased clarity provided to the application on the appropriate NOC type for their particular circumstances. It also allowed for the introduction of automated approvals in instances where the work was either minor or it did not impact on a specific section within the DoT.

### Process Mapping

The initial step in this work component was to map the current work-flow related to ROW within the various DOT sections. The analysis included identifying challenges and areas for improvement with an aim to increase efficiency and streamline the overall process.

One common theme that was identified early on in the process mapping work was that there were multiple inconsistencies between each section with the existing processes – an example of one section's "As Is" map is shown on the following page.

Once each of the "As Is" maps was determined a set of initial consolidated generic macro Process Maps were identified for each Stage Type known as the "To Be" processes. Within each of these macro process maps a further divisional process was developed which identified the processes to be followed within each of the sections.

In total 8 macro process maps and 5 divisional process maps were developed which collectively represented the generic process required to process over 1000 potential scenarios. These maps were as follows:

- Notice of Intent and Request for Information NOC: Macro Process
- Notice of Intent and Request for Information NOC: Divisional Process
- Design NOC: Macro Process ☐ Design NOC: Divisional Process
- Trial Trench NOC: Macro Process

- Trial Trench NOC: Divisional Process
- Construction NOC: Macro Process
- Construction NOC: Divisional Process
- Final Clearance Certificate Process
- Non Stage Specific NOC: Marco Process
- Non Stage Specific NOC: Divisional Process
- Emergency Process
- Site Monitoring Process

The base framework for the Process Maps is defined as shown below.

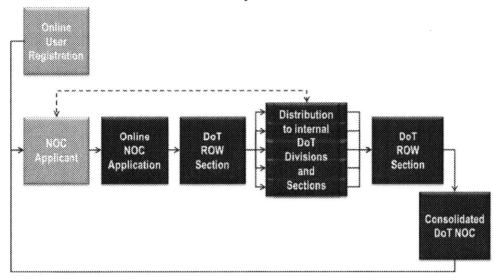

### Organisational Development

In order to achieve the objectives of the project the DOT needed to implement a section to take on the overarching role of having responsibility for the ROW and the approvals process associated with it.

Using the process mapping and information gathered, particularly through the international study tours, the team formulated an organizational structure which identified the Roles within the ROW Section and the function of the ROW team overall. As part of this organisational design process it was particularly important to take cognizance of the existing skill set within the other DOT sections and identify suitable job descriptions for the team moving forward.

These job descriptions were considered on two fronts:

1) Job Specification
   a) Organisational Relationships
   b) Key Responsibilities and Duties
   c) Key Accountabilities

2) Person Specification
   a) Key Knowledge and Skills Areas
   b) Preferred qualifications
   c) Preferred professional registration
   d) Preferred experience

Furthermore a set of guidance manuals was developed to support the entire system for both internal and external use – in both English and Arabic – including an NOC User Guidelines, an Online NOC System Operating Manual and an NOC Procedure manual.

### Online NOC System

The implementation of an Online NOC System formed a key component of the overall project. The objectives of the system were to:
- provide a single point of contact for NOC applications via the web;
- distribute application to relevant DOT sections based on Stage Type and Work

Type and answers to questions asked of the applicant;
- ensure appropriate individuals complete NOC tasks;
- assign and monitor required response time;
- provide back up if response time is not met and elevate for internal DOT action;
- track and monitor the overall progress of an NOC application.

Furthermore the online system was required to be integrated into the wider DOT GIS platform.

The Online NOC system included the following key functions:
- General conditions are available for assessors to select from drop-down menus;
- Generates lists of required supporting documents based on Stage Type and Work Type
- Provides management information by monitoring processing activities and producing reports;
- Flexibility to incorporate future changes, enhancements and expansion
- NOCs can be: Modified/Updated -Revalidated -Cancelled -Reopened
- Site monitoring inspections can be scheduled for approved Construction NOCs;
- Initiated by DoT (ad-hoc or planned) or Contractor;
- Issue Final Clearance Certificates upon completion of work and once all NOC conditions have been satisfied.

The system followed the generic base process framework map as previously shown with the following key attributes per step:

Online User Registration:
- Register as a Company
  - One username and password per company
  - Multiple Contacts per Company
- Validity linked to company Trade Licence
- Each Company will have access linked to the validity period of the Trade Licence
- ROW to provide final approval of applications NOC Distribution and Assessment:
- Applications are distributed to affected Divisions
  - Predetermined distribution depending on type of NOC
  - In response to questions posed to the applicant
  - As identified by DoT during the assessment process
  - Internal DoT Divisions review and process applications
- Internal DoT Divisions interact directly with applicants if required

- ROW Section collates Divisional responses
- ROW issues consolidated NOC on behalf of DoT
  - General and Particular Conditions
  - The final response can be provided in Arabic, English or both

Based on the information input into the system from both the applicant and the DOT processor a generic NOC letter is created by the system and sent out identifying whether or not the NOC application has been successful and also any conditions that may be applicable to the approval.

### 4.3 Organization & Social

The project involved the establishment of a new ROW section within the wider DOT establishment and therefore all the roles associated with the project were developed as new roles and for the most part these individuals were recruited into their roles. Where existing staff were available and suitably skilled, these staff were reassigned to the new section so that there was as much existing DoT knowledge within the team as possible.

During the organizational design process an organization structure was developed and a series of job descriptions put in place in order to provide the ROW section with a sound platform on which to build a team. A portion of the team was hired and in place for the launch of the system whilst the remaining members of the team continue to be identified and recruited as use of the system increases.

Much of the organizational development work undertaken during this phase was undertaken using the knowledge gained as part of the international study tours. In particular the organizational set up within the New York City Department of Transport was seen as a foundation on which a suitable and similar section could be implemented within the DoT.

## 5. HURDLES OVERCOME

### 5.1 Management

To ensure successful implementation of the new system and the ROW team it was important to gain buy-in from all the other sections with the DOT. In some areas this included getting buy-in from other sections whose own levels of responsibility, in respect to ROW management, where being diluted by the introduction of the system.

In order to mitigate the potential political issues that could come from this problem the team opted to develop very clear business flow maps outlining clear benefits of the proposed organizational model that could be appreciated by all.

By representing the changes to the organization model in a positive and clearly defined way the team were better equipped to have the often difficult discussions with individuals or teams who would inevitably lose some element of control over their existing work portfolio due to the introduction of the ROW team.

Another approach the ROW team opted for was to reach out to any existing DOT staff who were currently involved in or interested in work within the realm of ROW management and see if they were suitable for transfer from their existing Section into the newly created ROW team. The advantage of this approach was twofold – on one hand you gain support and trust of teams who may have otherwise been threatened by the change but also you acquire resources with inherent knowledge of your business already.

## 5.2 Business

One of the main driver's behind the implementation of the ROW section and eNOC system was to see a vast improvement in the timeline required for the processing of approvals related to NOCs. Many of DoT's external stakeholders, who effectively saw themselves as the DoT's customers, believed that the process times for obtaining NOCs from the Department were lengthy and arduous. In order to therefore ensure that the implementation of the system would achieve the key goal of reducing process time, it was critical to develop a series of key performance indicators for the new ROW section to ensure accountability and defines suitable progress targets relating mostly to processing of applications.

This posed some key challenges with regards to how dependent the ROW team were on other sections within the DoT throughout the application process. In some examples the team were highly dependent on other DoT sections (for example where an application had a unique technical component related to it) and it other examples there was almost no dependency (for example where an application was basic in nature and impacted very few sections).

In the end the key performance indicators were implemented firstly at a management level reaching further than just the direct ROW team. This allowed for a procedure to be introduced whereby the ROW team could elevate issues within the system to the direct attention of another sections line management in order to seek assistance in expediting any perceived issues.

## 5.3 Organization Adoption

Another significant challenge of the project was the roll out of the system and in particular building awareness of the new processes and procedures throughout both the internal sections of the DOT and the external stakeholders who would be reliant on the system for their NOC approvals going forward.

The new ROW section team took charge of building awareness of their new team structure and the new processes to be rolled out throughout the wider DOT community. Part of this was running a series of workshop and training sessions to show the new systems capabilities and run through the new process for NOC application.

A series of guidebooks were also established, in both English and Arabic, to help sup-port people looking to utilize the new system and the ROW team encouraged interaction with both internal and external stakeholders to ensure everything possible was done implement the new system successfully.

## 6. BENEFITS

## 6.1 Cost Savings / Time Reductions

Because of the nature of the services provided by the DOT and the fact that this project has also introduced a new section into the Department cost savings are not directly assessable. That said, the time reductions and productivity improvements – as noted in the following sections – generally result in considerable cost savings particularly to the Contractors and Consultants using the new system.

One of the clearest and most measurable benefits of the new online NOC system is in the time reductions for both users, in submitting applications, and the Department's staff, in assessing and responding to applications.

Furthermore, the additional control and overview provided by the NOC team ensures that each of the departments and sections within the DOT undertake their responsibilities within a timely manner. One of the main benefits reported by the individual staff within the DOT is that they have found that simply with the implementation of a fixed consistent process they are having to do less rework.

The tables below represent the response time before and after implementation of the system. The response time continues to improve.

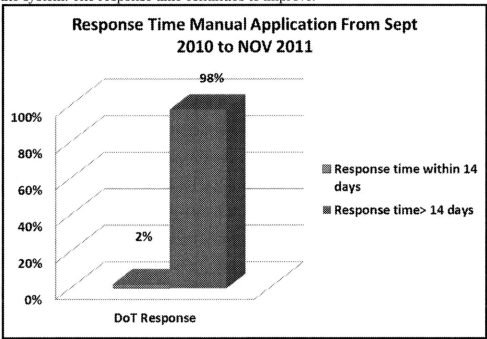

*Total Number Of Nocs Processed By Department Of Transport- Before & After*

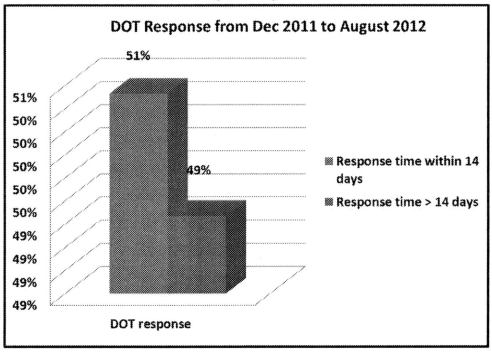

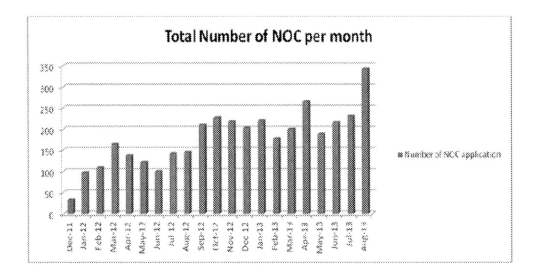

**Percentage of increase of online eNOC's per month:**

December 2011 to August 2012 – 300% increase from 50 to 150 December 2011 to August 2013 -700% increase from 50 to 350

These graphs indicate that in the initial 6 months of the new system being in place a significant improvement in response time had occurred. Prior to the system 98% of the NOC applications received took in excess of 2 weeks to be processed. Within the first 6 months this dropped to below 49%.

These figures have continued to improve mostly because the ROW team is still growing and working towards resourcing at full level. In the initial 6 months of processing the team itself had only employed 50% of its full quota of staff making this achievement all that much more impressive.

### 6.2 Increased Revenues

At present, the DOT does not collect fees relating to NOC processing. It should be noted that this was not a key focus objective for the project.

### 6.3 Quality Improvements

The quality improvements realised by the project are associated with the clear and streamlined processes, clear and consistent requirements and the consistency of their application.

External stakeholders now have a clearly defined path that they follow and requirements in order to obtain approval from the DOT to undertake work on the Department's assets. They also have visibility on the progress of their applications and access directly to a Project Manager who is responsible for that progress. Applicants know exactly what is required for each type of NOC and the system provides consistent feedback based on fixed DOT policies.

Within the ROW team the NOC process defines roles and responsibilities which empower each staff member to make the necessary decisions and take action to process approval in a timely efficient and consistent manner.

The nature of the system also encourages a paperless environment where, in addition to the obvious environmental benefits this initiative will provide savings associated with paper and printing for NOC applicants, archiving time and storage for archiving.

The automated nature of the system allows the team to process the more simplified NOCs with little time and effort whilst being able to concentrate on ensuring that the major works NOCs are given due consideration by all impacted parties.

## 7.   BEST PRACTICES, LEARNING POINTS AND PITFALLS

### 7.1 Best Practices and Learning Points

During the first 6 months of implementation the ROW Section, along with rest of the internal Division members, executed a series of enhancements to the on line system:

### 7.2 Pitfalls

During the implementation of this project a few issues arose, mostly around collaboration:

- ×   *Wider collaboration between the DOT and other government organisations would have proven particularly useful. A significant number of government organsiations were consulted during stakeholder engagement but there was potential for a single system to be implemented incorporating approvals for all government organisations.*
- ×   *Some additional prelaunch system testing may have improved the initial experience for users on the system initially as the first couple of months involved some system fixes that slowed down the processing time.*

## 8.   COMPETITIVE ADVANTAGES

The potential impact of the project on a wide range of both internal and external Stakeholders was recognised during the early planning stages and the need for close collaboration and consultation between the Consultants, the proposed NOC Team and the various stakeholders throughout Abu Dhabi in order to identify and accommodate the varying needs of the target user groups.

This interaction was a focus point at every stage of the project beginning with inviting participation from internal DoT stakeholders which was initiated through a series of Questionnaires being sent to each of the sections specifically designed to solicit information which may be relevant in achieving the project objectives. The questionnaires were followed up with a host of workshop sessions and meetings.

Similarly external stakeholder participation was initiated with questionnaires, followed up with interaction on a one on one basis and continued in the form of written (letters and e-mail) and telephonic communication. In all, approximately 40 external stakeholders were identified for interaction and included Service Authorities, developers, consultants and contractors active in Abu Dhabi.

The core interaction between the DOT project team and the key stakeholders throughout the early stages of the project allowed the team to fully understand the main issues and concerns regarding the various existing NOC procedures as well as gain insight into per-ceived opportunities for improvement and enhancement.

Other than the benefits outlined throughout this document one of the clear advantages that the system has is the multi-lingual nature of both the input and output documentation. Users can apply for an NOC in either English or Arabic and their NOC will subsequently be issued in that language. This capability makes the system stand out from many other systems that already exist and makes it certainly the first multi-lingual system of its kind in the Middle East.

The DOT continues to enhance their system and learn from global best practice to ensure they stay at the front of the pack not only in the UAE, but in the Middle East and the world. The team recently embarked on another International study tour to visit other like-minded organisations with similar systems to establish opportunities for continual improvement and value adding.

Due to the success of the system within the Emirate of Abu Dhabi other government entities in the Emirate, and also in other Emirates and other Middle Eastern Countries; are currently showing interest in developing similar systems.

## 9.  TECHNOLOGY

The Online NOC System was built on the Department of Transport's existing network using the Business Process Management Suite (BPMS) tool, FlowCentric. FlowCentric is built on the Microsoft .NET framework, uses a SQL database, and can integrate with a number of different systems using connectors or iAdapters.

The FlowCentric Process Suite allows users to design forms by using drag-and-drop facilities. All underlying business rules and routing for the Online NOC System are de-fined in the process suite. Completed processes are then rendered and presented to the users via browsers on their computers or mobile devices. The users only need to interact with the Online NOC system using their Internet browser – they do not require any other installations.

The FlowCentric BPMS allowed easy deployment of the Online NOC System to external users as well as internal ADDOT users. By configuring the site within FlowCentric, the different users were presented slightly different views – allowing the users to complete only the actions that they are required to do, and also ensuring that users only see what they had access to. FlowCentric makes use of notifications and escalations to ensure that users are notified via emails that they had tasks they need to complete, and that these tasks are to be done by a specific date.

FlowCentric was integrated with the following two systems:
- GIS – this integration used information from FlowCentric and used it when digitising the area of work on the DOT's GIS maps. The information was stored as metadata in GIS to ensure that a link between FlowCentric and the GIS system was kept – allowing users to view all NOC's submitted via FlowCentric in GIS.
- DOT's SMS service – this integration allowed FlowCentric to send updates to users via a SMS to their cellular phone. This ensured that a user was kept informed regarding the progress of their application.

Benefits provided by the use of the FlowCentric BPMS are:
- A drag and drop tool allowing users to update forms if required.
- A single point of access for all users interacting with the system.
- Predefined forms ensuring users complete NOC Applications by provided all the required information – thereby ensuring the standard of each application is the same as previous applications.
- Notifications and escalations – ensuring users are informed of work that they need to do.
- Tracking of application progress.
- Integration with different systems to increase functionality.

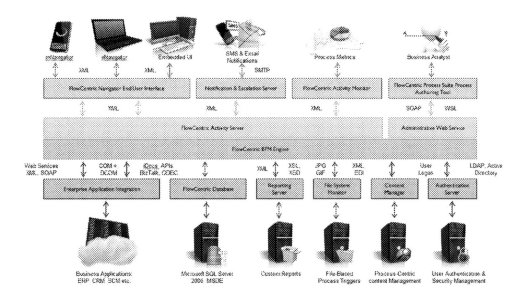

FlowCentric Processware is a Business Process Management Suite built on top of the Microsoft product stack. The latest offering of the FlowCentric suite includes a mixture of web applications, services, Windows applications and repositories; targeting the Microsoft.NET framework and leveraging Microsoft Office and Share-Point, SQL Server and IIS (Internet Information Services).

The FlowCentric Process Suite, a .NET 3.5 (SP1)-based Windows Forms application, provides users with a Microsoft Office Visio-driven process designer that, through the aid of ASP.NET (ASMX)-based web services, realises an internet-enabled solution for configuring and administering workflow-enabled solutions. The resulting solutions are accessible to users via many (role-driven) client interfaces.

The FlowCentric Process Suite has been tested to meet all of the technical requirements to be Compatible with Windows® 7.

FlowCentric Classic Navigator, FlowCentric Web 2.0, FlowCentric Event, FlowCentric Configuration Manager, FlowCentric Notification and Escalation Service have been tested to meet all of the technical requirements to become Works with Windows Server® 2008 R2 certified.

## 10. THE TECHNOLOGY AND SERVICE PROVIDERS

AURECON (www.aurecongroup.com)

Aurecon provides engineering, management and specialist technical services for public and private sector clients globally. The group, with an office network extending across 24 countries, has been involved in projects in over 80 countries across Africa, Asia Pacific, the Middle East and the Americas and employs around 7 500 people throughout 11 industry groups. Aurecon provided lead consultancy services for the project as well as technical and organization design support services.

FLOWCENTRIC (www.flowcentric.com)

FlowCentric Technologies is a trusted global provider of Business Process Management (BPM) Solutions. The company has a global presence servicing Africa, Asia, the United Kingdom, Europe and Australasia. The company provided specialist BPM and IT services for the project.

TROWERS & HAMLINS (www.trowers.com)

Trowers & Hamlins is an international law firm with offices throughout the UK, Middle East and South East. Trowers relied on years of experience working in the Emirate of Abu Dhabi to provide legal consulting services for the project.

# Swiss Federal Railways SBB

## Award: Transportation and Logistics, Agile Development
## Nominated by ti&m AG, Switzerland

EXECUTIVE SUMMARY / ABSTRACT

The Swiss are world champions in using their railways - on average a Swiss citizen travels 2258km per year on the railway network. As a consequence the railway system is heavily used and the quality of service has to be high according to Swiss standards which also means the processes for rail network operation have to be efficiently controlled.

The BPM project 'SIP' (SBB Infrastructure Portal) automates incident processes with a workflow system. In the project, one unified BPM system was used for very diverse process management and we would like to emphasize how we managed complexity. Imagine a tree that has fallen on a railway track. It damages rails, power lines and even telecom wires. A complex mixture of processes and organizations (civil engineering, power services, IT, external companies) has to be mastered by different technical control centers in order to efficiently react to the incident and finally make the joint decision to give the green light once all impediments have been resolved.

We used agile methods (Kanban & Scrum) to homogenize processes and disambiguate contradictory system requirements, and used innovative concepts like "heat maps" to implement flexible and self-learning processes. The BPM system allows us to coordinate different domains within the company and facilitates financial reporting, control and planning of preventative measures. Ultimately the system leads to a higher usage of the existing railway network, which means redundant infrastructure is not required thus saving costs in building and maintaining the railway network.

## 1. OVERVIEW

Switzerland has about 8 million inhabitants, the most of them use and love their rail network. The biggest state owned Railway Company is called "SBB" – the Swiss Federal Railways[1]. Swiss are proud of their accurate watches and the trains mostly leave on time.

But for SBB punctuality means efficiency. Handling less exceptions and efficiently handling incidents leads to a higher usage of the rail network. The better you are able to use existing rail tracks the less rails have to be build and maintained.

---

[1] http://en.wikipedia.org/wiki/Swiss_Federal_Railways

This leads us to the BPM project "SIP" – the "SBB Infrastructure Portal". All business processes of SIP are aligned on top of the SBB infrastructure, which is necessary to run the network.

So let's take a look at the infrastructure of Swiss Federal Railways (SBB):
- 9159 employees
- 30000+ of external employees
- 3005 km rail network
- 757 stations
- 6027 bridges
- 305 tunnels
- 559 signal boxes
- 30 066 signals
- 14 105 points
- 5 power plants
- IT infrastructure like servers, routers, etc.

All these "items" of SBB infrastructure can be managed either
- Reactive: Incident Management and process management
- Proactive: Management of the infrastructure – e.g. each asset needs a "patient record" – a history what has happened in the past of the asset.

According to this distinction, the business can be roughly separated between planned or unplanned changes to the infrastructure – in ITIL you would call them Changes and Incidents (http://en.wikipedia.org/wiki/ITIL). But in sense of the business process there is a huge difference between a change on a router for IT networks, which can be done remotely in seconds or a change which affects hardware rails in a remote location which may cause high safety measurements like closing the track.

We faced plenty of challenges; some of them are:
1. We had to integrate each part of the infrastructure in the same business process implementation. So we had to align for example the IT incident process with the process of civil engineering. The IT process followed the ITIL standard which had nothing in common with the civil engineering processes - which were themself executed differently in areas of Switzerland.
2. Switzerland hosts 3 languages. The software, the business analyst and the meetings had to deal with three languages and also different cultural background.
3. Besides languages barriers we had to deal with different maturity of their processes. IT process were highly standardized and somewhat the lighthouse. But you cannot tell a civil engineer, who has done his job reliable and error-free for the last 30 years to follow a certain process in order to improve the quality of his work.

Nevertheless the overall aim was to use "one process" for all its infrastructure. Benefits are to enable homogenized cost accounting, use process data for preventive measurements and to efficiently manage domain crossing processes especially for big incidents.

## 2. BUSINESS CONTEXT

What is happening on an incident?

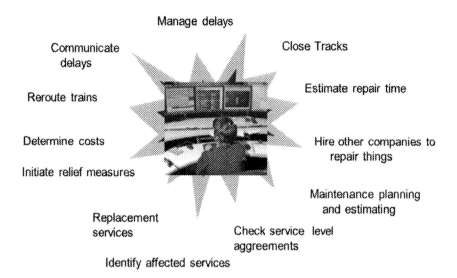

Manage delays

Communicate delays

Close Tracks

Reroute trains

Estimate repair time

Determine costs

Hire other companies to repair things

Initiate relief measures

Maintenance planning and estimating

Replacement services

Check service level aggreements

Identify affected services

All these things have to be done in parallel by different divisions. Without a homogenized process, imagine how difficult it is to determine the cost of an incident or to tell the railway customers "OK, incident is under control, all trains are ready to go!".

Behind the scenes the management of infrastructure is categorized by the classification of the assets:

- IT infrastructure: Servers, routers, etc.
- Signaling infrastructure: Light signals, ECTS beacons, etc.
- Electrical equipment and more.

Each asset class has its own organization, processes, terminologies and technical control centers which take care of the incidents on the affected infrastructure. Each of them have to be aligned so that the target can be applied to all asset classes:

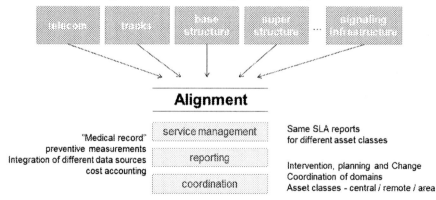

The alignment cannot be done on paper. Aligning processes means to affect people's daily life in their jobs. It has to be done carefully and step by step with small increments. The alignment will change the whole system. It was totally unclear how to system and the people will react on the process changes. We had to think about the process on how we going to achieve a common requirements on their processes.

## 3. The Key Innovations

### 3.1 Business

The main innovation was, that we heavily used agile methods for the alignment of business and their processes. The agile approach was communicated openly – it was not just an "IT thing". We used Scrum for development and Kanban for the business alignment. We had common understanding and the commitment all divisions to use agile methods. Everybody was aware that this would mean that we all have to work close together with equal rights "at one round table".

Another innovation was, that we used standardized ITIL terminology for non-ITIL areas. Instead of finding a common language with everybody, we tried to introduce an "intermediate" language. For example there is no "3rd level support" for civil engineering; but they have a "field force". Spoken in technical terms we introduced a common message bus with ITIL terminology and replaced the need for point-to-point communication and synchronization.

As a consequence it is worth to point out, that after each iteration every two weeks the customers had literally to sign the new functionality.

### 3.2 Case Handling

Here the process of the alignment is in focus, not the customer process of incident and change management. You also should have some basic knowledge of agile methods like Scrum and Kanban – if not, use Wikipedia before you go ahead, the information presented here is very condensed and does not introduce Scrum or Kanban.

We used following key procedures:

- two-week sprints
- Fully functional software every two weeks
- Customer workshops every two weeks
- Backlog is generally sufficient only for a sprint
- Fully automated regression testing executed by the development team

Following picture summarizes the alignment process which is repeated every two weeks and has a total cycling time of four weeks:

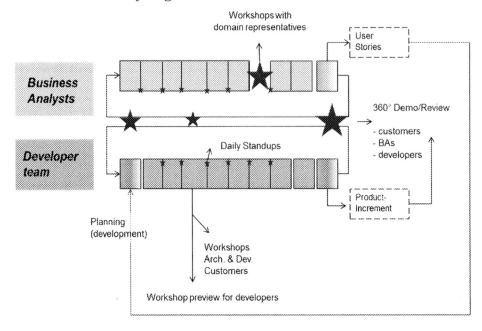

The 2-week cycle starts with the light-blue stream (the business analysts). At the end of their 2-weeks they created the user stories which are the input of the next cycle for the developer team. The user stories are implemented in the next 2-week cycle.

At the end of the cycle you find the customer review – which is where business analysts, customers (domain representatives) and business analysts come together to review and sign the product increment.

The two teams "business analysts" and "developer" worked closely together in one room. The red stars: show where extensive/planned communication between the teams happens. Every working day is represented by a square.

The most important feature next to extensive communication is that customers will see results within four weeks. There is no extensive document review and negotiations over BPMN notations – they immediately see what they get. Somewhat the software became its own specification.

### 3.3 Organization & Social

The project team consisted of

- The Product Owners – approx. 15 people which represent their field – the "customers"
- The Business Team – 5 people who talked to Product Owners and wrote the user stories
- The development Team – 7 people including developers, architects and testers

The self-management of the groups took place on two physical boards. Post-it notes were used to manage and track tasks. Most of the tasks had their counterpart in an IT system – we used a test tool (HP QTP) to specify the tasks. But other tasks were managed on the board only - especially the important ones. Every problem or idea, every question from developers to the business or vice-versa, every suggestion for a process improvement was made visible on the board. Thus the whole change and development process was made visible and accessible for all groups.

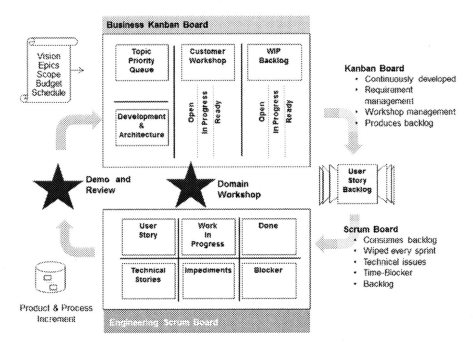

Some features of this approach:
- The business team and the development team worked in one office close to each other.
- Daily stand up meetings in front of the boards – members of other teams were invited to join.
- The engineers know what happened at the customer front and joined business workshops if necessary.
- The two boards represented "the gap" between the current status of the process and the vision of how it should be.

Every two weeks the alignment literally took place by showing current status and discussing the next issues. Big issues were consumed little by little and finally solved without big discussions and without making big trade-offs.

## 4. HURDLES OVERCOME

### 4.1 Management

We had to introduce agile methodologies to the management and demonstrate their advantages as well as their disadvantages. For the management the most important information on a projects was status of budget, schedule and quality. This is where agile methods have their strengths. The development process is highly transparent and you get exact project status including customer feedback every two weeks. It was crucial to demand commitment from the management for this approach – later on we could count on their support. Overall the management appreciated the agile approach – especially immediate transparency was essential. On the other hand, there were concerns that there may be cost overruns because it represents the scope of the requirements management as a major challenge.

### 4.2 Business

The biggest challenge and hurdle was not only to standardize or align the business process, but also adjust and consolidate the requirements of the various departments.

### 4.3 Organization Adoption

The biggest change was in the business. It was not just standardize their business processes and changes, but also so physically centralize control centers. This reorganization was an ongoing process - so we could not count on a stable organization for the process definition and implementation.

Both processes of product development and organizational change had to be continuously improved. To bring the agile process models in the business world takes time. It needs experienced people who are able to convince management and affected people to follow the agile path.

Of course, not all projects in SBB will be done agile in the future. For example, building a railway bridge will require less agility than building software or transforming an organization.

## 5. BENEFITS

### 5.1 Cost Savings / Time Reductions

Measurable cost savings were not the goal of this project. Also the agile development methodology did not save any costs during development. But the quality and user acceptance of the software is far better than in other workflow projects. We developed major improvements and optimizations in the business process.

We could automate, abolish or parallelize certain process steps. For example, the reaction time was reduced from infrastructure disruptions around 50% through the "heat map" functionality (see Chapter Best Practices).

### 5.2 Increased Revenues

The project has no impact on the company's turnover. The project business goals such as customer satisfaction or punctuality are supported.

### 5.3 Quality & Productivity Improvements

Through automation and optimization of processes efficiency improvements could be achieved. The goal of the project was to keep the ever increasing complexity and additional requirements of the railway infrastructure in control.

## 6. BEST PRACTICES, LEARNING POINTS AND PITFALLS

### 6.1 Best Practices and Learning Points

✓ **Look for strong agile leaders:** You cannot learn agile from Wikipedia or through certification. Your Agile Coach should have a strong record with agile methods.

✓ **Use a lighthouse process:** We never asked the customers what they wanted. We presented our understanding of the process and tried to adapt.

✓ **Look for process parameters:** Find a process design which allows to customize the process for the different asset categories. This drastically reduced the amount of processes and we automatically used a common language right from the start.

✓ **Use milestones to model a common process:** We used a fixed, predefined set of milestones instead of fixed or common processes. It is much easier to ask "when do you think is the right time to say the incident is closed?" instead of mapping processes. The next picture should give you an idea (e.g. "3" means "incident closed"):

✓ **Use dynamic "heat maps" for role mapping:** One though problem lead to a process innovation. We had thousands of different asset types which somehow map to teams, which are responsible for this assets. Due to the dynamics in the organization we could not rely on mapping rules. Our solution to this problem was to use heat maps: Initially the mapping of the affected asset to the manager role occurs manually by a dropdown list. But the system remembers the choice. Next time someone else is managing an incident on this asset the last role in the drop-down list will be on top on the list. So with every new process the system learns to support users to make the right choice by sorting of the drop down list. This had following benefits:

- High usability and flexibility of the process: For the user the system knows who is responsible for an asset and selects it as a default entry. But the user may always override the system by selecting an arbitrary role, which leads to high flexibility.
- We also brought agility to our business processes. The system is immune against reorganizations. If there is a new role or the responsibilities of a role change, the heat map will learn it without the necessity of process modifications.
- Roles which are recently never used (or deactivated roles) lose their high ranking or will not be shown.

### 6.2 Pitfalls

- × **Agile methods are expensive:** *Agile methods do not offer free lunch. The result was stunning but also quite expensive. We hat over 50 (!) full-day customer workshops and as many product reviews which took approx. 2 hours. Make sure you have commitment before you start.*
- × **Use an experienced Agile Coach:** *Projects which "try to be agile" may fail easily. Make sure you have enough experience and commitment of customers, business analysts and developers before you start.*
- × **Beware of Agile Architecture:** *We had a very strong developer team. It knew the product well and it was not necessary to re-invent the overall architecture of the project – so we were on the safe in sense of architecture.*

## 7. COMPETITIVE ADVANTAGES

Nothing much to mention here. But we had the benefits that with ti&m we had an experienced partner in agile methods and business process management.

## 8. TECHNOLOGY

The BPMS @enterprise is the standard and strategic BPM product of SBB. The decision of using @enterprise was made prior to the project. Nevertheless it turned out, that the tool was very powerful and the project team liked the product. For more information on the BPMS @enterprise see www.groiss.com.

This case study does not focus on technology. It emphasis the procedure how to gain high customer satisfaction and high consensus among very diverse groups of people and find a common ground for diverse processes. Although the project could probably have done with any workflow product, following properties of the product turned out to be key features:

- Strong user interface oriented workflow engine allowed us to use a prototype from the start.
- A lot of functionality came out-of-the-box which was very beneficial for the 2 week releases cycle:
  - Overall UI, menues, forms, worklists, access rights and security.
  - Fully fledged DMS is part of the workflow engine.
  - Reporting engine.
- Usage of standard technologies Java, SQL, HTML, Javascript, CSS and tools made it easy for the development to work with the tool.
- The tool was highly customizable and we were not bound to use provided widgets.

@enterprise is written in Java using JEE web profile. We use Jetty to run it with two cluster nodes and with an Oracle database (oracle appliance).

## 9. THE TECHNOLOGY AND SERVICE PROVIDERS

The technology (Java, @enterprise, Oracle) was given by SBB company strategy & IT architecture. Technology for interfaces to other system was chosen by the developer-team and approved the IT architecture. Business team and development team was formed by members of Swiss Federal Railways and ti&m.

Swiss Federal Railways was more on the business side and ti&m more on the development and consulting side. ti&m is a service provider and did the overall consulting for the agile methodologies and supported the teams with business analysts, workflow/process know how, architecture and programmers.

# U.S. Department of Veterans Affairs, USA

## Award: Public Sector, Benefits Enrolment
## Nominated by Living Systems Technologies, USA

### INTRODUCTION

This case study details the experience of transforming a highly political, over-burdened and mostly manual governmental claims processing system into a highly efficient and effective system via the application of world-class solution architecture and information technologies products. It examines the direct benefits of following a structured approach that effectively decomposes the business layer into a collection of requirements backed by BPMN 2.0 process models, followed by the subsequent composition of the solution through the application and technology layers.

An emphasis on correctly positioning layered architecture principles is crucial to the formation and evaluation of an appropriate solution architecture. Of particular importance, once a layered architectural perspective is adopted, it becomes possible to cleanly abstract a process layer, whose functionality can be fulfilled via model-driven execution. In this case, this functionality is provided by the Living Systems Process Suite (LSPS) from Whitestein Technologies, a recognized visionary product in Gartner's intelligent Business Process Manage Suite (iBPMS) Magic Quadrant.

This case study is structured as follows – first, it provides necessary background which serve as a backdrop to the problem, revealing issues of size and scope. Next it provides insight into the initial BPM-focused analysis that was conducted. This discussion is followed by an examination of a collection of transitional solution architecture diagrams that illustrate the evolutionary approach taken to delivering the full capabilities of the automated claims processing solution. Finally, the last section presents both results and concludes with a summary of lessons learned.

### BACKGROUND

Legislative and regulatory changes are typically passed without full consideration of their downstream impact regarding how they will be effectively implemented. This case study details how the US Department of Veterans Affairs (VA) staged and managed the implementation of the Post-9/11 Veterans Education Assistance Act of 2008, which expanded the educational benefits for military veterans who have served since September 11, 2001. The culmination of this implementation effort delivered world-class claims processing automation capabilities, while leveraging existing technologies and legacy assets. The capabilities delivered by this solution were recognized as a finalist for the prestigious PEX Awards in the Best BPM Project category for 2013.

One of the hallmarks of successful transformation initiatives is strong executive support and organizational recognition as to the importance of an initiative. The automated processing of veteran educational claims was performed in alignment with the VA's strategic plan. The automation of GI Bill benefits was identified as one of the VA's major initiatives and was denoted as a High

Priority Performance Goals (HPPG) program. The HPPG program was established by the White House as part of the US President's Accountable Government Initiative. As a high stakes program, the VA was determined to achieve the key goals that were set for this program. This is important as it provides a means to tie the initiative and its associated measureable results back to organizational goals and strategies.

When the legislation was enacted, a short-term solution for claims processing was put in place. This featured the hiring and training of hundreds of Veterans Claims Examiners (VCEs) who work in four geographically dispersed offices. The rapid on-boarding of staff presented many training challenges related to VCE competency development. It proved difficult to quickly gain intimate knowledge of the details and application of a complex government benefits program, established by legislative decree. Although the VCE resources were all performing the same business role, differences in interpretation of business rules and workflow presented compliance issues. Thus, the short-term, manual processing solution was ineffective due to the hand calculation of benefits and a lack of standard operating procedures across the four Processing Offices (RPOs). In effect, the lack of a runway to launch the program created a large backlog of claims that could only be overcome in the last stages of the long-term solution (LTS) implementation.

The scale of this benefits program presents a key challenge to the development and transition to an automated solution. Since the Post-9/11 GI Bill rolled out in 2009, more than $35.6 billion in benefits to over 1.1 million individuals has been awarded. As recently as October of 2012, it was reported that the total number of unprocessed claims had not dipped below 100,000 since July of 2011. This of course is untenable and creates undue hardship on the veteran. Besides creating difficulties when registering for classes, the benefits include a housing allowance. Not getting paid in a timely manner creates dire consequences when veterans cannot pay their rent. Notably, the volume of claims continues to increase due to the troop draw down in Iraq and Afghanistan. In 2013 approximately 3.4 million claims were handled by the system.

ANALYSIS

The human-based paper-claims processing solution was the baseline system which was studied. This analysis took the form of understanding the existing and desired operating model, and an assessment of the efficiency (Lean) and effectiveness (Six Sigma) of business service delivery.

The operating model relates business and technology alignment. From the business perspective one can assess the level of business process standardization, whereas the technology perspective is represented by the level of business process integration. The short-term solution exhibited characteristics of a diversified operating model – each of the RPOs had some variation and localization of claims processing rules and since the workload was divided geographically, there was no perceived need to integrate backend IT systems like The Image Management System (TIMS), which was replicated at each RPO. Clearly this operating model had direct, undesirable impact on claims processing effectiveness.

When considering the efficiency of claims processing, Lean's focus on waste identification provided useful guidance for targeting changes that could be made via IT enablement. The following five wastes were identified:

1. Transportation: paper forms and mail service

2. Inventory: backlog of claims on desks represents excessive WIP (Work In Process)
3. Defects: additional approval processes for awards above a certain threshold; necessary for detecting possible errors in calculation
4. Over Processing: human desk checks validating consistency between multiple VA systems
5. Human Capital: under-utilizing VCEs analytical capabilities due to routine work that could be automated

Given that the goal of Six Sigma is to reduce sources of error and minimize variability, the operating model needed to change to one that enforced standard operating procedures across RPOs. The effectiveness of the solution could also be increased by eliminating manual benefit calculations to further reduce error and insure consistency across VCEs and RPOs.

## SOLUTION DELIVERY

The initial phase of the long-term solution design took into consideration the identified issues that were related to operating model, efficiency and effectiveness. This resulted in the delivery of a private cloud-based infrastructure that delivered a Software as a Service (SaaS) application to the VCEs via the browser on their desktop computers. This same application was now accessible and in use at each of the RPOs. Thus the software provided a common standard operating procedure for VCEs to process claims via the structured screen flow of the model-view-controller architected web application. One of the key architectural decisions made at this stage of solution delivery was externalizing and separating the claims processing rules and calculations from the web application itself.

Though this first phase addressed issues of business process standardization; the solution simply overlaid the on-premise IT assets rather than integrating them across RPOs. As such, the operating model was transitioned from one that was diversified, to one that was replicated. The level of efficiency was raised dramatically due to the fact that a parallel effort enabled the electronic submission of claims, as well as student verification notifications from academic institutions. These electronic interfaces greatly reduced the amount of physical paper that was being moved through the system. From an effectiveness perspective, benefit calculation is now performed by a rules engine, which not only ensures consistency; architecturally it helps the solution accommodate further legislative changes without having to re-code and deploy the entire application. Encapsulating and accessing a rules engine via a service call was the start of what would become a robust service inventory.

Although the rules service was cleanly separated, the business layer and application layer remained entangled by the traditional approach to web application development. Of course it was recognized that having a clean separation between the business functions and their satisfying application services would have been initially desirable, the development team responsible for the web application was driven by a sense of expediency, rather than architectural purity. In the technology layer, an application server platform was hosted by the private-cloud's infrastructure to support the deployment of the SaaS delivered application. Figure one highlights key architectural dimensions of the solution delivered by the initial phase of development.

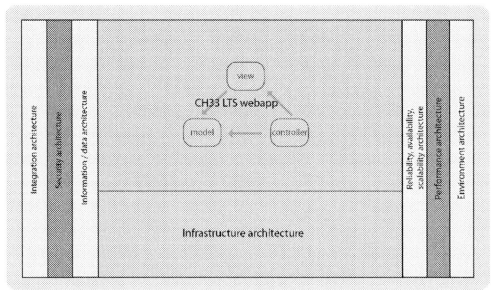

*Figure one: Solution Architecture associated with the initial phase of development.*

Although significant benefits were derived from the initial deployment of the SaaS application, educational were still being manual processed, albeit with software assistance. Thus an analysis activity was conducted for the purposes of exposing and capturing the business process found within the SaaS application. These process models served multiple purpose: they provided independent documentation of the process used for the adjudication of a claim, they were leveraged to identify candidate software services and ultimately via a process of continuous refinement they became executable artifacts within the LSPS platform.

Figure two presents a high level BPMN 2.0 diagram of the claims adjudication process.

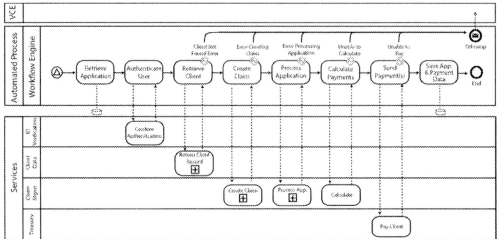

*Figure two: High-level Process Model for Claims Adjudication*

The initial solution was insufficient at addressing the quickening pace of claims backlog growth. In an effort to enable future adoption of an automated claims-processing solution, an interim, transitional architecture was put in place. The changes leveraged industry leading practices to cleanly separate the business process activities and flow from the application services that implemented the required functionality. This change had spill-over onto the information and data architecture which evolved to support multiple layers and models:

- a logical model exposed to the web application (i.e., information objects),
- a physical model (i.e., data objects) written to the databases hosted by the infrastructure,
- and a mapping layer between the two provided by a collection of data services.

The creation of application and data services, along with models and mapping related to information and data objects required the establishment of a governance architecture. The governance of services and the capabilities they exposed is crucial, especially when the transformation follows an evolutionary trajectory across transitional architectures. Figure three illustrates the interim solution architecture as described.

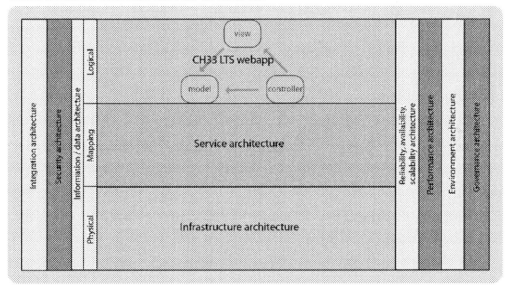

*Figure three: Interim solution architecture preparing for fully automated capability.*

The other major integration challenge was to establish the web services to external systems. These systems need to be integrated for the automated solution to be effective; in essence they provide access to information assets that VCEs manually check for consistency. Thus the complexion of the existing IT landscape and required integration of legacy assets demanded detailed planning and careful study. Figure four depicts the five major external systems that the LTS solution integrates.

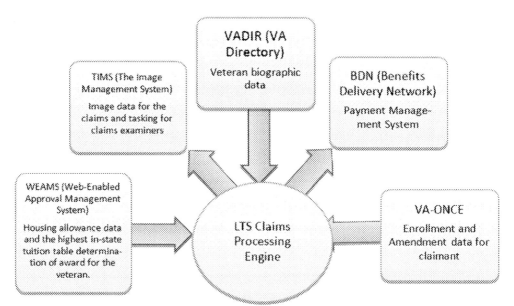

*Figure four: External systems for which Application Services were created.*

Many integration and performance architecture decisions needed to be made during the establishment of the interim solution. A key requirement for the establishment of a service layer, is that it could not adversely impact the performance of the web application. As such, a hybrid services architecture was established that leveraged SOAP-based web services for external consumption and EJB-based component services for internal consumption. In this way, the best of both worlds could be obtained – vendor and implementation decoupling for external services via the open standards of XML, XSD, WSDL and SOAP and the desired performance via optimized local calls to EJBs from the web application.

It is important to note that the changes required to establish the interim solution architecture were thoroughly explored via the establishment of a Proof-of-Concept (POC) environment. As illustrated in Figure five, this environment was simplified by the fact that many of the supporting architectural layers were considered out of scope – for example performance and environmental architecture. This POC facilitated detailed planning of required work, to include methods and procedures for data migration, software developer skill-set acquisition, and early establishment of the process orchestration engine as a means to rapidly compose and test application and data services that were developed.

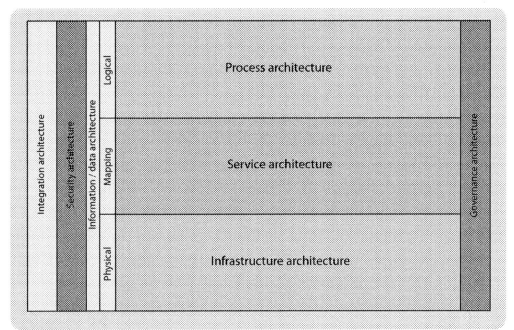

***Figure five: Base architecture for a Proof-of-Concept***

The POC phase began with an Analysis of Alternatives (AoA) for the selection of a process engine which would support model-driven execution and was compatible with the existing technology stack and experience base of the development team. The AoA compared both open source and commercially available technologies. Some of the driving considerations were cost, performance, capabilities and compatibility with the VA's Technical Reference Model (TRM). It was determined that the LSPS was the best fit for the stated goals and objectives of the automated claims processing solution. The below list provides insight into some of the key advantages that are presented by the chosen platform:

- LSPS is BPMN model-driven and JAVA centric. It is Eclipse-based and developer friendly.
- LSPS leverages traditional source code control and maven build scripts making its integration into the continuous integration build pipeline possible.
- LSPS is compatible with Weblogic Application Server technology which is the VA's standard app server as defined in their Technical Reference Model (TRM).
- LSPS developed applications deploy as a J2EE Enterprise Archive (EAR file) making it compatible with existing deployment scripts.
- It is easy to integrate LSPS Custom Tasks with internal EJB services or external SOAP-based service technology.
- LSPS has specific functionality that eases persistence concerns of Personally Identifiable Information (PII).
- The LSPS administration application, process management console and dashboard reporting functions are available to operators via a web browser, facilitating remote diagnostics.
- LSPS was integratable with the existing security used for operation-level authentication and authorization.

- The security mechanisms for accessing the LSPS applications integrate out-of-the-box with active directory for authentication and identity management.
- LSPS supports standard J2EE container-based transaction management which was already being used by the LTS SaaS delivered Web App.

Figure six is a screen grab of the LSPS Process Development Environment. The top window in the figure shows the Goal-Oriented extension to BPMN, which drives the selection of plans that are specified in BPMN 2.0 based process models (bottom window). Goal-based modeling gives the platform enormous flexibility in regards to designing process models that execute with a high-level of dynamism.

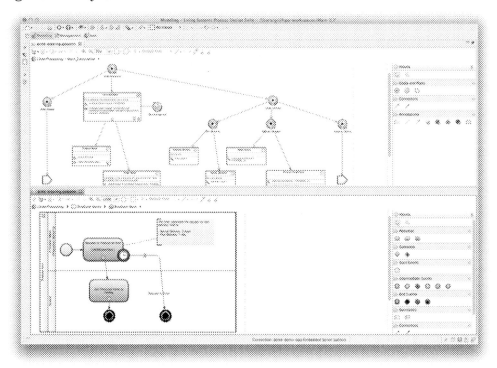

*Figure six: Living Systems Process Suite's process design environment*

In the final transitional phase, the LSPS product was introduced into the production system to fulfill the requirements for an automated claims processing engine. Naturally, the VA was cautious in rolling out automated claims processing; thus, they requested the ability to dynamically tune the claims processing. The tunable parameters became known as "knobs and switches" and serve to off-ramp claims from automation for manual processing by VCEs if a claim does not meet all conditions for automated handling. The switches allow settings to be enabled or disabled, whereas the knobs allow for dynamic thresholds to be established. An example switch is to off-ramp a claim if a change of student address is submitted by a school, whereas an example knob is a threshold that controls the maximum award size allowed to be automatically authorized. When the system was first deployed, conservative settings were used and 30% of the supplemental claims were fully automated. As comfort and familiarity with the capabilities of the system increased, changes were made to the tuning and by the six month mark, 53% of the claims were fully processed by automation.

In figure seven, the Process architecture block represents the automated claims processing channel. It is important to point out that both the automation engine and the web application are sharing the same inventory of services and rules engine. This is vital from a regulatory compliance perspective because it is provable that both application channels compute benefits using the same sets of computational assets; therefore, the results are consistent regardless of which channel is exercised.

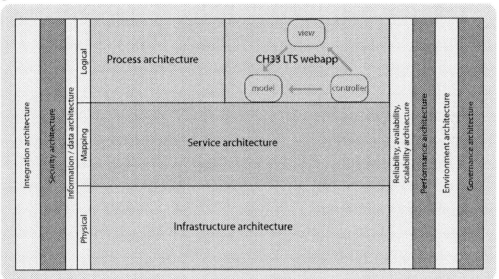

***Figure seven: Final architecture which supports automated claims processing.***

The automation capability served to promote the LTS database as the official authoritative source for information related to the processing of educational claims. As such, it facilitates an increased level of business process integration, moving toward a unified operating model. This will allow work to be more easily moved from one RPO to another based upon variations in workload and capacity. From an efficiency perspective, moving a full 50% of claims to hands-off, fully automated processing has eliminated the backlog. An added benefit was realized by reducing routine work, which allows VCEs to focus on claims that truly require more time and human judgment to process.

Figure eight depicts key architectural components of the two claims processing channels, manually processed claims leverage VCEs and the SaaS delivered web application, whereas, automated claims use the process engine. All supplemental claims are first directed to be processed in an automated fashion; however, in the event they are off-ramped, they proceed to the software supported, VCE based processing channel.

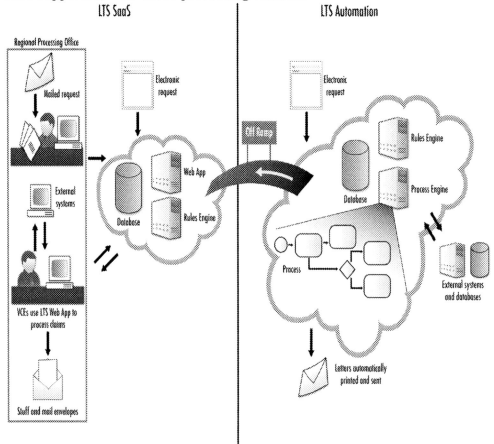

***Figure eight: Linkage between full automation and manual processing.***

## Conclusion

The automated claims processing capabilities were deployed in September of 2012. In first 6 months of operation, 1.2 million supplemental claims were evaluated by the claims processing engine. Of these 560,000 were fully automated without human touch. Another 520,000 claims were partially automated before being off-ramped for VCE verification. Effectively, through automation, a virtual RPOs worth of claims processing capacity has been added to resource pool. Claims processing times have been reduced from nearly 3 weeks to 8 days on average.

Besides impressive raw performance numbers, this solution also met a key objective that was defined in the VA's strategic plan. This objective was to use the LTS development to effectively create a model for future VA software systems development and acquisition. In other words, the Post-9/11 GI Bill LTS program defines an approach and technological foundation upon which the VA will build future systems and drive improvement across all programs. Lessons were learned from both technological and systems and software engineering perspectives. The two lists below highlight several key takeaways:

From a technological perspective:

- cloud-based infrastructure provided the underpinnings that allowed a change in the operating model
- the rules engine enabled the system to more readily adapt to policy and legislation changes
- the BPMS and its reliance on explicit process models helped increase the transparency of the solution to users
- using a shared inventory of services between the SaaS and Automation solutions ensures consistent claims processing
- finally, the approach of having configurable off-ramps to manual processing allowed the system to be tuned after deployment, allowing the VA to control that automation of claims to a level that they were comfortable with

Systems engineering and software development processes used during the creation of the solution that are influencing future software acquisition by the VA, are as follows:

- BPMN model-based development of system requirements allows requirements to be grounded within the context of a business process
- use of Application Lifecycle Management (ALM) tooling to support agile Scrum based software development at scale
- accelerated development via the use of a continuous integration build pipeline with automated regression testing
- the development and use of service governance processes to ensure the vitality and sustainability of the delivered solution

In closing, the success of this program was recognized in a recent press release from the VA (found here: http://1.usa.gov/1gu7w16) in which Under Secretary for Benefits Allison A. Hickey states that "This automation has not only improved education benefits processing, it has allowed us to shift resources to other priorities, like improving timeliness of disability compensation decisions. It's a great example of how technology is helping us to transform the way we do business and better serve Veterans."

## Technology Providers

Living Systems Technologies, LLC brings Whitestein's flagship Intelligent Business Process Management Suite, the **Living Systems Process Suite (LSPS)**, to North America.

LSPS Goals provide amazing options for designing in intelligence and flexibility into applications. It allows for the alignment of a business's strategic and operational policies with the processes themselves, providing governance and agility while optimizing process execution flow.

http://www.livingsystemstechnologies.com/

## Paper Author

Dr. Paul Buhler, Scientist at Modus21. See Appendix for full bio.

# Vitens, the Netherlands

## Award: Public Sector- Customer-centric Transformation
## Nominated by You-Get, the Netherlands

### EXECUTIVE SUMMARY / ABSTRACT

With over 5M customers, Vitens is the largest water company of the Netherlands, with the goal to be the best service provider of the Netherlands and additionally have the lowest integral costs per connection.

The Customers department of Vitens, responsible for all communication (including invoicing and collection) realized that the key in achieving this lies in more efficient and effective business processes, and entered into a partnership with You-Get, the BPM partner.

Vitens implementation followed the BPM Maturity Model steps, in combination with proven Best Practices.

The starting point has been the business processes documentation and optimization, followed by a BPMSuite automation project (IBM BPM) and completed with an organization structure adjustment. First the organization is made process aware, then (to secure the proactive and continuous improvement of the processes) Process Improvement teams and a BPM CoE (Center of Excellence) has been set up, including defined KPIs.

At that point the connection was made between business and IT (including integration to SAP) by developing an innovative process application in a BPMSuite, providing real-time visibility of the process performance.

Vitens now has a flexible and efficient matrix organization, with real-time process monitoring and continuously visible process performance, and is working towards all end-to-end processes being visible, in control and continuously improving.

Results:
- Go-Live within budget and planning;
- almost 20% in FTE Reduction;
- Huge Reduction of Handover Moments;
- Work in progress: from 5 months into daily/weekly stock;
- Transaction time Reduction from, for example, 4 min to 20 seconds;
- 40% Reduction in number of Transaction activities;
- Complete customer centric / focused organization;
- Process is leading, not system;
- Knowledge / decisions inside BPMsuite (BPMS), not inside employee heads.

## 1. OVERVIEW

### The Challenge

Vitens wants to be the best service provider of the Netherlands and additionally have the lowest integral costs per connection. Vitens realizes that the key in this lies in more efficient and effective business processes, and looks for a partner specialized in setting up, implementing, analyzing, automating and improving of Business Process Management projects.

### *The approach*

Vitens has followed the steps from the BPM Maturity Model, in combination with proven Best Practices, in order to come to the most optimal results. The starting point has been the guidance, management and education of the business and afterwards automation with the support of a BPM Suite.

### Step 1: Process Aware

The first step taken by Vitens is to make the organization process aware instead of system and department oriented. Vitens has created a process organization that is fully deployed with own employees. The expressed and proven commitment of both management and employees is crucial for the success of the project. Next to the process organization also a process architecture has been created. With these process organization and –architecture as a basis, the core processes have been described in this phase. Companywide training was a significant part for the success of this first step.

### Step 2: Process Improvement

The next step was to secure the proactive and continuous improvement of the processes within the Vitens organization. To come to process improvement, Process Improvement team have been established and a BPM Center of Excellence has been set up. KPI's have been defined within Vitens, building a bridge between strategy and processes. This makes the organization aware and focused on the improvement of its processes.

### Step 3: Process Focused

The third step Vitens has made is the step towards a process focused organization. In this step Vitens has made the connection between business and IT by deploying a BPMSuite. This BPMS provides real-time visibility of the process performance and in each defined process step the processes can be improved quickly and pro-actively. By means of training and workshops the organization now is completely transformed into a transparent organization where cooperation and process focused way of working is leading.

### Step 4: Process innovative

With the implementation of automated processes for the customer processes, the Vitens organization now is set up flexible and efficient. Processes are monitored real-time and the performance of the processes is continuously visible. By now the process teams have become autonomous and self-controlling, and they analyze the process performance for ways of optimization. The BPMSuite will also be deployed for the other primary business processes.

This is the situation that Vitens is currently in. The next and final step is the step towards a Dynamic Business structure. This step will make a completely mature BPM organization out of Vitens.

### Step 5: Dynamic Business structure

The ultimate goal of Vitens is to develop into a Dynamic Business structure. At that moment all end-to-end processes are visible and in control. The complete business structure (organization, processes, IT, etc.) is focused on been able to apply fast and continuous process improvements into the full process chain. The business culture has developed into a Dynamic Business structure entirely focused on continuous improvement.

### *Conclusion*

Because of the chosen BPM total approach, in which BPM has been implemented in every thinkable aspect and at every level, together with employees, process managers, management and the right external parties, this BPM project has become an enormous success and exceeded the results of the ambitious business case agreed at the start of the project.

## 2. BUSINESS CONTEXT

Together with our BPM implementation partner You-Get a consultancy advice and report was setup, including a preliminary business case. One of the key advices from the report is, separate from the tooling, to start with focusing on the methods, techniques, standards and governance regarding BPM. First a method needs to be formulated and formalized on architecture and processes, and afterwards a tool should be selected that fits this method. Conclusion from the report was that within Vitens there is certainly BPM knowledge available, but at that moment it lack coherency in that knowledge.

The initial organization is depicted above. The size of the organization was 335 FTE,

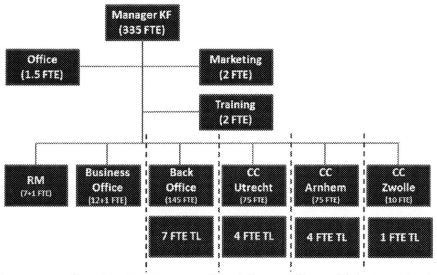

and set up along functional and geographical lines, with multiple team leaders (TM). The management numbers and layer are relatively big.

The maturity of the organization was largely in line with the lowest level in the model, i.e. conscious of inefficiency. However because of a lack of process awareness there was not enough insight where these inefficiencies were.

There was no clear and concise process architecture, and the processes where only partly documented but not in a uniform way, and not integral based on an architecture.

Vitens had some sort of 'local hero' culture, with improvement initiatives depending on individual actions. The work was also department orientated, the end-to-end process was not managed.

On top of that there was a lot of everyday hectic, with a SAP implementation and M&A activities.

## 3. THE KEY INNOVATIONS

### 3.1 Business

Since Vitens is a public utility company, the rates towards the end customers are regulated, and cannot be raised. The BPM(S) implementation project and activities have been made possible because of cost reductions coming out of the BPM projects.

One of the key innovations is that the uniformity in the processes (and with that the way of working, methodology) leads to a bigger uniformity towards the end customer. This is done by means of fixed templates for customer communication in writing.

The key result is that, guided by First Time Right / First Time to Fix principles, the entire end-to-end process can now be overseen, managed and controlled by one single employee. This leads from a quality and efficiency perspective to more insights and therefore more control on backlog and executed work: lower backlogs and shorter throughput time, and with fewer errors and waste because of the uniformly documented processes.

Another business innovation is the blending of activities, this leads to a better way of servicing the customers from a quality and time perspective.

### 3.2 Case Handling

**Before the project**

Customer cases were handled without any uniformity, and without documented end-to-end processes, with SAP as the leading system. SAP is not a process-oriented system, the employee needs to decide him- or herself how certain items are handled, but then limited by the system boundaries. Since the employee decides every step in the process to be followed (i.e. which SAP transactions need to be executed in which order), a customer case cannot be supported by the system from start to finish.

**After the project**

The processes have been documented and based upon that the new system has been built up. The system supports the required process completely and therefore enforces a process oriented way of working towards the employee: the BPMS implementation acts as a layer in between the employee and SAP, with the employee working according to the documented process in BPMS, and BPMS arranging the underlying SAP actions (in the right order and proper way).

Every customer case now triggers the right process and shall be managed and handled according to that predefined process. This leads from a transaction-driven system to a real process-driven system.

### 3.3 Organization & Social

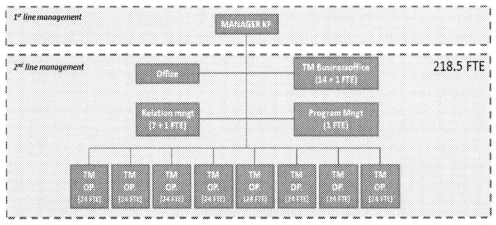

The picture above shows how the Vitens organization is now setup, with equally sized Operations team, all with a team manager (TM), capable of self-controlling within a team the entire process, and thus – with scaling up and down teams - bringing a lot of organizational flexibility and agility into the organization.

To achieve this, the commitment and day-to-day involvement of the senior management of Vitens has been crucial for the success of this project.

For the employees themselves the biggest change is that there is a lot less focus on system knowledge, and a lot more focus on *process knowledge*. The teams are really self-controlling, and each person has the knowledge, ability and opportunity to initiate process improvements. This can be done via process improvement teams and the also for the purpose of this project created Center of Excellence (CoE).

The scope of the CoE is the content-driven competence over the processes, as well as the authority to (initiating) process changes in the BPMS system and implementation of new processes. This entails the competence of the complete PDCA (Plan-Do-Check-Act) cycle applicable to the business processes, including the supporting systems. The biggest challenge was the alignment between CoE and line organization, this challenge was mainly covered by putting the right roles into the CoE and communication. This also applies to the self-controlling and –supporting teams, who also have their presence in the CoE.

## 4. HURDLES OVERCOME

The most important hurdle to overcome was creating a firm level of commitment towards BPM within the entire Vitens organization. This has been realized and covered by focusing on management level commitment, communication and training.

### 4.1 Management

The commitment and day-to-day involvement of the senior management of Vitens has been crucial for the success of this project. BPM has been embedded in the strategy and as a means to achieve long-term goals. This includes connecting organizational goals to BPM goals (with specific targets on cost savings and 'tilting' the organization towards process oriented).

### 4.2 Business

An important business hurdle to overcome was the difference in approach to the new way of working for the Frontoffice (FO), compared to the Backoffice (BO). It was easier for the FO, since the delta as well as the variety on additional activities was less than with the BO people. Especially the direct customer-engagement aspect for BO was a new experience. This has been covered by focusing on soft skills, communication and training.

### 4.3 Organization Adoption

Also from an organizational adoption perspective, the topline management commitment and sponsorship from day one has made all the difference.

The IT department was used to being in the driver seat, especially with the big influence the IT driven SAP implementation projects taking place. The move for the IT department from driver seat towards a role of being an enabler for the business, has been crucial for the success. The continuous focus on active involvement of IT and in a joint effort moving away from the "SAP unless" mentality was pivotal.

From a people and organization perspective, certainly regarding the CoE implementation and set-up of the process teams, it has been very important to encourage as much as possible all the different people to participate and let them hear their voice.

Also making the results visible as soon as possible, in order to continue to show successes, have contributed largely to the success of the project. A continuous flow of organized communication around this was used to achieve this.

## 5. BENEFITS

### 5.1 Cost Savings / Time Reductions

- An FTE Reduction of 17% (the BPMS project itself leads to a reduction of 52 FTE, from 300 FTE to 248 FTE);
- 1 person can do entire case management: transfer moments between departments or people / teams are hardly needed anymore;
- Significant reduction in the number of Transaction activities;
- 5 months of backlog reduced to a daily backlog;
- Transaction time has been reduced from an average 4 min to 20 seconds;
- Less manual activities;
- Reduction of "Swivel chair" waste: no need any more to operate different systems;
- ICT reduction: less SAP investments and a lot less tailor-made work.

### 5.2 Increased Revenues

Since Vitens has a regulatory assigned geographic area in which the services are delivered, it is not possible to grow the number of customers based on services. The customer base is fixed (over 5 million customers), as well as the rates towards these end customers. Therefore the project has no impact on revenue or top-line growth.

### 5.3 Quality Improvements

The most important quality improvement is the switch from functional case management to a process driven case management, making it possible for one person to manage the entire case end-to-end. This is supported by the complete 'tilting' of the Customer & Invoicing organization (refer to 3.3), making the process leading instead of the system, and focusing on getting the knowledge into the BPMS instead of in the heads of people.

The project has led to less manual activities, less tailor-made work and a substantial reduction of "Swivel chair" waste (i.e. no need any more to operate different systems), all greatly contributing to improvement of the quality.

## 6. BEST PRACTICES, LEARNING POINTS AND PITFALLS

### 6.1 Best Practices and Learning Points

Over the last years, Vitens and You-Get as BPM partner have built up a lot of experience in business process management. The complete approach with all its dimensions have been optimized with best practices, developed during a large number of projects.

- ✓ *Continuously emphasize BPM is a means to come to efficiency, quality improvement and cost savings. Not a goal in itself.*
- ✓ *Successful implementations and improvements come from a continuous iteration and process adaptation.*
- ✓ *Not only keep an eye on current requirements and wishes, but also anticipate on needs of next years and/or iterations.*
- ✓ *Get beforehand a firm commitment from the business and its stakeholders.*
- ✓ *In the steering group all departments need to be represented.*
- ✓ *Make sure Senior Executive level and management truly understand capacity and capabilities BPM, as well as implications on strategy and management.*
- ✓ *There must be consensus on the business strategy and project priorities.*
- ✓ *Controlling and commenting on process performance is one of the key management disciplines.*

- ✓ *Setting up a communication plan as part of change management strategy early in the project, continuously checked.*
- ✓ *Setting up a clear plan to roll out new documentation (training on new processes and procedures of the business).*
- ✓ *A clear test strategy with clearly defined test expectations (incl agreed test scenarios set up by the business) must be available before start test.*
- ✓ *Vitens needs to have multiple moments (pre-defined in project phasing and planning) to assess and decide on project and approach.*
- ✓ *Operations and/or process team need to balance activities in the CoE.*
- ✓ *Good and integrated planning for complete roadmap. Ownership and direct involvement of project / steering group.*
- ✓ *Connect process team members per process to each developer. Escalation to process manager and business project manager. Eventual clarity on scope through RFC procedure.*
- ✓ *Tight control on scope. Starting point are approved requirements documents. With deviations or disagreement use change procedure, to be judged on time and budget.*
- ✓ *Develop in different work environments and import per process in test environment. Then proper regression testing on newly imported functionality.*
- ✓ *Phased implementation BPMS and direct controls on performance during Build.*
- ✓ *Early monitoring and proper implementation of technical application operations. Proper decision making process for web services change control.*
- ✓ *Thorough preparation including clear agreements and rules throughout the entire business are crucial for the success.*
- ✓ *Evaluation moments at the right time in the projects are very important to keep control on direction, scope and momentum of the activities in the project.*

### 6.2 Pitfalls

With the before mentioned best practices approach there has also been a continuous learning curve of topics and items to be improved, or not completely judged to the proper value. This has led to a number of potential pitfalls concerning the introduction, maturity growth and implementation of BPM, of which the prevention is a key part of the best practices approach.

Generic

- ✗ BPM becomes a goal in itself.
- ✗ Assuming first time right. You cannot create a perfect system in the first iteration, continuous improvement is the way.
- ✗ Omitting to keep an eye on the future wishes, functionality and only focusing on the here and now of a fitting BPM solution.
- ✗ Not following up on the improvement potential achieved or within reach, will leave the organization otherwise with a lot of open ends and unfinished activities.

Governance

- ✗ Assume without checking that the business is committed to the project.
- ✗ Certain business sections are not represented in the steering group.
- ✗ Understanding of Senior Executive level and management of capacity and capabilities BPM.
- ✗ Indistinctness or disagreement on the business strategy and project priorities.

Communication

- ✘ Not showing advantages of BPM at regular intervals.
- ✘ insufficient, inconsistent or untimely communication

Execution

- ✘ Insufficient training on new processes and procedures of the business
- ✘ Unclear or missing test-expectations and –scenarios.
- ✘ Not enough go/no-go decision moments
- ✘ Operations and Project work on 1 environment (technical and functional (application) operations).
- ✘ Large project with many dependencies.
- ✘ Indistinctness in design documents during Build phase.
- ✘ Because of new insights during implementation (build) phase continuously new requests to or deviations from the scope occur.
- ✘ Parallel implementation of processes in the development environment is risky.

Performance

- ✘ Performance: Stability of infrastructure, BPMS, Performance
- ✘ Performance: performance can decrease with too big web services.

## 7. COMPETITIVE ADVANTAGES

Since Vitens has a regulatory assigned geographic area in which the services are delivered, it is very difficult to describe the competitive advantage.

It is regulatory set how the water companies are benchmarked on peer-to-peer level, based on quality, price and performance. If Vitens is performing on these elements higher than average, the other water companies shall be stimulated to do it better.

On an employee perspective the average Vitens employee has become a much more complete, flexible and involved person, making Vitens as a company much more agile and customer focused.

## 8. TECHNOLOGY

Below architecture brings the strong combination of Business Process Management (BPM) together with Services Oriented Architecture (SOA). BPM means the offering of the most optimal process towards the organization of Vitens.

This is done through the deployment of the BPMS of IBM. This product makes it possible to implement the optimal process, and offers functionality in the areas of process monitoring and control.

This is supported by SOA through distributed reusable services from underlying systems like SAP. The services are set up as modular as possible in order to be reused at different places in the process and even can be offered to other systems. For the SAP part the choice was made to use SAP PI as a connection between the BPM layer and the SAP service layer.

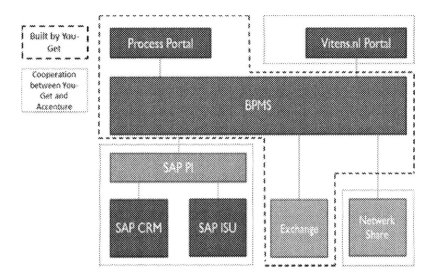

In essence the BPM product is connected to any system where – from an ideal process perspective – there is a need. This means that the BPM product is connected to other systems, like for example Exchange and a network share for file exchange. Also these systems are connected by means of reusable services, in this case developed in the BPM system itself (without an integration layer in between).

A future improvement on this could be the addition of a service bus (for example with IBP BPM Advanced), which means also the services for the non-SAP systems can be offered to other systems.

## 9. THE TECHNOLOGY AND SERVICE PROVIDERS

### You-Get – BPM partner

You-Get is the BPM partner for Vitens. You-Get has advised and executed a BPM approach according to the in-house developed 360° Business Services Approach™.

In this approach a clear growth path is followed via different dimensions: process management, strategy, culture, organization, ICT and BPM Governance. This BPM approach is realized through iterations with support of advice, training, tools, best practice methodology and project management, and has been successfully applied by You-Get numerous times.

In the software track You-Get has eventually implemented the IBM BPM software (Websphere Lombardi Edition) with success.

### IBM – BPMS / Service provider:

IBM has provided the BPMS software for the project implementation.

After pre-defined blocks of the project have gone live, IBM also has been involved in health checks of the full application, including tool kits. Within the health checks best practice follow-up and generic architecture and set-up have been checked. You-Get has taken the results of these health checks to incorporate these into the continuous cycle of process optimization and improvement.

### Accenture – SAP implementation party:

Accenture is responsible for the SAP ERP system and software integration, implementation and support services to Vitens.

# Section 3

# Appendix

# WfMC Structure and Membership Information

## What is the Workflow Management Coalition?

The Workflow Management Coalition (WfMC), founded in August 1993, is a non-profit, international organization of BPM and workflow vendors, users, analysts and university/research groups.

The Coalition's mission is to promote and develop the use of collaborative technologies such as workflow, BPM and case management through the establishment of standards for software terminology, interoperability and connectivity among products and to publicize successful use cases.

## Workflow Standards Framework

The Coalition has developed a framework for the establishment of workflow standards. This framework includes five categories of interoperability and communication standards that will allow multiple collaboration products to coexist and interoperate within a user's environment. Technical details are included in the white paper entitled, "The Work of the Coalition," available at www.wfmc.org.

## Achievements

The initial work of the Coalition focused on publishing the Reference Model and Glossary, defining a common architecture and terminology for the industry. A major milestone was achieved with the publication of the first versions of the Workflow API (WAPI) specification, covering the Workflow Client Application Interface, and the Workflow Interoperability specification.

In addition to a series of successful tutorials industry wide, the WfMC invested many person-years over the past 20 years helping to drive awareness, understanding and adoption of XPDL, now the standard means for business process definition in over 80 BPM products. As a result, it has been cited as the most deployed BPM standard by a number of industry analysts, and continues to receive a growing amount of media attention.

### Workflow Reference Model

The Workflow Reference Model was published first in 1995 and still forms the basis of most BPM and workflow software systems in use today. It was developed from the generic workflow application structure by identifying the interfaces which enable products to interoperate at a variety of levels.

All workflow systems contain a number of generic components which interact in a defined set of ways; different products will typically exhibit different levels of capability within each of these generic components. To achieve interoperability between workflow products a standardized set of interfaces and data interchange formats between such components is necessary.

A number of distinct interoperability scenarios can then be constructed by reference to such interfaces, identifying different levels of functional conformance as appropriate to the range of products in the market.

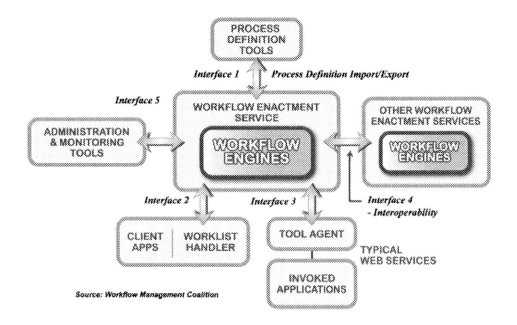

**WORKFLOW REFERENCE MODEL DIAGRAM**

### XPDL (XML Process Definition Language)

An XML based language for describing a process definition, developed by the WfMC. Version 1.0 was released in 2002. Version 2.0 was released in Oct 2005. The goal of XPDL is to store and exchange the process diagram, to allow one tool to model a process diagram, and another to read the diagram and edit, another to "run" the process model on an XPDL-compliant BPM engine, and so on.

For this reason, XPDL is not an executable programming language like BPEL, but specifically a process design format that literally represents the "drawing" of the process definition. Thus it has 'XY' or vector coordinates, including lines and points that define process flows. This allows an XPDL to store a one-to-one representation of a BPMN process diagram.

For this reason, XPDL is effectively the file format or "serialization" of BPMN, as well as any non-BPMN design method or process model which use in their underlying definition the XPDL meta-model (there are presently about 60 tools which use XPDL for storing process models.)

In spring 2012, the WfMC completed XPDL 2.2 as the *fifth* revision of this specification. XPDL 2.2 builds on version 2.1 by introducing support for the process modeling extensions added to BPMN 2.0.

### BPSim

The Business Process Simulation (BPSim) framework is a standardized specification that allows business process models captured in either BPMN or XPDL to be augmented with information in support of rigorous methods of analysis. It defines the parameterization and interchange of process analysis data allowing structural and capacity analysis of process models.

BPSim is meant to support both pre-execution and post-execution optimization of said process models. The BPSim specification consists of an underlying computer-interpretable representation (meta-model) and an accompanying electronic file format to ease the safeguard and transfer of this data between different tools (interchange format).

### Wf-XML

Wf-XML is designed and implemented as an extension to the OASIS Asynchronous Service Access Protocol (ASAP). ASAP provides a standardized way that a program can start and monitor a program that might take a long time to complete. It provides the capability to monitor the running service, and be informed of changes in its status.

Wf-XML extends this by providing additional standard web service operations that allow sending and retrieving the "program" or definition of the service which is provided. A process engine has this behavior of providing a service that lasts a long time, and also being programmable by being able to install process definitions.

## AWARDS

The Workflow Management Coalition sponsors three annual award programs.

1. The **Global Awards for Excellence in BPM & Workflow**[1] recognizes organizations that have implemented particularly innovative workflow solutions. Every year between 10 and 15 BPM and workflow solutions are recognized in this manner.
   WfMC publishes the case studies in the annual Excellence in Practice [2] series.

2. WfMC inaugurated a Global Awards program in 2011 for **Excellence in Case Management**[3] case studies to recognize and focus upon successful use cases for coordinating unpredictable work patterns. Awards are given in the category of Production Case Management and in Adaptive Case Management which are both new technological approaches to supporting knowledge work in today's leading edge organizations. These awards are designed to highlight the best examples of technology to support knowledge workers.
   Several books[4] have been published recognizing the winning teams. In 2013, WfMC updated the program to "WfMC Awards for Excellence in Case Management" to recognize the growing deployment of Production Case Management.

3. The **Marvin L. Manheim Award For Significant Contributions** in the Field of Workflow is given to one person every year in recognition of individual contributions to workflow and BPM standards. This award commemorates Marvin Manheim who played a key motivational role in the founding of the WfMC.

---

[1] BPM Awards: www.BPMF.org

[2] *Delivering BPM Excellence:* Published 2013 by Future Strategies Inc. http://futstrat.com/books/Delivering_BPM.php

[3] Case Management Awards: www.adaptivecasemanagement.org

[4] *Empowering Knowledge Workers:* Published 2013 by Future Strategies Inc. http://futstrat.com/books/EmpoweringKnowledgeWorkers.php

*How Knowledge Workers Get Things Done.* Published 2012 by Future Strategies Inc. http://www.futstrat.com/books/HowKnowledgeWorkers.php

*Taming the Unpredictable:* Published 2011 by Future Strategies Inc .http://futstrat.com/books/eip11.php

The Workflow Management Coalition gives you the unique opportunity to participate in the creation of standards for the workflow industry as they are developing.

Your contributions to our community ensure that progress continues in the adoption of royalty-free workflow and process standards.

THE SECRETARIAT

Workflow Management Coalition (WfMC)

www.WfMC.org

# Author and Contact Appendix

## Paul Buhler

### *Chief Scientist, Modus21*

Dr. Paul Buhler is a seasoned professional who has worked in commercial, government and academic environments. He is a respected researcher, practitioner, and educator of service-oriented computing concepts, technologies and implementation methodologies.

Dr. Buhler has authored over 20 published papers in the subjects of SOA, agent-based computing, and service composition. His expertise has been sought in the areas of enterprise architecture, open source middleware, complex event processing, and semantic web technologies. Most recently he has been working toward closing the gap between business strategy and process execution. To accomplish this he is leveraging responsive design principles and a goal-based approach to enable continuous alignment across a corporation's strategic, tactical and operational levels.

In his position of Chief Scientist at Modus21, Dr. Buhler is responsible for aligning corporate strategy with emerging trends in business architecture and process execution frameworks. He also holds an Affiliate Professorship at the College of Charleston, where he teaches both graduate and undergraduate computer sciences courses. Dr. Buhler earned his Ph.D. in Computer Engineering at the University of South Carolina. He also holds an MS degree in Computer Science from Johns Hopkins University and a BS in Computer Science from The Citadel.

## Lloyd Dugan

### *Chief Architect, BPM, Inc.*

Lloyd Dugan is the Chief Architect for BPM, Inc., and is a widely recognized expert and thought leader in the development and use of leading modeling languages, methodologies, and tools, covering from the level of Enterprise Architecture (EA) and Business Architecture (BA) through Business Process Management (BPM) and Service-Oriented Architecture (SOA).

He specializes in the use of the standard language for describing business processes, the Business Process Model & Notation (BPMN) language from the Object Management Group (OMG), having developed and delivered BPM and BPMN training to the Department of Defense (DoD) and contractors from several IT consulting companies, presented on it at national and international conferences, and co-authored the seminal BPMN 2.0 Handbook, chapter on Making a BPMN 2.0 Model Executable, sponsored by the Workflow Management Coalition.

He is also an Advisory Board Member of the Business Architecture Guild. In addition, he is a Co-founder of Semantic BPMN, which is dedicated to proving the proposition that realizing BPMN's full potential lies in leveraging semantic technologies to address BPMN model data.

## CHARLES FARINA

### *Manager, Business Process Improvement, Essroc Cement Corp.*

Responsible for driving the implementation of BPM capabilities at Essroc, the North America business unit of Italcementi Group, one of the leading global suppliers of construction materials (cement, concrete, and aggregates). Prior to joining Essroc in 2007, he was involved in BPM initiatives at Air Products and Chemicals, Inc. with his first involvement in process excellence during the mid-1980s. He holds a B.S. in Chemical Engineering and an M.B.A., both from Lehigh University in Bethlehem, PA.

## LAYNA FISCHER

### *Publisher, Future Strategies Inc., USA*

Ms Fischer is Editor-in-Chief and Publisher at Future Strategies Inc., the official publishers to WfMC.org. She was also Executive Director of WfMC and BPMI (now merged with OMG) and continues to work closely with these organizations to promote industry awareness of BPM and Workflow.

Future Strategies Inc. (www.FutStrat.com) publishes unique books and papers on business process management and workflow, specializing in dissemination of information about BPM and workflow technology and electronic commerce. As such, the company contracts and works closely with individual authors and corporations worldwide and also manages the renowned annual Global Awards for Excellence in BPM and Workflow and the new annual Adaptive Case Management Awards.

Future Strategies Inc., is the publisher of the business book series *New Tools for New Times*, the annual *Excellence in Practice* series of award-winning case studies and the annual *BPM and Workflow Handbook* series, published in collaboration with the WfMC. Ms. Fischer was a senior editor of a leading international computer publication for four years and has been involved in international computer journalism and publishing for over 20 years.

## MARIA HOVE

### *Thought-Leader*

International recognized researcher and thought-leader in the field of business model, performance modelling and in the field of value identification, value design, value modelling and value realization. She has worked for many fortune 500 organizations and for government s around the world, She leads multiple researches in the Global University Alliance (GUA), the largest non-vendor academic platform for academic collaboration. As a part of the GUA work he she been involved of developing multiple Enterprise Standards as well as Industry Standards. Within the field of BPM her speciality is

- Align business processes to business goals
- Process Innovation & Transformation Enablement (PITE)
- BPM & Operating Model
- BPM Change Management
- BPM Portfolio Management
- Continuous process improvement

Author of multiple publications among them the IEEE publication "How to integrate Enterprise Architecture and BPM". From Elsevier and Morgan Kaufman: "The Complete Business Process Handbook" as well as for Future

Strategies Inc. and the Workflow Management Coalition (**WfMC**) "Passports to Success in BPM"

She is certified Process eXpert & LEAD Process Architect as well as Business Architect Certified.

## FRANK F. KOWALKOWSKI
### *President, Knowledge Consultants, Inc*

Frank Kowalkowski is President of Knowledge Consultants, Inc., a firm focusing on business performance, business/IT architecture and business analytical techniques. He has over 30 years of management and consulting experience in a wide variety of industries. He has been involved with many projects including business analysis, process management, business performance measurement, business and competitive intelligence and knowledge management. In addition to being a keynote speaker at international conferences as well as a conference chair, he has written numerous papers and spoken at conferences on a variety of subjects. He is the author of a 1996 book on Enterprise Analysis (Prentice – Hall, ISBN 0-13-282-3365) and numerous papers. Frank is currently working on a both a BPM book for managers and a new edition of the enterprise analysis book. He conducts frequent seminars nationally and internationally on a variety of business management and information technology topics. He is co-author of a quarterly column on architecture for the website TDAN.

## NATHANIEL PALMER
### *Vice President and CTO, BPM, Inc.*

Rated as the #1 Most Influential Thought Leader in Business Process Management (BPM) by independent research, Nathaniel is recognized as one of the early originators of BPM, and has the led the design for some of the industry's largest-scale and most complex projects involving investments of $200 Million or more. Today he is the Editor-in-Chief of BPM.com, as well as the Executive Director of the Workflow Management Coalition, as well as VP and CTO of BPM, Inc.

Previously he had been the BPM Practice Director of SRA International, and prior to that Director, Business Consulting for Perot Systems Corp, as well as spent over a decade with Delphi Group serving as VP and CTO. He frequently tops the lists of the most recognized names in his field, and was the first individual named as Laureate in Workflow. Nathaniel has authored or co-authored a dozen books on process innovation and business transformation, including "Intelligent BPM" (2013), "How Knowledge Workers Get Things Done" (2012), "Social BPM" (2011), "Mastering the Unpredictable" (2008) which reached #2 on the Amazon.com Best Seller's List, "Excellence in Practice" (2007), "Encyclopedia of Database Systems" (2007) and "The X-Economy" (2001).

He has been featured in numerous media ranging from Fortune to The New York Times to National Public Radio. Nathaniel holds a DISCO Secret Clearance as well as a Position of Trust with in the U.S. federal government.

## PEDRO ROBLEDO
### *Editor and BPM Networker, BPMteca.com, Spain*

Pedro Robledo is Editor-in-Chief, Publisher and BPM Marketing Advisor and trusted Networker at BPMteca.com, who publishes unique books on business process management and the e-magazine "World BPM Magazine"; it provides services of translation of BPM documents from English to Spanish, and it provides marketing services oriented to lead generation for BPM providers and trusted Networking for all people who is interested on BPM. Robledo has more than 24 years of professional experience in Enterprise Software Market with a complete background and skills in sales, marketing and business development, focused on the company strategy, lead generation and oriented to objectives with the commitment and consecution to results. He is one of the most influential Spanish thought leader in BPM, as for 8 years has been dedicated to promote industry awareness of Business Process Management in Spain and Latin America. Pedro has over 21 years of experience as Professor in University with strong skills in eLearning for 14 years in Universitat Oberta de Catalunya (UOC). He is currently the academic Director of online BPM Technologic Master in Universidad Internacional de la Rioja (UNIR) as well as BPM professor of Project Management Master in Universidad Pontificia de Salamanca (UPSAM) and BPM Professor of IT Service Management for Universities Expert Course in Universidad Castilla La Mancha (UCLM).

He writes his Blog "The White Book on Business Process Management": http://pedrorobledobpm.blogspot.com.es/

You can reach Pedro Robledo at Linkedin: es.linkedin.com/in/pedrorobledobpm and you can follow him on Twitter: @pedrorobledobpm

## PETER SCHOOFF

### Managing Editor, BPM.com, USA

Peter Schooff is Managing Editor at BPM.com, where he oversees the BPM.com Forum as well as other content and social media initiatives. Peter has over 15 years' experience in various enterprise IT fields, including serving as Director of Marketing for email security company Message Partners. Most recently he served as Managing Editor for ebizQ, for which he created and ran the ebizQ forum. Peter is known world-wide for his views and contributions to BPM, and was named among the Top 12 Influencers of Case Management through independent market research.

## KEITH SWENSON

### Vice President of R&D, Fujitsu America Inc., USA

Keith Swenson is Vice President of Research and Development at Fujitsu America Inc. and is the Chief Software Architect for the Interstage family of products. He is known for having been a pioneer in collaboration software and web services, and has helped the development of many workflow and BPM standards. He is currently the Chairman of the Workflow Management Coalition. In the past, he led development of collaboration software MS2, Netscape, Ashton Tate and Fujitsu. In 2004 he was awarded the Marvin L. Manheim Award for outstanding contributions in the field of workflow. His blog is at http://social-biz.org/.

## MARK VON ROSING

### BPM and Enterprise Architect Guru

Prof. Mark von Rosing is in every way an innovator impacting developments, standards, frameworks, methods and approaches around the world. For over

15 years he has taught in different universities around the world. He founded in 2004, the Global University Alliance (GUA), the largest non-vendor academic platform for academic collaboration. As a part of the GUA work he has been involved of developing 94 Enterprise Standards and 51 Industry Standards, both with ISO, OMG, LEADing Practice, NATO and many more. Furthermore founding LEADing Practice, the fastest growing community with +3900 practitioners.

Some of the major focus areas are among others:

- Academic research focus on Enterprise DNA, Business Model, BPM, EA, Value Modelling, Case Management and Social Media
- Member & Co-developer of the OMG-Object Management Group standards, focusing on:
    - Value Delivery Modeling Language (VDML)
    - Business planning and motivation modeling (BMM)
    - Business Process Modeling Notations (BPMN)
    - Semantics of Business Vocabulary and Rules (SBVR)
    - Decision Model and Notation (DMN)
- Researcher and developer of ISO Enterprise Architecture standards
- Research collaboration and developer with IEEE standards.
- Member & Co-developer of the Global TOGAF Business Architecture Methods & Certification Development Group
- Development member of the NATO standards, including EA, BPM, Capabilities and joint mission execution.
- Built the BPM and EA curriculum for the SAP University Alliance (+ 900 universities).
- Developer of SAP Business Process Expert (BPX) and SAP LEAD Enterprise Architecture certification program.
- SAP AG Method developer e.g. ASAP, SAP Agile, BPM, Enterprise Architecture (EAF).
- Author of multiple publications among them the SAP Press bestseller: "Applying real-world BPM in an SAP environment" and the IEEE publication "defining the profession of the Business Architect" as well as the publication "How to integrate Enterprise Architecture and BPM"

## HENRIK VON SCHEEL

### CEO, LEADing Practice

International recognized thought-leader and the driving force behind the Enterprise Modelling revolution and a pioneer in linking strategy with operational execution. For most Fortune 500 and public organizations, Henrik von Scheel is synonym for a visionary, game changer and a challenger striving to defy outmoded business models.

Recognized as a strategy and business process management thought leader, advisor, mentor and co-author of SAP Press bestseller book: Applying real-world BPM in an SAP environment. He has made a significant contribution to the enterprise modelling discipline—whether by driving standards, expanding the technology, or pushing process improvement in new direction.

Together with Global University Alliance, he has evolved mainstream process thinking, approaches and styles through his efforts in standards bodies, books, academic publications and published reference content, such as extended BPMN, Object Modelling (Business, Service, Process, Information &

Data) BPM enabled Innovation & Transformation, BPM Centre of Excellence, BPM Alignment, Social BPM, BPM & Enterprise Architecture, BPM Change Management, BPM Lifecycle, BPM Maturity, Value BPM, Goal Oriented Process and BPM Industry Accelerators etc.

Henrik is the CEO of LEADing Practice - #1 Enterprise Standard provider, setting the agenda for 56 Industries. He serves as Advisory Board Member at Google EMEA, Gazprom, Global University Alliance and Chairman of Capital Investment Partners. AWARDED "The NEXT 100 Top Influencers of the European Digital Industry in 2012" among the most important Europeans shaping our digital future.

Advising executives how tackle THE BLIND SPOTS or "change gap" - discover the WHY, define the WHAT and deliver the HOW. Enabling executives to transform and innovate existing business models and their service model to design tomorrow's enterprises. His trademark is the unique ability to help organizations master the rare discipline of developing their core competitive and differentiated aspects. Translating the "Big Picture" into operational execution using layered architectural rigor and applying leading practice, industry- and best practice with the IT team.

# Award-winning Case Studies

AWARD: BANKING AND FINANCIAL SERVICESLOAN ORIGINATION

**Company: *Bank Dhofar, Sultanate of Oman***

Nominated by:

**Company:** Newgen Software Technologies Limited

**Contact:** Ankita Sinha, Senior Executive- Products & Solution, ankita@newgen.co.in

**Website:** www.newgen.co.in

AWARD: BANKING AND FINANCIAL SERVICESBACK OFFICE OPTIMIZATION

**Company: *HCL IBS, United Kingdom***

Nominated by:

**Company:** Corporate Modelling

**Contact:** Alex Allan, COO, alex.allan@corporatemodelling.com

**Website:** www.corporatemodelling.com

FINALIST: FINANCIAL SERVICES

**Company: *HML***

**Contact:** Paul Swinson, Program Manager, Paul.Swinson@hml.co.uk

**Website:**www.hml.co.uk

Nominated by:

**Company:** IBM

**Contact:** Claire Lynam, Marketing Manager, claire.lynam@uk.ibm.com

**Website:**www.uk.ibm.com

FINALIST: EDUCATION
**Company: *Liberty University***
Nominated by:
**Company:** BizFlow
**Contact:** Garth Knudsen, gknudson@bizflow.com
**Website:**www.bizflow.com

FINALIST: HEALTHCARE
**Company: *Prince Sultan Military Medical City***
**Contact:** Dr. Adnan A. Al-Tunisi,CIO, aaltunisi@rmh.med.sa
Website: www.rmh.med.sa
Nominated by:
**Company:** Bizagi
**Contact:** Jolanta Pilecka, CMO, jolanta.pilecka@bizagi.com
**Website:**www.bizagi.com

AWARD: BANKING AND FINANCIAL SERVICESSERVICE REQUEST MANAGEMENT
**Company: *PSCU***
**Contact:** Dan Rosen, Director of the Center for Process Excellence, drosen@pscu.com
**Website:**www.pscu.com
Nominated by:
**Company:** OpenText
**Contact:** Brian Wick, Director of Product Marketing, BPM, bwick@opentext.com
**Website:**www.opentext.com

FINALIST: MANUFACTURING
**Company: *Refinery of the Pacific Eloy Alfaro***
Nominated by:
**Company:** AURA - AuraPortal
**Contact:** Pablo Trilles, VP Commercial, pablo.trilles@auraportal.com
**Website:** www.auraportal.com

AWARD: PUBLIC SECTOR PLANNING AND PERMITTING
**Company: *Right of Way, Abu Dhabi DoT***
**Contact:** Jahfar Mohamed Ismail,, jahfar.ismail@dot.abudhabi.ae
**Website:** www.dot.abudhabi.ae
Nominated by:
**Company:** Abu Dhabi Department of Transport
**Contact:** Khamis Al Dahmani, Head of Right of Way Section, khamis.aldahmani@dot.abudhabi.ae
**Website:** www.dot.abudhabi.ae

AWARD: TRANSPORATION AND LOGISTICS AGILE DEVELOPMENT

**Company:** *SBB - Swiss Railroad*

**Contact:** Jacob Archana, Project leader, archana.jacob@sbb.ch

**Website:**www.sbb.ch

Nominated by:

**Company:** ti&m

**Contact:** Walter Strametz, CTO Bern, walter.strametz@ti8m.ch

**Website:**www.ti8m.ch

AWARD: PUBLIC SECTORBENEFITS ENROLLMENT

**Company:** *US Department of Veterans Affairs*

Nominated by:

**Company:** Living Systems Technologies

**Contact:** Dan Neason, , dan.neason@livingsystemstechnologies.com

**Website:**www.livingsystemstechnologies.com

AWARD: PUBLIC UTILITY CUSTOMER-CENTRIC TRANSFORMATION

**Company:** *Vitens NV*

**Contact:** Geuje van Dijk,, geuje.vandijk@vitens.nl

**Website:**www.vitens.nl

Nominated by:

**Company:** You Get

**Contact:** Erik van Krevel, Manager Customer & Billing Department, evankrevel@you-get.com

**Website:**www.you-get.com

HOW TO WIN AN AWARD

The annual WfMC **Awards for Global Excellence in BPM** are sponsored by WfMC.org and BPM.com. The prestigious annual Awards are highly coveted by organizations that seek recognition for their achievements. These awards not only provide a spotlight for companies that truly deserve recognition, but provide tremendous insights for organizations wishing to emulate the winners' successes.

General information and guidelines for submissions are at www.bpmf.org.

# Index

agile methods, 191, 197, 198

Analysis Latency, 36

Analysis of Alternatives (AoA), 205

analysis, 84, 90, 91, 94, 95

architecture principles, 199

assessment, 84, 88, 92

Associations, 90

automated procedure, 85

baseline, 87, 96

best yield, 87, 96

BPM capabilities, 58, 61

BPM discipline, 67

BPM initiatives, 58, 59, 61

BPMN XML, 71

Brooks' Law, 54, 55

business architecture, 25

Business Model, 73

Capability, 74, 75, 76, 77, 78, 80

CMIS, Content Management Interoperability Services, 30

company politics, 23

complexity, 84, 88, 89, 90, 91, 92

Continuous Improvement., 165, 167

credit union services, 157

cycle time, 85, 86, 91, 94

DAD (Dynamically Activated Divisions), 169

Data Latency, 36

Decision Latency, 36

Decomposition, 75

Digital Business, 64

Digital Economy, 63, 71

Digital Enterprise, 65

disruptive technologies, 70

disruptive technology trends, 68

Dynamic Business structure, 212

enablers, 85, 90, 91, 92, 95

End States, 75

enterprise analysis, 84

Enterprise Content Management (ECM)., 37

Exchange Interfaces, 75

failure, risk for, 23

First Time Right, 214

fraud management, 159

function, 87

Hard-Dollar Benefits, 49, 53

Heat Map, 80, 81

High Priority Performance Goals (HPPG), 200

iBPMS, 27, 32, 37

improvement, 84, 85, 86, 89, 90, 91, 95

Infrastructure Portal, 191, 192

Intelligent BPM Systems, 27

matrices, 88- 96

Net Present Value (NPV), 48, 53

No Objection Certificates (NOCs), 175

Operating Model, 73

process aware, 211, 212

Process Classification Frameworks (PCFs), 77

public utility, 213

Resource Description Format (RDF), 81

Return on Equity (ROE), 48

Return on Investment (ROI), 48

SMACT – Social, Mobile, Analytics, Cloud, Things, 68

SMACT, 64

Soft Benefits, 49

Span of Control, 74

Strategic BPM, 57, 61

Strategic or Operational Benefits, 49

Strong decomposition, 79

subjective, 86, 87, 91

The Mythical Man-Month, 54

Total Inquiry Management System, 158

touch points, 84, 89, 96

Trigger, 75

Value Stream, 75, 76, 78, 80

waste identification, 202

Weak decomposition, 79

Web Ontology Language (WOL), 81

weight factors, 87, 90

Weighted Average Cost of Capital (WACC), 48

# Additional Reading and Resources

**NEW!**

**e-Book Series ($9.97 each)**

*Download PDF and start reading.*

### Introduction to BPM and Workflow
http://store.futstrat.com/servlet/Detail?no=75

### Financial Services
http://store.futstrat.com/servlet/Detail?no=90

### Healthcare
http://store.futstrat.com/servlet/Detail?no=81

### Utilities and Telecommunications
http://store.futstrat.com/servlet/Detail?no=92

EMPOWERING KNOWLEDGE WORKERS:

New Ways to Leverage Case Management

http://futstrat.com/books/EmpoweringKnowledgeWorkers.php

ACM allows work to follow the worker, providing cohesiveness of a single point of access. Case Management provides the long-term record of how work is done, as well as the guidance, rules, visibility and input that allow knowledge workers to be more productive. Adaptive Case Management is ultimately about allowing knowledge workers to work the way that they want to work and to provide them with the tools and information they need to do so effectively.

**Retail $49.95 (see discount online)**

TAMING THE UNPREDICTABLE

http://futstrat.com/books/eip11.php

The core element of Adaptive Case Management (ACM) is the support for real-time decision-making by knowledge workers.

Taming the Unpredictable presents the logical starting point for understanding how to take advantage of ACM. This book goes beyond talking about concepts, and delivers actionable advice for embarking on your own journey of ACM-driven transformation.

**Retail $49.95 (see discount on website)**

### HOW KNOWLEDGE WORKERS GET THINGS DONE

http://www.futstrat.com/books/HowKnowledgeWork-ers.php

*How Knowledge Workers Get Things Done* describes the work of managers, decision makers, executives, doctors, lawyers, campaign managers, emergency responders, strategist, and many others who have to think for a living. These are people who figure out what needs to be done, at the same time that they do it, and there is a new approach to support this presents the logical starting point for understanding how to take advantage of ACM.
**Retail $49.95 (see discount offer on website)**

### DELIVERING BPM EXCELLENCE

http://futstrat.com/books/Delivering_BPM.php

Business Process Management in Practice

The companies whose case studies are featured in this book have proven excellence in their creative and successful deployment of advanced BPM concepts. These companies focused on excelling in *innovation, implementation* and *impact* when installing BPM and workflow technologies. The positive impact includes increased revenues, more productive and satisfied employees, product enhancements, better customer service and quality improvements.
**$39.95 (see discount on website)**

### DELIVERING THE CUSTOMER-CENTRIC ORGANIZATION

http://futstrat.com/books/Customer-Centric.php
The ability to successfully manage the customer value chain across the life cycle of a customer is the key to the survival of any company today. Business processes must react to changing and diverse customer needs and interactions to ensure efficient and effective outcomes.

This important book looks at the shifting nature of consumers and the workplace, and how BPM and associated emergent technologies will play a part in shaping the companies of the future. **Retail $39.95**

### BPMN 2.0 Handbook SECOND EDITION

(see two-BPM book bundle offer on website: get BPMN Reference Guide Free)
http://futstrat.com/books/bpmnhandbook2.php

Updated and expanded with exciting new content!

Authored by members of WfMC, OMG and other key participants in the development of BPMN 2.0, the BPMN 2.0 Handbook brings together worldwide thought-leaders and experts in this space. Exclusive and unique contributions examine a variety of aspects that start with an introduction of what's new in BPMN 2.0, and look closely at interchange, analytics, conformance, optimization, simulation and more.
**Retail $75.00**

### BPMN MODELING AND REFERENCE GUIDE

(see two-BPM book bundle offer on website: get BPMN Reference Guide Free)

http://www.futstrat.com/books/BPMN-Guide.php

**Understanding and Using BPMN**

How to develop rigorous yet understandable graphical representations of business processes.

Business Process Modeling Notation (BPMN) is a standard, graphical modeling representation for business processes. It provides an easy to use, flow-charting notation that is independent of the implementation environment.
**Retail $39.95 See special 2-book offer online**

### iBPMS - INTELLIGENT BPM SYSTEMS

http://www.futstrat.com/books/iBPMS_Handbook.php

"The need for Intelligent Business Operations (IBO) supported by intelligent processes is driving the need for a new convergence of process technologies lead by the iBPMS. The iBPMS changes the way processes help organizations keep up with business change," notes Gartner Emeritus Jim Sinur in his Foreword.

The co-authors of this important book describe various aspects and approaches of iBPMS with regard to impact and opportunity. **Retail $59.95 (see discount on website)**

### Social BPM

http://futstrat.com/books/handbook11.php

Work, Planning, and Collaboration Under the Impact of Social Technolog y

Today we see the transformation of both the look and feel of BPM technologies along the lines of social media, as well as the increasing adoption of social tools and techniques democratizing process development and design. It is along these two trend lines; the evolution of system interfaces and the increased engagement of stakeholders in process improvement, that Social BPM has taken shape.
**Retail $59.95 (see discount offer on website)**

# Get 25% Discount on ALL these Books
Use the discount code **SPEC25** to get 25% discount on ALL books in the store; both Print and Digital Editions

## Digital Edition Benefits:
Enjoy immediate download, live URLs, searchable text, graphics and charts in color. No shipping charges. Download from our website now.

### Future Strategies Inc.

### www.FutStrat.com